CW00570998

Ideology and Ireland in the Nineteenth Century

Ideology and Ireland in the Nineteenth Century

EDITED BY

Tadhg Foley and Seán Ryder

FOUR COURTS PRESS

Set in 10.5 on 12 point Bembo for
FOUR COURTS PRESS
Fumbally Lane, Dublin 8, Ireland
e-mail: info@four-courts-press.ie
and in North America
FOUR COURTS PRESS
c/o ISBS 5804 N.E. Hassalo Street, Portland, OR 97213.

© Four Courts Press and the various authors 1998

A catalogue record for this title
is available from the British Library.

ISBN 1–85182–330–1 cased
1–85182–360–3 pbk

All rights reserved. No part of this publication may be
reproduced, stored in or introduced into a retrieval
system, or transmitted, in any form or by any means
(electronic, mechanical, photocopying, recording or
otherwise), without the prior written permission of
both the copyright owner and the publisher of this book.

Printed in Great Britain
by MPG Books, Bodmin Cornwall

Contents

III IDEOLOGIES OF NATION AND IDENTITY

Preface

Versions of the essays in this book were delivered at the 'Ideology and Ireland in the Nineteenth Century' conference which took place in the National University of Ireland, Galway, in June 1996. We are grateful to all of those who participated in that conference and to the Society for the Study of Nineteenth-Century Ireland, under whose auspices the conference was held. In particular we would like to acknowledge the support and encouragement of the Society's officers Richard Hayes, Margaret Kelleher, Leon Litvack, and James Murphy, and pay tribute to the two preceding volumes based on the Society's annual conferences, *Fearful Realities: New Perspectives on the Famine*, edited by Chris Morash and Richard Hayes (1996) and *Gender Perspectives in Nineteenth-Century Ireland*, edited by Margaret Kelleher and James Murphy (1997). Having such models to follow made our work very much easier.

Vital financial support for this conference and volume of essays was made available from the following people and institutions: Professor M. F. McCarthy, former Registrar, NUI, Galway; an tOllamh Nollaig MacCongáil, Dean of Arts, NUI, Galway; Professor Kevin Barry, English Department, NUI, Galway; the board of the Culture and Colonialism programme, NUI, Galway; and Mr Harold Fish of the British Council. We would like to express our particular gratitude to the School of Irish Studies Foundation for a timely and generous grant towards the preparation of the volume for publication.

We are indebted to Fiona Bateman for her invaluable help in proofreading and indexing the volume, and to the infinitely patient Michael Adams, Martin Fanning and staff at Four Courts Press, who have brought their usual talents and professionalism to bear on the book's production.

We also wish to thank the editors of *Journal X: A Journal in Culture and Criticism* for permission to reproduce a version of Marjorie Howes' essay on Lady Wilde.

Tadhg Foley
Seán Ryder

National University of Ireland, Galway

Introduction

TADHG FOLEY & SEÁN RYDER

Their alleged allergy to ideas notwithstanding, it appears that the Irish were enthusiastic participants in the ideological strife which characterised the economic, social, political and cultural domains of the nineteenth century. In the essays collected in this volume we see some of this activity in a variety of fields – moving from the controversies over aesthetics and representation in art and literature; to the contests associated with the public discourses of science, popular culture, state policy, economics and philosophy; to the contribution made by Irish writers and thinkers to international debates about nationality, race and identity.

In many cases, Ireland appears to have functioned as an testing-ground for those ideologies developed within and utilised by metropolitan imperial cultures such as Great Britain. The aesthetics of classicism, the economics of *laissez-faire*, the gender ideology of 'separate spheres', and the discourse of Aryanism, to name but a few ideological discourses which feature in the following pages, were all challenged, modified or deconstructed when exposed to the conditions of nineteenth-century Ireland. The reasons for this are various, but have much to do with the inescapable effects of the 'unfinished business' of colonialism and imperialism in nineteenth-century Irish culture. The unresolved contests between Gaelic and English cultural values, between modernity and tradition, between peasantry and gentry, between Protestant and Catholic – all were such highly visible conflicts in nineteenth-century Ireland that ideology found itself continually in a state of exposure and confrontation, unable to 'naturalise' itself and achieve hegemonic invisibility. The failure or crisis in Ireland of those ideas and practices which had become hegemonic or at least dominant in the metropolitian imperial culture of Britain could in fact be understood in quite diametrically-opposed ways. Such failures were, from an imperial point of view, a mark of Ireland's hopelessly recalcitrant primitivism. On the other hand, from an anti-imperial position one might see such 'failures' quite differently, as positive evidence of the ideological and self-interested character of those supposedly 'natural' or 'progressive' imperial values.

Yet the picture is not a simple one of polarised conflict between competing British and Irish, or imperial and nationalist ideologies. Some of these essays demonstrate that the relations between Irish culture and metropolitan ideologies were occasionally more collusive than confrontational. Bourgeois Irish nationalism, for instance, adopted wholeheartedly the ideological forms of public commemoration, the discourses on gender and the theories of national identity which originated in the metropolitan imperial 'centres' of European culture. Even more intriguingly, there is evidence that at certain moments the discourses of Gaelic popular culture and British state policy overlapped quite comfortably, as Niall Ó Ciosáin's paper suggests. Peter Gray too reminds us that personal and historical circumstances were often as influential as ideological debates in shaping the political and cultural relationships between Britain and Ireland in the nineteenth century.

The essays in the volume are arranged in three general categories. The first five papers, under the rubric of 'Ideology, Art and Representation', show how the literary and artistic representations of Ireland often complicated those ideological assumptions about the nature of art which imperialism (and purist forms of nationalism) tended to take for granted. Terry Eagleton, in his paper on 'Fr Prout' (Francis Sylvester Mahony), sees in the carnivalesque discourse of Mahony, Maginn and Mangan a form of subversion and resistance to the ideologically-saturated discourses of metropolitan imperialist culture. The plagiaristic, inbred, fragmentary, frequently hilarious writing produced by these nineteenth-century Hibernian *bricoleurs* was 'so doggedly, brilliantly peripheral', argues Eagleton, that it had the potential to deconstruct the very distinction between the 'peripheral' and the 'central'. For Eagleton, this mirrors a similar deconstructive process at work in O'Connellite politics. Yet all is not necessarily a matter of joyful discursive play under such conditions. Eagleton draws attention to the fact that such positions of resistance may have oppressive aspects too, as they did for Mahony and Wilde, where the 'pains of exile' became a kind of counterweight to the 'pleasures of the polyglottic'. In a general sense, it appears that the 'directionless', 'self-involved' and sectarian society produced by colonialism leaves its destructive marks upon even its most brilliant talents.

Luke Gibbons, in his discussion of Lady Morgan, Thomas Moore and Daniel Maclise, also focuses on the inescapability of politics and ideology in considering aesthetic problems in nineteenth-century Ireland. Gibbons shows how, when it came to the subject of Ireland, artistic representation was inevitably imagined and mobilised in terms of politics, even at the most fundamental level of aesthetic form: 'the difficulties in establishing a framing narrative, ordering the disparate elements in a story or picture and subjecting them to a unifying point of view, presented itself not simply as an aesthetic difficulty but as an intractable political problem'. Thus, certain works of art, like Maclise's *The Installation of Captain Rock* (1834), become politically subversive through their 'formal instability', particularly where such formal strategies 'disturb the composure of the viewer' rather than conform to the controlled aesthetic distance demanded by imperialist ideology. Like Eagleton's Bakhtinian revellers, an Irish artist like Maclise, in attempting to represent the 'truth', makes visible

the ideological nature of representation itself. The problems of truth and transparency, and their effects on the political culture of Ireland, is a theme
addressed also by Willa Murphy, whose discussion of Maria Edgeworth shows
how the latter's writings deconstruct the Enlightenment opposition between
openness and secrecy. In a fascinating account of Edgeworth's double-sided
discourse, Murphy argues that in a colonial society, 'there is at once too much
secrecy and not enough – too much among Irish tenants for Ascendancy rulers
to unmask; and not enough for the Ascendancy itself to hide behind. To an
anxious and exposed Ascendancy, Ireland is at once a deeply opaque and
painfully transparent place'. Judith Hill's essay turns to the commemorative
monument as a form of representation, and sees it as a means of very explicitly
'putting culture to political use', in accordance with the theories of Thomas
Davis as much as those of Victorian imperialism. The questions again of what
(or who) is to be represented, and whose interests are being served by such
representations, are shown to be central to the ideologically-inflected debates
over the subjects, style and siting of Ireland's public urban monuments. Yet
behind these factional disputes over whether to commemorate O'Connell or
Prince Albert, Fr Mathew or Lord Gough, lies a deeper ideological unity,
where all sides appear to share certain basic ideological assumptions – assumptions about the value of these specific forms of representative art, for instance,
or shared assumptions about the nature of history (something propelled by a
series of 'great men'). Irish art of this type challenges the values of the ruling
ideology at one level (choosing an Irish hero rather than an English one, for
example), while embracing those ruling values at another level. In this way,
ironically, such nationalist art seems less challenging than the work of Mahony,
Maclise, or even Edgeworth. Finally in this section, Sandra Siegel, in arguing
against the simplistic view of Wilde as an apolitical dandy, shows how the
material circuits of exchange, donation and reception of a literary work (in this
case Wilde's *Poems*) can in fact reflect something of the imperial relation
between Ireland and Britain – and show up the discrepency between ideology
as professed and ideology as practiced.

   The second group of essays, under the rubric 'Ideology and Public
Discourse' examines a variety of discourses, and considers their relation to ideological conflicts in nineteenth-century Ireland. Angela Bourke and Niall Ó
Ciosáin both consider Gaelic popular culture and its relation to ideologies
associated with modernisation and British political administration. The two
writers show very different aspects to these relations: Bourke argues that Gaelic
folklore constituted a 'vernacular cognitive system', the value of which was
unrecognised by the 'modernising' linear ideology of the nineteenth century,
an ideology associated with science, with English culture and with the official
discourse of the state. In this case the English and Gaelic cultures represent
radically alternative methods of understanding, with the latter being gradually

undermined by the former throughout the nineteenth and twentieth centuries. Ó Ciosáin's discussion of the Poor Law Commission, on the other hand, shows that when it came to specific areas of knowledge and ideology, such as making discriminations between 'deserving' and 'undeserving' poor, 'the gap between official and popular views was not as complete as the commissioners themselves imagined or as a historian might assume'. Margaret Preston, like Ó Ciosáin, looks at attitudes to the Irish poor – in this case the world of Dublin charities – but finds that in this particular arena the state's ideological discourse on poverty, intertwined with discourses on gender, race and class, did indeed serve a hegemonic function, whereby philanthropy for the most part reflected the interests of the ruling class.

In a very wide-ranging essay, Thomas Boylan and Terrence McDonough consider the ways in which the economic condition of Ireland was understood in the nineteenth century itself, but also show how certain types of twentieth-century analysis, such as dependency theory, were foreshadowed by Irish political economy in the post-Famine period. The work of Irish political economists such as John Kells Ingram (author of 'The Memory of the Dead'!), T.E. Cliffe Leslie, and Hancock and Richey demonstrated that English economic analysis based on liberal classical political economy was inappropriate when applied to Irish conditions, particularly in the wake of the Famine. In fact Irish political economists were 'disproportionately' central to the development of various alternative forms of economic analysis, such as institutionalism. Yet again, Ireland proved a location where the authority of dominant metropolitan or imperial ideologies was difficult to maintain. At the same time, Peter Gray's detailed account of the thinking of Nassau Senior during the Great Famine provides a salutary reminder to scholars that theory is not everything, and that the concrete political and social effects of ideology cannot be read from a set of historical circumstances in a simple or mechanistic way. 'In the complex relationship between economic thinking and public policy', he argues, 'it is inadequate and distracting to turn primarily to the most theoretically sophisticated and articulate statements of economic theory to account for governing practice. Rather it is vital to turn to a broader range of sources – the press and popular pamphlets, sermons and private correspondence – to build up a picture that … more accurately reflects the gamut of conflicting forces operating on political protagonists'. Thomas Duddy, in his intriguing and thought-provoking essay on Thomas Maguire, similarly presents a complicated picture of the relations between the personal, the professional and the ideological in the case of a nineteenth-century Irish academic. The apparent contradiction between Maguire's intellectual 'high-mindedness' (he was an idealist philosopher), and his involvement in the sordid Pigott forgeries affair, which was intended to discredit Parnell, was, according to Duddy, less the result of a moral flaw than of 'the pressure that historical developments can place on individuals who happen to occupy particularly sensitive ideological positions at a crucial moment'. Duddy's argument raises fundamental questions about the position of intellectuals in relation to culture and ideology generally, and the necessity for intellectuals in marginalised or postcolonial situations to maintain critical distance – not only from their local cultures, but also from powerful neighbouring cultures, especially those which may appear at first glance to be attractively 'Other'.

The volume's final five essays deal in different ways with ideological questions of identity and nationality. In a detailed reading of the popular nationalist poetry of Speranza (Lady Wilde), Marjorie Howes shows how, in spite of itself, Young Ireland's bourgeois nationalism sometimes produced 'unsettling versions of national subject constitution', brought on especially by its wildly ambivalent feelings about the Irish 'masses'. Looked at critically, the tensions in Wilde's work seem to imply that 'signs of national feeling are ambiguous, their meanings contingent and shifting', rather than possessed of the transparency demanded by ideology. Howes also connects this aspect of Wilde's work to her gender: 'as a woman writer engaging with a deeply masculinist tradition', she argues, 'Wilde had cause to be particularly sensitive to the impulses in Young Ireland nationalism which emphasized disjunction, distrust and hierarchy'. Eva Stöter, on the other hand, writes of much less fraught ideological links between Young Ireland nationalism and the writings of German romantics, particularly Herder and Lessing, whose secularisation of religious discourse and theories of nationalist pedagogy were important and direct influences on Thomas Davis.

In her disturbing account of women's unappreciated involvement in the Land League, Niamh O'Sullivan draws attention to the way many nineteenth-century Irish women remained resistant to ideological and material pressures to domesticate them. 'At a time when the separation of the spheres was being consolidated in advanced metropolitan countries', she writes, 'women in Ireland were still not fully domesticated within the home, as is clear from the numerous images of women outworkers found in popular illustrations of the period'. The boundaries between political and domestic, between (masculine) activity and (feminine) passivity were clearly difficult to police – literally – in nineteenth-century rural Ireland.

Theories of racial identity and difference were prominent in European culture generally in the nineteenth century, and Edward Hagan and Chris Morash each give particular attention to the impact of Aryanism among Irish intellectuals. For Hagan, the myth of Aryanism is 'a touchstone for seeing the nature of the Protestant-Catholic divide – political, social, and religious – as it played itself out in the nineteenth century'. Focusing on the figure of Standish O'Grady, Hagan argues that the Anglo-Irish Ascendancy's interests in the occult and in Aryan myth are signs of the insecurities of a class under threat: 'it is not hard to see how these fascinations indicate that the Ascendancy was compensating for its loss of power, purpose, and ideology'. Chris Morash approaches race theory from the opposite perspective of its impact on nationalist, rather than Ascendancy, culture, arguing that 'while it is certainly the case that any sort of axiomatic linking of nationalism and racialism is too crude, it is equally misleading to suggest that race is somehow a disposable accessory in nationalist discourse'. Morash suggests that Irish nationalism's utilisation of race theory produced contradictory effects, deconstructing as much as bolstering up the attempt to establish the nature of Irish identity, 'constitut[ing] a threat to the stability of the national unit, while at the same time helping to make possible the state's existence'. As with other essays in the volume, what becomes clear is that ideology functions in ways which are not always predictable or identical, being in fact closely shaped by differing historical, local and material contexts.

The essays in this volume all represent valuable, and in some cases, pioneering attempts to investigate the nature and impact of ideology in nineteenth-century Ireland. The multidisciplinary work here should help to illuminate aspects of the complex dynamics of Irish culture in ways which have not always, perhaps, been visible to conventional historiography.

Prout and Plagiarism

TERRY EAGLETON

The aim of this essay is to introduce the work of Francis Sylvester Mahony, wit, hack, toper, ruined priest, scholar and satirist, of whose prodigal array of pseudonymns 'Father Prout' is the one which posterity has preserved.[1] It is with this appellation that he has, to quote his own words, come 'floating triumphantly down the stream of time, secure and buoyant in a genuine "Cork" jacket'.[2]

Prout, so he tells us, was the offspring of a secret marriage between Swift and Stella, and was kidnapped at a tender age by the Englishman William Wood, in vengeance for the savaging which he had received in the Dean's *Drapier's Letters*.[3] The villainous Wood left the child exposed on the bleak summit of Watergrasshill near Cork, identifiable only by a locket around his neck containing a lock of his mother's hair and inscribed with the motto *Prout Stella Refulges*, '*Prout*' meaning literally 'to the extent that'. Father Prout, then, is Father-up-to-a-point, an accurate enough description of Mahony's dubious clerical status as a defrocked priest still in holy orders. It was the brutal abduction of the child which was the cause of his father's madness, though the story turned out well enough for the lad himself. Taken into the Cork foundling hospital, the young Prout escaped from the institution hidden in a wooden churn, to end up as the erudite clergyman of Watergrasshill whose papers have descended to us by the good offices of his editor Oliver Yorke, also *alias* Frank Mahony. Prout is hot in defence of his father's reputation, and asserts of the bare-faced political self-promotor Swift that he 'sought not the smiles of the court, nor ever sighed for ecclesiastical dignities' (p. 115). We read all this in Prout's essay 'Dean Swift's Madness, or the Tale of a Churn'.

1 Mahony stole the name from a real cleric, parish priest of Arnagehy, Co. Cork. There are some comments on the real Prout in William Le Fanu, *Seventy Years of Irish Life* (London, 1893), pp. 179-80, a work which also contains some observations on Sheridan Knowles and Sergeant Frank Murphy of the Fraserian circle.
2 *Reliques of Father Prout* (London, 1873), p. 104. All subsequent references to this work are given in parentheses. There is a reference to 'prouts' in James Joyce's *Finnegans Wake* ([New York, 1939] p. 482), followed closely by one to 'the bells of scandal' (cf. Prout's poem 'The Bells of Shandon').
3 Robert Mahony points out that Prout's defence of Swift as an Irish patriot, in the period of Catholic Emancipation, was quite unusual. It is clearly among other things an attempt to marginalise O'Connell. See his *Jonathan Swift: The Irish Identity* (New Haven and London, 1995), pp. 82-7.

Prout, then, has an illicit pedigree, like forged literary texts or false ety-mologies. The word 'kidnapping', so he informs us, is cognate with the word 'plagiarism', since in Cicero's day kidnappers were known as *plagiarii*, after the lash or *plaga* which they could expect if apprehended. (This is itself a false ety-mology: *plagiarius* actually derives from *plagium*, a net to catch game.) To steal an infant is a kind of plagiarism, appropriating what is not your own, rather as Prout's father Swift does with his assumption of literary personae, a tendency inherited by his son. Prout is a protean impersonator, a literary ventriloquist whose 'soul is multilateral, his talk multifarious' (p. iv). He is an odd mixture of the conservative and the carnivalesque, 'a rare combination of Socrates and Sancho Panza, of Scarron and the venerable Bede' (p. 167). The reactionary Prout is one of the 'polished and high-born clergy of the old Gallican church' (p. 5), deeply contemptuous of the vulgar herd of petty-bourgeois Corkonians with whom it is his lot to mingle. These, in his essay 'The Watergrass Carousal', include a down-at-heel fashion journalist who though not well-dressed him-self is the cause of dress in others, and who, as the editor of a local newspaper, keeps on eye on Russia in his columns vigilant enough to annoy the Tsar.[4] There is also a dentist who finishes his dinner parties with especially hard nuts, thus profitably converting his guests into patients.

Despite his conservatism, however, Prout is a kind of cultural studies expo-nent *avant la lettre*, whose chief field of scholarly inquiry, so he tells us, is popu-lar song; indeed Mahony himself has survived on the strength of one such bal-lad, 'The Bells of Shandon'. It is true that the Cork Fraserians practised along with their anti-plagiarising a kind of anti-popularising, translating ephemeral works into more durable linguistic media, as with William Maginn's rendering of 'Old King Cole' in Hebrew. Maginn's persona O'Doherty dreams of land-ing the office of Embalmer General, commissioned to turn living languages into dead ones for their better conservation. The danger, he reflects, would be to beautify the original to the point where it would be made better than itself, and so encourage readers to value inferior modern products by the allure of the linguistic wrapping he lends them. In his essay 'The Songs of France', Prout gives us a commendable French version of the anonymous eighteenth-century Irish verse 'The Night before Larry was Stretched'. But since the point of this project is to help preserve the ephemeral as well as antiquate it, it could be said to be popularising enough in its perverse way.

A supposed correspondent to *Fraser's Magazine* (in fact Mahony himself) describes Prout as being a 'rare combination of the Teian lyre and the Tipperary bagpipe ... of the Ionian dialect blending harmoniously with the Cork brogue; an Irish potatoe [*sic*] seasoned with Attic salt, and the humours of Donnybrook

---

4 We have here a version – perhaps even the origin – of the old Irish anecdote about the
   editorial in the *Skibbereen Eagle* which declared that the newspaper was keeping a close
   eye on the Tsar, or in another version on the Treaty of Versailles.

wed to the glories of Marathon' (p. 66).Or as another commentator has it, 'a piquant mixture of toryism, classicism, sarcasm and punch'.[5] Mahony, in short, is the very essence of carnival, with his abrupt lurchings from the erudite to the everyday, from pokerfaced pedantry to knockabout humour. In his essay 'The Painter, Barry', the Cork artist James Barry, painting at dead of night in the Vatican for fear (significantly enough) of snooping would-be plagiarists, is disturbed by a shadowy figure who, once wrestled to the ground, turns out to be the pope.[6] The two then proceed to conduct a learned conversation. Dinnertable conversation, of which there is much in Mahony's writing as well as in his life, is itself a carnivalesque mode, combining the intellectual and biological, semantic and somatic, while exploiting the comic tension between the two.[7]

Mahony, who was kicked out of the Clongowes seminary because of a gargantuan bash which got grotesquely out of hand, was never actually suspended from the priesthood – he was, as his editor Blanchard Jerrold remarks, 'a halfpay soldier of the Church, minus the half pay'.[8] Though he was a pious rightwing Catholic, his notions of temperance, as a friend put it with exquisite diplomacy, were 'too liberal for the Church'.[9] Ironically, however, he was a close friend of Father Mathew, commissioned a bust of the friar, and was commended by Mathew for the selfless courage he displayed while attending the poor as a young curate during the Cork cholera epidemic of 1832. As Mahony himself commented of his priestly status, he flirted openly with all nine Muses, since his vow of celibacy prevented him from forming a permanent liaison with any one of them. He was a bohemian backwoodsman who moved with aplomb from Horace to claret, a polyglot of enormous erudition who seemed with deliberate perversity to trivialise his own talents and cultivate an assiduous hackery.

In carnivalesque mode, Mahony deranges the proportions between central and peripheral, with a multifunctional style of writing like 'the proboscis of an elephant, that can with equal ease shift an obelisk and crack a nut' (p. 33). His art, so he informs us, is 'to magnify what is little, and to fling a dash of the sublime into a two-penny-post-communication' (p. 134); and this upending of literary hierarchies, this scrambling of the mighty and the myopic, can be seen as the aberrant colonial's smack at the literary categories of the metropolis.

---

5 Quoted in Ethel Mannin, *Two Studies in Integrity* (London, n.d.), p. 149.
6 Mahony might have been influenced here by Samuel Ferguson's knockabout piece 'Father Tom and the Pope' (*Blackwood's Magazine*, May 1838), which Yeats misattributed to William Maginn. See Peter Denman, *Samuel Ferguson: The Literary Achievement* (Gerrards Cross, 1990), p. 53.
7 There is today a Father Prout restaurant in Cork's Watergrasshill.
8 *The Final Reliques of Father Prout*, ed. Blanchard Jerrold (London, 1876), preface. Jerrold was the son of Mahony's friend Douglas Jerrold, editor of *Punch*.
9 Mannin, *Two Studies in Integrity*, p. 150.

Indeed he and William Maginn were such superlative hacks that they seemed
to raise that lowly status to the second power, and so to transcend it. Like
Oscar Wilde, Mahony is a major kind of minor writer, so doggedly, brilliantly
peripheral that he ends up troubling the very distinction between that and
centrality, as one might claim that the O'Connellite politics of his day did in
their own way too. There is a cross-grained, perverse streak in his writings, as
in those of Maginn,[10] which is evident elsewhere in Irish letters, and which is
closely linked to colonial eccentricity.

The line between the trivial and the substantial, then, is as hair-thin for
Prout as the border between madness and sanity, or drunkenness and sobriety.
He has some Foucauldian reflections on madness in the case of Swift, or
should one say Swiftian reflections, musing that the frontier between the sane
and the crazed is utterly indeterminate, not least for want of a 'really solid sen-
sible man' to act as a norm by which to measure deviations. In similar spirit, he
is fascinated by the precise metaphysical point at which sobriety passes over
into inebriation. As far as authenticity goes, was Mahony himself entitled to be
called 'Father', suspended as he was in some limbo between orgy and ordina-
tion? His very existence was liminal, his authority undecidable, his identity
aporetic. The whole odious, gimcrack world of Benthamism and Whiggery
struck him as hollow, parasitic, entirely intertextual: 'all I read now', writes
Prout, 'strikes me as but a new version of what I have read somewhere before
… I'm sick of hashed-up works' (p. 137). This of course is pretty rich, coming
as it does from a master plagiarist whose whole selfhood is merely a recycled
version of a derivative fiction. As with the practice of anti-plagiarism, the Tory
Prout deplores the death of authenticity at the very instant that he saps away at
the whole illusion of it. Fearful less forged Prout papers, or a 'false paper currency', might begin to circulate, his 'editor' Oliver Yorke solemnly gives notice
to his readers that 'no "Prout paper" is the *real* thing unless with label signed
"OLIVER YORKE"' (p. 232). We are not told how we are to determine whether
this signature itself is forged or genuine. One is reminded of the man in
Ludwig Wittgenstein's *Philosophical Investigations* who bought extra copies of
the morning newspaper in order to assure himself that what the first copy said
was true. What, in any case, is an original signature, since a signature can be
authentic only by virtue of being a repetition? That a piece of writing can be
fraudulently detached from its authorial source is constitutive of the act of
writing, for both Jacques Derrida and Andrew Prout: 'nothing so truly serves a
book', as the latter (though it could be the former) remarks, 'as the writer's
removal from the sphere or hemisphere of his readers' (p. x).

---

10 Maginn remarks himself how he is accused by some of 'maintaining always the untenable side of any question', just to demonstrate his logical dexterity (*Works* [New York,
   1856], vol. iii, p. 155).

Enraged that Thomas Moore ('this Anacreontic little chap') has accused Henry O'Brien of plagiarism in his study of Irish round towers,[11] Prout turns the charge back on Moore himself, a detestable self-publicising Whig in any case in Mahony's eyes. He does so by himself composing the French troubadour ballads of which, so he maintains, Moore's *Irish Melodies* are imitations, thus constituting them as a brand of 'petty larceny'. For good measure, he also arraigns Moore for having transmogrified his own 'Bells of Shandon' into his 'Evening Bells', and claims that some lines from Moore's 'Lalla Rookh' originally appeared in the Mogul language over the audience chamber of the king of Delhi. As it happens, Prout's own anti-plagiarising tactics are themselves plagiarised: he derives them, as he admits, from a French Jesuit who held that Horace's odes were written by a twelfth-century Benedictine monk. Generously enough, however, he acknowledges that some of Moore's 'translations' are very nearly as fine as the originals. The real-life Mahony, if that is not too strong an epithet, finds his fictional equivalent in the literary dilettante Joe Atlee of Charles Lever's novel *Lord Kilgobbin*, whose delight is 'to write Greek versions of a poem that might attach the mark of plagiarism to Tennyson, or show, by a Scandinavian lyric, how the laureate has been poaching from the Norsemen' (chapter 4). With Atlee, an Irish nationalist of sorts, this textual dialogism is turned against the most revered figure of the English literary pantheon.

The poet Béranger's father was a tailor, so Prout informs us, whereas Tom Moore's 'juvenile associations were of a grocer sort' (p. 259) – the reason why his compositions, with their 'mock-turtle pathos', are so highly spiced. This kind of word-play is second nature to Mahony, who likes to pronounce the word 'morale' as 'more ale', claims that 'Jupiter' is a corruption of 'Jew Peter', ruminates on the female root of the name of a fish ('Ann Chovy'), and finds in the Latin *dignitate* an inescapable echo of 'diggin' taties'. Etymology concerns the exchange-value of words, and one of Mahony's most abiding metaphors is that of exchange-value/commerce/translation, a constant analogising of signs and commodities. This, in its own muted way, is a carnivalesque tactic, deflating the idealist pretensions of the spirit in Swiftian style by stressing its kinship with humdrum material life. It is also an appropriate metaphor (literally: transport, traffic) for one who sells words as commodities on the metropolitan market.

It is no wonder that the materiality of the signifier should have been a popular theoretical doctrine on Grub Street. Both Mahony and Maginn were fascinated by the material circulation of texts, the happenstance of literary transmission and reception. Translation, like the trade between colony and metropolis, involves a sort of unequal exchange, 'the interchange in vocabulary showing at times even a balance in favour of the substitute (language), as happens in the ordinary course of barter on the markets of the world' (p. v). (One

---

11 There are some comments on this controversy, and on Prout's part in it, in Joep Leerssen, *Remembrance and Imagination* (Cork, 1996), pp. 121-6.

is reminded that for the poet Mangan the link between commerce and translation could be embarrassingly direct: he occasionally translated on the spot for
cash in John O'Daly's shop in Dublin.)[12] There can be no exact translation, so
Prout maintains: 'the *tradottore* differs from the *traditore* only by a syllable' (p.
396), ringing a variation on the familiar Irish cognates of tradition, translation
and treason. The Irish, one might say, are a kind of translation or mimicry of
their colonial masters, but the line between this and political treachery is never
well-defined. All translation for Prout is a kind of false etymologising, just as all
tradition is a sort of illegitimacy and all meaning contaminated. As he stoically
puts it, 'there is ever a cankerworm in the rose; a dactyl is sure to be mixed up
with a spondee in the poetry of life' (p. 7).

As a cosmopolitan conservative, Prout is in favour of intellectual free trade
but commercial protectionism, a universality of the spirit but a nationalism of
the economy; and this, one might note, was a fairly unique position in the
Ireland of his day, offensive at once to Irish cultural nationalism and British
political economy. His translations are a way of 'promoting the interchange of
national commodities': by translating from the French he has 'enriched England
at the expense of her rival, and engrafted on her literature the choicest products
of Gallic culture', so that the inhabitants of these islands may now whistle his
'Songs of France' 'duty free', in their native language (pp. 201-2). In translating
Homer, Alexander Pope 'works the mineral ores of Greece with the abundant
resources of English capital' (p. 395). William Maginn writes in his turn of translation as a kind of imperialism, admiring the poet who 'having explored the
mines of foreign intellectual ore, devotes himself to the glorious task of enriching his country's treasure of words and thoughts – HER LANGUAGE – with the
brightest and the rarest gems, the diamonds which his own hands have raked
from their native beds, and washed in the streams of Helicon'.[13]

Maginn approvingly quotes from one of Pope's letters which argues that 'A
mutual commerce makes poetry flourish; but then poets, like merchants,
should repay with something of their own what they have taken from others'.[14] Translation, in other words, is at once purchase and sale: by extending
your own language with a foreign engraftment, you enrich the translated language too, disclose a depth within it, so that your profit can seem like payment.
Dryden, claims Maginn, is right to hold, in his *Essay on Dramatic Poesie*, that
Ben Jonson 'invades authors like a monarch, and what would be theft in other
poets, is only victory in him'. It is a kind of genius which according to Maginn
'does but assert its own prerogative in rendering the intelligence of past ages
tributary to its success'[15] – an excellent résumé of anti-plagiarist practice. The

12 See C.P. Meehan (ed.), *Poets and Poetry of Munster* (Dublin, 1906), p. xxv.
13 William Maginn, *Miscellaneous Writings* (New York, 1857), vol. v, p. 145.
14 Ibid., p. 146.
15 Ibid., p. 132.

problem lies in the undecidable distinction between this form of 'creative' borrowing and the petty pilfering of a Moore, who, Maginn believes, says nothing
which has not been said before but does not say it half so well.[16] When does
inspirational influence become plain theft? Perhaps, Maginn considers, genuine
imitation consists in so mixing the gold of the ancients with one's modern
materials that the difference between them disappears; but how is this not just
to claim that the finest poem is the most deviously derivative, the most cun-
ningly plagiaristic? The anti-Whig conservative in Maginn wishes to enforce a
distinction between authentic and inauthentic which his own metaphors
unwittingly deconstruct.

Mahony, who rambled aimlessly as far as Asia Minor, rejects all provincial-
ism of the mind in the name of exchange, hybridity, cosmopolitan cross-breed-
ing; yet he denounces any economic version of such spiritual *laissez-faire* as
injurious to the poor and unprotected. Free trade, then, is for him just a cultural trope; but since Mahony, along with Maginn, no doubt as a stout Tory
endorses imperialism as a fact as well as a literary strategy, this would not be
wholly compatible with the economic protectionism he also favours. The distinction can only be kept in place by insisting on the purely figurative force of
one of its terms (imperialism), which threatens nonetheless to intrude its 'liter-
al' meaning and so to undercut the protectionist case. Mahony, in any case, is
like his colleague vehemently opposed to economic *laissez-faire*: if you're going
to dismantle protective commercial barriers, why not, he enquires, do away
with the quarantine laws while you're at it and permit a free trade in plague?

Moore steals supposedly from the French troubadours, but there are built-
in security devices against such expropriation: 'Unfortunately for such
attempts, the lays of the Norman troubadours, like the Government rope in
the dock-yard at Portsmouth, have in their texture a certain twist by which
they are recognised when they get into the possession of thieves' (p. 247).
Writers who pillage foreign produce are really smugglers, as opposed to those
who pay the customary duty of acknowledgement. The god Mercury derives
his name from *merx* or merchandise,[17] and he is also of course, so Prout
reminds us, the god of wit, messages, eloquence, mediation, highways, commerce, diplomacy, mobility, secrets, translation, interpretation – and robbers.[18]
(He might have added: borders.) Mahony's own work is entirely mercurial and
hermetic – though he notes the oddness of this deity of locomotion and rapid-
ity being also the protector of fixtures, milestones, permanence, and – an
unfortunate phrase for a cleric – 'monumental erections' (p. 401).

16 See his essay 'Poetical Plagiaries: Thomas Moore', *Works*, vol. v, p. 145. Moore considered
    challenging Maginn to a duel over this article.
17 Perhaps another false etymology; the point is evidently controversial.
18 Susan Mitchell describes George Moore as 'a born literary bandit' (*George Moore*
    [Dublin, 1916], p. 103).

Maginn also observes that Mercury, said to be the inventor of written characters, was the patron of thieves, and explains this connection mock-pedantically by claiming that Mercury was the prototype of Moses, also associated with letters and in Egyptian eyes a thief . 'He who could make a pun would pick a pocket', he quotes Dr Johnson as proclaiming.[19] As a conservative quick-change artist or antiquarian modernist, however, Mahony resolves this apparent conflict of change and conservation in his own person. Like Maginn, he was the best sort of Tory, the Johnsonian variety who believes that Whiggish liberalism will simply injure the poor. O'Connell – the 'bog-trotter of Derrynane' – was his predictable *bête noire*, a man who, so he scathingly remarks, never put a Latin hexameter together in his life. In his late reports from Italy for Dickens's *Daily News*, in which the land of Sardinia figures as a thinly veiled allegory of Ireland, O'Connell appears as Dandelone, the champion of 'immaculate emancipation', and Thomas Moore as Thomaso il Moro.[20] The Whigs are 'Perukes', and the Irish Famine the great chestnut rot. But Mahony's anti-O'Connellite animus is less red-neck reaction than the old canard that the Liberator was ripping off the poor.

Indeed in his own tongue-in-cheek or tongue-in-glass way, Mahony was a kind of nationalist. His 'Poetical Epistle from Father Prout to Boz' admires Dickens's concern for the poor but urges him also to 'Think of the poor / On t'other shore, / Poor who, unheeded, perish, / By squires despoiled, by "patriots" gulled, / I mean the starving Irish'.[21] His 'Apology for Lent' commends the 'Celtic and Eastern races' (which mysteriously includes Greeks, Arabs and Irish) for the lightness of their diet, in contrast to the Teutonic craving for heavy meat, or the 'gross, carcase-eating propensities of John Bull' (p. 16). 'We are in truth a most abstemious race' (p. 25), he comments without twitching an eyebrow, casually poking his finger through an anti-Irish stereotype. When he adds later that the Irish are 'the most ill-fed people on the face of the globe' (p. 25), one registers the political animus lurking behind the bland iconoclasm. It is curious, Prout reflects, that no monument exists to that demographic hero Sir Walter Raleigh, who by importing the potato has fed more families and provided a greater impulse to procreation than any other benefactor of humanity.

What Prout is up to in this essay, in fact, is a kind of dietary theory of history,[22] one centred like so much from Swift to Samuel Beckett on the body, and

---

19 Maginn, *Miscellaneous Writings*, vol. v, p. 223.

20 See, for Mahony's correspondence from Rome and Paris, *The Final Reliques of Father Prout*. Like James Joyce, Mahony when abroad was interested in what was afoot in Ireland, and was proud of the tombs of the fled earls O'Donnell and O'Neill in Rome, which John Hogan took it upon himself to repair.

21 *Final Reliques*, p. 234. If one is to judge by Dickens's satirical portrait in *Bleak House* of Mrs Jellyby, busy with overseas charity but careless of want at home, he would not perhaps have responded to this appeal with wholehearted enthusiasm.

22 As opposed to the tobacco theory of history expounded in 'A Tavern in the Town', in James Stephens's *Here Are Ladies* (London, 1913). Stephens speculates that our ancestors'

the starving body at that. Ancient Rome having 'burst of its own plethory', it was fasting which, in a kind of culinary version of the Freudian doctrine of sexual sublimation, 'originated civilisation and commerce'. This theory of the rise of an ascetic anti-materialism is, like Freud's, a thoroughly materialist one. 'In the progress of maritime industry along the shores of southern, and subsequently northern Europe', Prout maintains, 'we find a love for freedom to grow up with a fondness for fish' (p. 20). Indeed it is Lent, of all things, which cements the union between Britain and Ireland, since if fasting were abolished in Ireland the natives would eat rather than export their meat, and Repeal of the union would quickly follow. Conversely, were Lent to be revived in England, the consequent fall in the price of cattle and the flourishing of the fishing industry would 'eventually harmonise the jarring interests of agriculture and manufacturing industry' (p. 24). Mahony adds for good measure a few notes on the pig-based parallel betwen the Irish and the Israelites: in both cultures the pig is a sacred object, and the mass export of the creatures from Ireland resembles nothing quite so much as the rush to the sea of the Gadarene swine. Shortly after these musings, Prout expires on Shrove Tuesday, having consumed a particularly indigestible pancake.

Prout describes British rule in Ireland as 'oppressive', and is not slow to sing the praises of Irish history. In 'A Plea for Pilgrimages', he lectures Sir Walter Scott, who has come to kiss the Blarney stone, on that object's venerable pedigree. It was, so he claims, brought to Cork by the Phoenicians, who cleared the pillars of Hercules and landed with it in the Cove of Cork. (Carthage, he informs us, is 'Tarshish' in Hebrew, which means 'valuable stone'.) The Blarney stone beggars all rivals: 'the long-sought *lapis philosophorum*, compared with this jewel, dwindles into insignificance' (p. 50), along with the Luxor obelisk, the treaty-stone of Limerick and the Elgin marbles. Without the eloquence and 'splendid effrontery' which it affords, how, he asks, could Dan O'Connell have come to con the world? But Irish history extends back still further: the Nile was so named after the tribe of O'Neils, its aboriginal inhabitants, who threw up a few pyramids before they set sail for Ireland. The poet Richard Milliken's 'The Groves of Blarney', so Prout has ascertained through his researches, was originally an ancient Greek lyric, and the industrious cleric has compared Greek, Latin, Norman-French and Irish manuscript versions of the poem, all of which, apart from the Irish, he duly gives us, while rejecting as spurious the Arabic, Armenian and Chaldaic fragments which survive.[23] Moreover, since it

---

lack of pockets, and consequently of the ability to carry around tobacco, was responsible for their diverting their energies into wars, revolutions and the like. He also reflects that what is unique to the human animal is brewing and shaving. There is much of Mahony's pokerfaced mock-erudition in Stephens's soberly expounded metaphysical fantasies.

23 W.J. Mc Cormack has some illuminating comments on the political subtext of Milliken's poem in *The Field Day Anthology of Irish Writing* (Derry, 1991), vol. i, p. 1102. 'Groves', he

was the Irish monks of Bobbio who counselled Dante not to write his *Divine Comedy* in Latin,[24] the Irish can take credit for the whole of Italian literature.

Mahony's antiquarianism is of course a send-up, but his backward glance is also genuine conservative nostalgia. Is the homesickness of 'The Bells of Shandon', with its ritual denigration of foreign exotica in favour of provincial Cork, straight, tongue-in-cheek or poised more likely at some undecidable in-between?[25] Bakhtinian revellers like Mahony and Maginn were in one sense free cosmopolitan spirits, heretically at odds with a chauvinist, parochial culture, their writing shamelessly mongrelised and macaronic in a way which constitutes a silent rebuke to the linguistic purism of a narrowly conceived Irish nationalism. But like the great nationless modernists who were to follow them, they paid the price of this deracination too, forced to cobble together styles, forms and idioms in the absence of a vigorous set of native English-language traditions. They are drudges, parodists and *bricoleurs* adrift between cultures, shuttling from one (sometimes) invented tongue to another, gifted wastrels who squander their extraordinary philological talents on poems in praise of port, wicked burlesques of Wordsworth and a pathology of punning.

This inbred, fragmentary form of writing then gives off all the resonance of a directionless, self-involved colonial society, not least in its virulent literary sectarianism. Though Prout loftily proclaims that there is no place for religious or political differences in the realm of Parnassus, he also characterises the *Edinburgh Review* as 'that ricketty go-cart of drivelling dotage' (p. 163), and brutally traduces a friend in print. He also writes that Attila king of the Huns, and Leigh Hunt king of the Cockneys, have both spread 'havoc and consternation' in Italy (p. 318). William Maginn almost lost his life for writing a vicious review, called Sheridan a 'buffoon' and Macaulay a quack and moral beggar. As with the great modernists, one needs to recall the pains of exile as well as the pleasures of the polyglottic, the oppressive as well as emancipatory aspect of colonial identities which are unstable, self-fashioning, intertextual. Mahony, like Wilde, died as a lonely expatriate in Paris. He was a potentially major writer striving very hard to become a minor one, and brilliantly succeeded. [26]

suggests, may be a family name. Mahony's father, a prosperous wool merchant, moved his factory to Blarney from Cork. Prout himself plans a university of Blarney, which would combine 'cultivated fun and the genial development of national acuteness' (p. 65).

24 There is apparently no evidence for this claim.

25 The disastrous effects of taking the poem entirely straight are betrayed in the earnest academicist comments of Cleanth Brooks and Robert Penn Warren in their *Understanding Poetry* (New York, 1938), pp. 133-6. I am grateful to Dr Tadhg Foley for this reference.

26 The protagonist of Graham Greene's *Travels with my Aunt* declares that he would have been content to be a poet in a quite humble station, like 'an English Mahony'.

Between Captain Rock and a Hard Place:
Art and Agrarian Insurgency

LUKE GIBBONS

> [Thomas Moore's *Captain Rock* was] to the
> struggle for Catholic Emancipation what *Uncle
> Tom's Cabin* was to the abolition of slavery.
>
> Daniel O'Connell

Writing about the difficulties in representing Irish life to polite sensibilities in
the metropolitan centre, a reviewer of the exhibition at the Royal Academy in
1834 commented that:

> It is true that, in depicting an Irish scene, a little wildness is necessary,
> for that facetious and singular people can do nothing – nay, not even
> woo a lass, or drink a glass of liquor – like the staid and philosophic
> English. So much the better for the painter or the novelist ...[1]

The implication here is that the artist comes to Ireland like an explorer to an
unknown territory, for no one has been there beforehand to raise the benight-
ed culture to the level of artistic representation. This presents a number of
problems at the outset, for according to the restricted codes of the late eighteenth or early nineteenth-century aesthetics, the further art ventures beyond
the pale of propriety, or reaches down the social scale, the greater its detach-
ment from those it represents. It was one thing for the lower orders, or 'lesser
races', to be noticed by the discerning eye of the artist: but for the subaltern to
have access to the means of representation, or to gain control of their own self-
images, was out of the question. For this reason, as Hugh Honour has
observed, the lofty ideal of reconciling artistic and political liberty, which
inspired so many of the leading figures in European Romanticism, was inherently contradictory. The main beneficiaries of extending the remit of art to
include hitherto objectionable or disreputable social strata were the artists
themselves, rather than those they aspired to represent:

---

1 'The Exhibition at the Royal Academy' (Second Notice), *The Athenaeum*, no. 342, 17
  May 1834, p. 378.

> The Romantic artist was primarily concerned with his own liberty –
> his freedom to express his genius, as much as his emancipation from the
> dictates of academies and the whims of patrons. Paradoxically, however,
> he achieved this less frequently in representations of subjects with polit-
> ical meanings than in those which had none – a scene of his own
> choice from literature or history, a portrait, a landscape or even a still-
> life ... [and] his obsession with his own work and personality and
> uniqueness was eventually to drive him to take refuge in the doctrine of
> *l'art pour l'art*.[2]

The democratization of artistic vision thus had the result of distancing the artist
further from society, accentuating the difference between those who, in Edward
Said's words, had permission to narrate, and those who were increasingly
deprived of the right to represent themselves, or to speak in their own voice.[3]

It is in the context of bridging this gulf, of preventing a fatal dissociation of
artistic and political liberty, that the utopian prospect presented itself to the
romantic imagination of the artist as outcast, or, conversely, of the dispossessed
themselves acquiring the tools of the trade, and achieving artistic expression. In
1824, two remarkable works were published by Irish writers which addressed
different variations on these themes, Lady Morgan's *The Life and Times of Salvator
Rosa* and Thomas Moore's *Memoirs of Captain Rock*. In the former, the artist
turns bandit: in the latter, the bandit becomes an artist. The publication of both
works incurred considerable political risks, drawing opprobrium from the dominant political factions of the day, but in the end they undermine their imaginary
transgressions, displacing the voices that lent them their radical appeal.

Lady Morgan's romantic biography of Salvator Rosa followed the *succès de
scandale* of her incendiary two-volume work on Italy, published in 1821. This
latter work, which indicted the nepotism and depravity of the petty absolutist
regimes in Italy, also condemned the corruption of the British government
which contrived to suppress the spirit of liberty in Italy. It was this attack on
British foreign policy which drew the wrath of reviewers in leading conservative organs such as the *Edinburgh Magazine*, leading to equally vehement replies
from the author. The book was also banned by both the papal and Austrian
authorities, with copies being seized and burned in Turin, and in 1824, the
Emperor took the grand step of issuing a decree which prohibited Lady
Morgan from visiting his dominions.[4] When, in her biography of Salvator, the

---

2 Hugh Honour, *Romanticism* (London, 1981), p. 244.
3 For a sustained analysis of the silencing, and silences, of subaltern cultures, see Gayatri
   Chakravorty Spivak, 'Can the Subaltern Speak?' in Cary Nelson and Lawrence Gross-
   berg (eds), *Marxism and the Interpretation of Culture* (London, 1988).
4 Lionel Stevenson, *The Wild Irish Girl: The Life of Sydney Owenson, Lady Morgan 1776-1859*
   (London, 1936), pp. 225-9.

turbulent artist is depicted as going over to the side of banditti and rebels in their struggles against injustice, it is difficult not to suspect that her hero is taking on many of the traits ascribed to romantic outcasts in her own Irish novels. Salvator, and the banditti he fell in with, were a thorn in the side of the Italian authorities, but Lady Morgan never omits an opportunity to draw analogies between Ireland and Italy, comparing Salvator to Ossian and even to O'Carolan, the last of the Irish bards, in the courtesy and respect they both received from liberal patrons.[5]

Yet, as Hugh Honour observed, the logic of this romantic cult of banditti is that the sympathies of the writer lie ultimately with the artist rather than with the low life in which he sought refuge. Commenting on the bold imagination and 'deep sagacious study of Nature' evident in Salvator's early work, Lady Morgan writes that:

> His 'Robber Chief' was always distinguishable from the ruffians he led, less by his habits than by those distinctions which high breeding on the human, as on the brute subject, rarely fails to impress ... A splendid illustration of this remark lies before the author, as she writes, in an etching of Salvator's. It is a single figure, of a Captain of Banditti. He is alone, near a rock; his hair floating wildly on the wind, his countenance marked by that deep melancholy, that pensive and meditative sadness, which the turbulent remorse of vulgar minds never produces.[6]

The cost of elevating the bandit to the solitary status of the artist is to erase entirely the social milieu which gave popular legitimacy to brigandage, and, indeed, to eliminate the collective sense of purpose of the bandits themselves. As Ranajit Guha explains, this attempt to divest peasant insurgency of that 'praxis called rebellion' lends itself to 'metaphors assimilating peasant revolts to natural phenomena: they break out like thunder storms, heave like earthquakes, spread like wildfires, infect like epidemics. In other words, when the proverbial clod of earth turns, this is a matter to be explained in terms of natural history'. Even when human explanations are advanced, they invariably tend to assume 'an identity of nature and culture, a hall-mark, presumably of a very low state of civilization' attained by the insurgents.[7]

---

5   Lady Morgan, *The Life and Times of Salvator Rosa*, vol. ii (London, 1824), p. 33. The thinly veiled comparison between Ireland and Naples pervades the work: 'In the year 1647, the kingdom of Naples exhibited a spectacle of rapacity and misrule in government, and of misery in the people, which even unhappy Ireland, in her worst days, has perhaps never surpassed' (vol. i, p. 265). See also vol. i, p. 391, and vol. ii, p. 147.

6   Ibid., vol. i, pp. 130-1.

7   Ranajit Guha, 'The Prose of Counter-Insurgency', in Ranajit Guha and Gayatri Chakravorty Spivak (eds), *Selected Subaltern Studies* (New York, 1988), p. 46. This univer-

Portrait of the Outlaw as a Young Artist

From this point of view, the choice of the sobriquet 'Captain Rock' for the most notorious insurgent movement in nineteenth-century Ireland seems ill-advised, but as if with this in mind, the fictive narrator of Thomas Moore's *Memoirs of Captain Rock* moves quickly to correct any misunderstanding of the group's political and ideological leanings:

> With respect to the origin of the family name, ROCK, antiquarians and etymologists are a good deal puzzled. An idea exists in certain quarters that the letters of which it is composed are merely initials, and contain a prophetic announcement of the high destiny that awaits, at sometime or other, that celebrated gentleman, Mr Roger O'Connor, being, as they fill up the initials, the following awful words, – R oger O C onnor, K ing! Others perceive in the name an indication of the design of the Papists to establish their own religion in Ireland, through the instrumentality of Captain ROCK, and quote in support of this conjecture the sacred text – 'On this *Rock* I will build my church'.[8]

For good measure, another apocryphal explanation is thrown in, connecting the movement to the alleged Semitic or Phoenician origins of the Irish through the Stone of Jacob which was brought to Ireland from Egypt before the time of Moses. This is now, we are told, under the coronation chair in Westminster Abbey, but its Irish provenance cannot be doubted since 'it is said to make a remarkable noise when any of the true descendants of Milesius sit upon it'! Notwithstanding the irreverent and whimsical tone, Moore's Captain Rock has run together in his own name three of the forces designed to strike fear in the heart of the Protestant Ascendancy: the Catholic cause in its most sectarian and millenarian forms; republicanism, of the maverick variety associated with the eccentric Roger O'Connor, brother of the leading United Irishman, Arthur, but also in the idiosyncratic form in which it percolated through popular culture; and finally, at a more recondite level, the Gaelic tradition in its distinctively anti-colonial Phoenician variant, associated also with

---

salizing thrust, removing all specific consideration of time and place, is, no doubt, that which led Sir Joshua Reynolds to praise the congruence between man and nature in Salvator's landscapes: 'What is most to be admired in him is the perfect correspondence which he observed between the subjects which he chose and his manner of treating them. Everything is of a piece: his Rocks, Trees, Sky, even to his handling, have the same rude and wild character which animates his figures' ('Discourse V', *Discourses on Art* [London, n.d.], p. 62).

8 [Thomas Moore], *Memoirs of Captain Rock, the Celebrated Irish Chieftain, with Some Account of his Ancestors, Written by Himself* (London, 1824), p. 6. Subsequent references parenthetically in text.

leading Catholic propagandists and, of course, with Roger O'Connor's own deranged foray into antiquarianism, *The Chronicles of Eri*, published in 1822.

In terms of its immediate causes, the Rockite movement which swept Munster in the early 1820s was motivated by economic issues having to do, firstly, with the agricultural crisis precipitated by the ending of the Napoleonic wars, and, secondly, with perceived injustices in the exaction of tithes for the Protestant church.[9] Religious grievances gained in intensity due to the refusal to grant Catholic emancipation as a trade-off for the Union, but acquired a lethal millenarian dimension as a result of the widespread influence of what came to be known as Pastorini's prophecies following the calamitous famine and typhus epidemic of 1817.[10] The notorious eighth chapter of Pastorini's prophecies, which predicted an apocalyptic destruction of the Protestant Ascendancy by 1825, was so dirtied by reading, presumably at the hands of menials, in one inn visited by a traveller that it was scarcely legible, and through hand-bills, ballads and other ephemeral matter, the prophecies circulated throughout Munster in tandem with the upsurge in Rockite activity.[11]

9 According to Joseph Lee, the immediate cause of the unrest of 1821-3 was a wave of evictions on the Courtney estate in Limerick, which occurred against a backdrop of potato crop failure and 25 to 30 per cent falls in grain prices ('The Ribbonmen', in T. Desmond Williams [ed.], *Secret Societies in Ireland* [Dublin, 1973], p. 27). Daniel O'Connell also mentions the enforcement of the practice of economic distrain, which prevented the peasantry from having access to their own subsistence crops such as the potato. (See Thomas Moore's report of his conversation with O'Connell, 11 August 1823 in *The Journal of Thomas Moore*, ed. Wilfred S. Dowden, vol. ii [Newark, 1984], p. 67.)

10 The so-called Pastorini prophecies were a turgid series of commentaries on the Book of Revelation, entitled *The General History of the Christian Church from her Birth to her Final Triumphant State in Heaven, Chiefly Deduced from the Apocalypse of St John the Apostle.* They were written by the Catholic bishop, Charles Walmesley (1722-97), vicar apostolic for the western district of England, under the pen-name 'Signor Pastorini', and first published in 1771. They predicted that Protestants would be wiped out in 1825, thus heralding the Second Coming. Pastorini's prophecies appeared in a Dublin edition as early as 1790, and were blamed by Richard Musgrave for stoking the embers that ignited in the 1798 rebellion. They acquired a new lease of life during the agricultural slump which followed the Napoleonic wars, attaining almost fever pitch in the years leading up to 1825 in Ireland. See James S. Donnelly, Jr., 'Propagating the Cause of the United Irishmen', *Studies*, lxix, 273 (1980), and 'Pastorini and Captain Rock: Millenarianism and Sectarianism in the Rockite Movement of 1821-4', in Samuel Clark and James S. Donnelly, Jr. (eds), *Irish Peasants: Violence and Political Unrest 1780-1914* (Dublin, 1983).

11 The date of Armageddon for the Protestant population varied from 1821 to 1825, but, in a rebuke to those sceptics who doubted the accuracy of the prophecies after they were found wanting in 1825, Charlotte Elizabeth, in her proselytizing novel *The Rockite* [1832], warned that the end was indeed nigh, for the real day of reckoning was rather in 1829: 'It is worthy of remark, that among the predictions of the noted Pastorini, he fixed the 14th day of April, 1829, for the first act towards the destruction of Protestantism. Let those who remember that on the 13th of April, 1829, the royal assent was given to the eventful Bill [i.e. Catholic Emancipation], say what inducement the votaries of Pastorini

The unrest reached proportions where it was declared by the authorities to be 'nothing short of rebellion', and an indication of the reprisals visited upon the insurgents may be deduced from the grim proceedings of one trial in February, 1823, in which thirty-six capital convictions were handed down, more than one in ten of the total number committed for trial.[12]

This was the political climate in Ireland when Thomas Moore returned in July 1823 on the visit that prompted his writing of the fictive *Memoirs of Captain Rock*. As soon as he arrived in Dublin, Moore called upon Lady Morgan whom, he noted, 'is just about to publish a life of Salvator Rosa'.[13] Passing through Kerry en route to Killarney a few days later, Moore muses on Lord Bellamont's description of the Kerry landscape that might have come straight from Lady Morgan's life of Salvator: 'All acclivity and declivity, without the intervention of a single horizontal plane; the mountains all rock, and the men all savages'. That Moore's thoughts were preoccupied with a different kind of rock formation is clear from a following sentence where he mentions his discovery that the name of Captain Rock was reputed to be derived from Roger O'Connor's initials. Subsequent journal entries describing his stay at Killarney, and the scenic splendours of the renowned lakes, are punctuated by ruminations on the Rockite movement, which show a determination on his part to understand the sources of their grievances, and a questioning of the existing colonial stereotypes of agrarian insurgency. Visiting Ross Island and Inisfallen on the Lakes, he notes that 'Never was anything more beautiful', but instead of being entranced by nature, his attention is directed at 'the peasants that live on the opposite bank' who come over with fruit when strangers appear, 'their appearance, with their infants, stepping from rock to rock, across the cascade, highly picturesque'. Moore then reflects on the small acts of hospitality practised by even the poorest cottiers, which leads him to observe that the Rockite movement, instead of being involved in mindless destruction, may operate as a cohesive force in their localities, attempting to control inter-communal violence such as faction fights at fairs.[14]

This impression is reinforced when he meets O'Connell, who, responding to his enquiry 'on the state of intellect and education among the lower orders, said they were full of intelligence'. O'Connell recounted the instance of a recent trial in which he defended a common gardener named Hickey, 'a sort of

will here find to praise in their triumphant career' (*The Rockite: An Irish Story* [London, 1836], p. 263).

12 Galen Broeker, *Rural Disorder and Police Reform in Ireland, 1812-36* (London, 1970), pp. 132-6.

13 [Journal Entry], 28 July 1823; Moore, *Journal* , p. 657.

14 [Journal Entry], 8 August 1823; ibid., p. 665. For the important integrative effects of the Rockite movement in forging solidarity among the Catholic population on the eve of the Catholic Emancipation campaign, see the 'Introduction', in Clark and Donnelly, *Irish Peasants*, pp. 33-4.

Captain Rock' who 'always wore feathers to distinguish him'. When O'Connell was attempting to shake the credibility of the young boy who was the main witness against him, Hickey 'asked him not to persevere, as it was useless, and his mind was made up to suffer'. By the end of August, Moore decided to interrupt the life of Richard Brinsley Sheridan which he was working on, and embarked on background reading for a short book on Ireland. By early October this had taken shape as the memoirs of the fictive Captain Rock, and the work was published in April of the following year. Its publication, as Moore was pleased to observe, created a sensation, the first edition of the work selling out on the day of publication. The book went into five editions in 1824, and spawned a whole genre of 'Captain Rock' memoirs, including a run of a weekly newspaper allegedly published by the Captain in London;[15] Roger O'Connor's own *Letters to his Majesty, King George the Fourth, by Captain Rock* (1827);[16] another account detailing the Captain's visit to Rome,[17] and, not unexpectedly, a vehement counter-offensive from the Protestant side, Mortimer O'Sullivan's *Captain Rock Detected: or, the Origin and Character of the Recent Disturbances, and the Causes, both Moral and Political, of the Present Alarming Condition of the South and West of Ireland, Fully and Fairly Considered and Exposed: by a Munster Farmer* (1824).

In his classic study of 'The Prose of Counter Insurgency', Ranajit Guha notes that, almost without exception, primary or contemporary documentation concerning agrarian insurgency is official in character:

> Even when it incorporated statements emanating from 'the other side', from the insurgents or their allies for instance, as it often did by way of direct or indirect reporting in the body of official correspondence or even more characteristically as enclosures to the latter, this was done only as a part of an argument prompted by administrative concern.[18]

---

15 *Captain Rock in London, or the Chieftain's Weekly Gazette* ran from 1825 to 1827, as a propaganda sheet for the Catholic cause, purporting to continue the Captain's memoirs, attacking leading anti-Catholic propagandists such as Robert Southey. It was edited, and a large part of it written, by the Wexford-born writer and journalist, Michael J. Whitty, whose *Tales of Irish Life*, 2 vols (1824), was illustrated by Cruikshank, and subsequently translated into German. Annual collections of *Captain Rock in London* were also published in book form.

16 For a discussion of O'Connor, in keeping with the tone of his own forays into print, see Joep Leerssen, *Remembrance and Imagination: Patterns in the Historical and Literary Imagination of Ireland in the Nineteenth Century* (Cork, 1996), pp. 82-5. O'Connor's work is discussed in the context of a perceptive appraisal of Moore's *The Memoirs of Captain Rock*.

17 *Captain Rock in Rome, Written by Himself in the Capital of the Christian World* (London, 1833).

18 Guha, 'The Prose of Counter-Insurgency', pp. 47-8.

Moore's *Captain Rock* parodies this containment exercise, for the 'memoirs', in typical gothic fashion, fall into the hands of an evangelical Protestant, who is sent to Ireland to raise 'that unfortunate race from the darkness'. This framing narrative attempts to re-assert its authority at the end by recounting how the Captain was eventually arrested and deported in an old green coat worn by no less than Napper Tandy, but in fact the Captain himself has the last word in the form of letter from Cobh, which looks forward to a prosperous future for 'the ROCK dynasty'(p. 375) on account of continual government oppression.

The difficulties in establishing a framing narrative, ordering the disparate elements in a story or picture and subjecting them to a unified point of view, presented itself not simply as an aesthetic difficulty but as an intractable political problem for the authorities of the day.[19] In his inquiry into *Local Disturbances in Ireland*, published in 1836, the eminently rational George Cornewall Lewis makes an observation which is worth quoting at length:

> when men's interests impel them to use violent and illegal means, and to form secret combinations, in order to gain certain ends, we are not to suppose that those ends are always directly conceived, or that the purposes of the Whiteboy association are as clearly defined, for example, as those of a geological or an astronomical society. Men are often concerned in the working of a system, nay, they may even contribute to its development, without presenting clearly to their minds the objects at which they are aiming, or the rules by which they are guided. The happy combinations of genius, accompanied with an obscure consciousness of the end in view, have produced some of the most perfect creations of art and poetry. If Homer and Shakspeare [*sic*] could be raised from the dead as they were in life, they would probably give but an imperfect idea of the processes by which they arrived at the perfection of epic and dramatic poetry. How much less are we to expect from an illiterate Whiteboy, that he should be able to express the ends of his association in a neat and precise formula, that he should be able to define with logical accuracy the objects of an union which he had joined only from a vague instinct of self-preservation.[20]

19 According to Patrick O'Sullivan the instability of the narration is a shortcoming in the work: 'Throughout the book there are problems of tone. Often in the main text, it is not clear whether Moore speaks with his own voice, as it were, or in the character of Captain Rock. And in the footnotes it is not clear whether it is Moore, Rock or the Missionary editor who speaks' ('A Literary Difficulty in Explaining Ireland: Tom Moore and Captain Rock, 1824', in Roger Swift and Sheridan Gilley (eds), *The Irish in Britain, 1815-1939* [Savage, MD, 1989], p. 244). It could be argued, however, that such oscillation in the narrative voice(s) is precisely the 'literary difficulty' in explaining Ireland, or subjecting it to one authoritative point of view.

20 George Cornewall Lewis, *Local Disturbances in Ireland* [1836] (Cork, 1977), pp. 139-40.

In this extraordinary statement, Lewis is suggesting in effect that such coherence as an agrarian society possesses is not unlike that to be found in a work of art – a kind of emergent unity held in place by the process of creating the work, rather than the clarity and self-consciousness of 'identity', personal or national, promulgated by the enlightenment. But when this process is confounded, and the unity is unresolved or incomplete, the dynamics of identity remain inscrutable. This is not to say that there is no ordering intelligence at work: the difficulty is that it does not yield itself up to a detached observer, or to external forms of control.[21] That the problem ultimately lies with the spectator, rather than those involved in the process, is clear from Lewis's admonition that 'we must ... guard against an error, not infrequently committed, of attributing to insurgents a fixed design'. It is we who are unable to 'fix the design': it is in the insurgent's interest not to make it so transparent that it can be read off at will, particularly for the purposes of government surveillance or counter-insurgency.

The Agitated Eye: Art and Agrarian Unrest

For an example of a work in which these issues are contested at both an aesthetic and political level, we can turn to Daniel Maclise's remarkable painting *The Installation of Captain Rock*, first exhibited at the Royal Academy to uncomprehending reviews in 1834 (see Plate 1). Its departure from Salvator-type conventions of isolated banditti deriving their mandate from their rugged environment is clear from the staging of the installation in a ruined abbey, a material embodiment of history in the Irish popular imagination. This setting – soon to become a trope in nationalist iconography[22] – derives perhaps from the opening scene of Moore's *Captain Rock* where the narrator,

---

21 The detached observer need not, of course, be external: in the form of an 'impartial spectator', it recommended itself to Adam Smith as a model for a higher, inner self which was in a position to command the flux of passions and bodily appetites. The equivalent of this in an agrarian organization was the alleged existence of a ringleader, usually from a superior, educated social background, manipulating the impressionable lower orders behind the scenes. Patrick O'Sullivan identifies this as the trope of 'the man in the gig' which lent itself to the more paranoid accounts of agrarian or urban unrest given by the ruling elites. It surfaces in Ireland in the submission of Major George Warburton to the Parliamentary committee on the Rockite disturbances established in 1824, which reported 'a person sent from Dublin, who came in a gig from Limerick' to stir up what could possibly be described as the first 'rock gig' in Ireland. ('A Literary Difficulty in Explaining Ireland', p. 255).

22 A midnight ruin also provides the setting for 'The Ruin: A Fragment', a narrative within a narrative contained in Mortimer O'Sullivan's *Captain Rock Detected* – though, on this occasion, it is presented in a more sinister, sectarian light.

under the influence of 'some genial "Mountain dew"', sallies forth at midnight to visit 'the ruins of a celebrated abbey, which stand, picturesquely enough, on the banks of a river'. As he approaches the abbey 'a dark cloud happened to flit over the moon' and obscure the abbey, but passing through 'its great portal':

> [I] found myself all at once, to my astonishment and horror (the moon at that moment breaking out of a cloud) in the midst of some hundreds of awful looking persons – all arrayed in white shirts, and ranged in silent order on each side to receive me! This sight sobered me completely – I was ready to sink with terror – when a voice, which I could observe, proceed from a tall man with a plume of white feathers in his hat, said, sternly, 'Pass on' ... . [It] was not long before I learned, from his own lips, that I actually stood in the presence of the great CAPTAIN ROCK.[23]

That the ruins of an abbey in this context do not refer to the wear and tear of time in the diffuse, metaphysical sense of some romantic poetry, but to actual historical events, is perceived by the reviewer of the painting in *Fraser's Magazine*, who writes under the pseudonym 'Morgan Rattler': 'The scene is laid in a ruined abbey – a very common sight in the south of Ireland, thanks to the old Fitzgeralds, and Butlers, and the more recent labours of Cromwell and Ireton'.[24]

Raising the spectre of Cromwell brings together the twin legacies of the Protestant Reformation and colonial rule in Irish history, and infuses the Rockite movement, as depicted in the painting, with overt political and religious leanings, transforming it into a proto-nationalist organization. The religious overtones are evident in the setting itself, particularly in the grim reaper-like figure of the monk, holding a crucifix, who comes to officiate at the wake of the dead insurgent leader. Related to both colonial and religious concerns is the demotic hedge schoolmaster, haranguing the assembly with a newspaper, or some other form of printed matter, protruding from his pocket. He is being listened to with reverential awe by an impressionable neophyte who is carrying some books, and if we revert to Moore's *Captain Rock*, it is likely that these edi-

---

23 Moore, *Memoirs of Captain Rock*, pp. xi–xii. As a footnote indicates, the head-dress refers to 'Hickey, a pseudo Captain Rock who was hanged last Summer at Cork, [and who] appears to have generally worn feathers on his nightly expeditions' (p. xii) – information derived, as we have noted above, from Moore's conversation with Daniel O'Connell on his visit to Kerry (see *Journal*, 11 August 1823, p. 667).

24 'Morgan Rattler', 'Some Passages on a Visit to the Exhibition of the Royal Academy', *Fraser's Magazine*, x, no. 55 (July 1834), p. 118. Subsequent references parenthetically in text.

Plate 1 Daniel Maclise, *The Installation of Captain Rock*

fying texts include *Pastorini's Prophecies* and, equally ominous for the political authorities, *Paddy's Resource*, the popular ballad collection of the United Irishmen.[25] As if with this subversive vignette in mind, James Donnelly notes in relation to the diffusion of seditious doctrines in the early nineteenth century:

> To the circulation of millenarian ideas in oral form schoolmasters made a major contribution. Schoolmasters, in fact, played an important role in the Rockite movement, as they did in other popular political and agrarian agitations before and after 1800. Many rural schoolmasters as a matter of course carried 'articles', the cant term for the Whiteboy oath and regulations, and presumably those of Captain Rock, which they used to enlist recruits when the occasion arose … Schoolmasters were also invariably well versed in the millenarian prophecies attributed to Colum Cille and Pastorini.[26]

As Moore's reference to *Paddy's Resource* as a set-text in hedge schools indicates, the schoolmaster was also a conduit of popular republicanism. This is elaborated by Thomas Crofton Croker in his *Researches in the South of Ireland*, written during the upsurge of Rockite activity in the early 1820s:

> In an evening assembly of village statesmen he [the schoolmaster] holds the most distinguished place, from his historical information, pompous eloquence, and classical erudition. His principles verge closely indeed on the broadest republicanism; he delivers warm descriptions of the Grecian and Roman commonwealths; the ardent spirit of freedom and general equality in former days – and then comes down to his own country, which is always the ultimate political subject of discussion.

25 With evident relish, the Captain lists some of the improving literature which had helped to form his impressionable mind, in the absence of formal schooling due to discrimination against Catholics: 'In History, – Annals of Irish Rogues and Raparees. In Biography, – Memoirs of Jack the Batchelor, a notorious smuggler, and of Freeney, a celebrated highwayman. In Theology, – Pastorini's Prophecies, and the Miracles of Prince Hohenloe. In Poetry, – Ovid's Art of Love, and Paddy's Resource. In Romance-reading, – Don Belianis of Greece, Moll Flanders. &c.&.' (pp. 187-8). So far from being a mischievous product of of Moore's imagination to alarm the authorities, this list would seem to have been derived from Hely Dutton's *Survey of Clare* (Dublin, 1808) where, among the reading books actually used in the 'schools', are (in Dutton's own description) ' – Irish Rogues and Rapparees. – Freney, a notorious robber, teaching them the most dangerous mode of robbing. – the most celebrated pirates. – Jack the Bachelor, a noted smuggler. – Fair Rosamund and Jane Shore, two prostitutes … – Ovid's Art of Love. – History of Witches and Apparitions. – The Devil and Doctor Faustus. – Moll Flanders – highly edifying, no doubt.' (cited in P.J. Dowling, *The Hedge Schools of Ireland* [Cork, 1968], pp. 64-5).

26 James Donnelly, Jr., 'Propagating the Cause of the United Irishmen', p. 120.

We are told, then, in a passage that must surely be a trial run for one of the Citizen's diatribes in the Cyclops chapter of James Joyce's *Ulysses*, that the demagogue:

> Praises the Milesians – curses 'the 'betrayer Dermod' – abuses 'the Saxon strangers'– lauds Brien [*sic*] Boru – utters one sweeping invective against the Danes, Henry VIII., Elizabeth, Cromwell, 'The Bloody' William 'of the Boyne,' and Anne; he denies the legality of the criminal code; deprecates and disclaims the Union; dwells with enthusiasm on the memories of Curran, Grattan, 'Lord Edward,' and young Emmet; insists on Catholic emancipation; attacks the *Peelers*, horse and foot; protests against tithes, and threatens a separation of the United Kingdoms![27]

Crofton Croker adds that the schoolmasters' political sentiments are not confined to 'mere declamation' but pass into print 'in the shape of popular ballads', and into political action through his planning of 'the nocturnal operations of the disaffected', writing their threatening proclamations with names 'studiously mis-spelled and pompously signed' such as 'Captain Moonlight' and 'General Rock'.[28]

The unresolved legacy of Lord Edward, Emmet and 1798 is discernible in the left background of the painting where a green shirted croppy is retrieving pikes, not from the proverbial resting place of the thatch, but from the ivy of the ruins above the schoolmaster's head – itself an ironic comment on the secretion of history in the antiquities which scar the Irish landscape.[29] In the left foreground, a number of the brotherhood make a pledge and join hands over the table in a manner reminiscent of the Swiss patriots in Fuseli's famous painting, the *Oath on the Rutli* (plates 2, 3 and 4) and, as if to complete the allusion to Fuseli's work, the new Captain Rock in the centre of the picture is cast in the image of its central heroic figure (plate 5).

27 Thomas Crofton Croker, *Researches in the South of Ireland, Illustrative of the Scenery, Architectural Remains, and the Manners and Superstitions of the Peasantry* (London, 1824), p. 328. It is likely that Maclise was acquainted with this book, as he illustrated other work by Crofton Croker, and drew a portrait of him.

28 The promotion of 'Captain' Rock to 'General' is also the distinguishing feature of the account of the leader who addresses the nocturnal gathering of Rockites in Mortimer O'Sullivan's *Captain Rock Detected*.

29 That Captain Rock brought this legacy with him to London is evident from Moore's lifelong sympathies with the United Irishman, dating from his early friendship with Emmet in Trinity College, Dublin. These sentiments found expression in his various homages to Emmet and Sarah Curran, in his later *The Life and Death of Lord Edward Fitzgerald* (1831), and *The History of Ireland* (1858) (for Moore and the United Irishmen, see Mary Helen Thuente, *The Harp Re-Strung: The United Irishmen and the Rise of Literary Nationalism* [Syracuse, 1994], chap. 6). Michael J. Whitty, the editor of *Captain Rock in London*, also printed eulogies to Wolfe Tone in the publication, and wrote a biography of Emmet.

Plate 2 Johann Fuseli, *The Oath on the Rutli*

Plate 3 Daniel Maclise, *The Installation of Captain Rock* (detail)

Plate 4 Daniel Maclise, *The Installation of Captain Rock* (detail)

This scene is described in the *Tipperary Tales*, which, according to the Royal Academy catalogue, provided Maclise with the inspiration for the work:

> Amid the tears and lamentations of women, Delaney advanced to the tomb on which the murdered man was laid, and placing his right hand upon the body, swore to revenge his death. Ere his solemn vow was thrice repeated, a hunchback mendicant had elevated himself upon the shoulders of one of the heterogeneous assembly, and with the old milking cap worn by the former leader of the faction, crowned Delaney as 'Captain Rock', muttering 'Upon this Rock I will build my church'.[30]

It was this endowment of what were perceived as Irish rabble with the dignity and noble bearing of classical heroes in a burlesque, sacrilegious setting which caused most offence to the reviewer in *Fraser's Magazine*, just as it did to Crofton Croker in his character sketch of the hedge schoolmaster. It was understandable, the reviewer in *Fraser's* wrote, that Maclise wished to make a 'perfectly Irish picture', yet, he adds, 'I deeply regret that [he] ... did not change the VENUE', and 'transfer the scene to some other country and some other age ... [and] persons in whom we might acknowledge some sympathy':

> Might not some such passage as is here represented be imagined in the history of Spartacus, that immortal slave and rebel? Might we not have him in the ruins of some ancient temple, vowing vengeance against imperious Rome and the Roman name, over the body of some fellow-slave, done to death by the cruelty of his Patrician master, and surrounded by the multitude of slaves, male and female, belonging to some great household? (p. 117)

The breach of the protocols of history painting was not just in the contemporary setting, but in the profusion of local details and ribald behaviour conventionally associated with representations of low life in Dutch or Flemish

---

30 Cited in W.J. O'Driscoll, *A Memoir of Daniel Maclise, RA* (London, 1871) p. 50. There is a remarkably similar scene in Charlotte Elizabeth's *The Rockite* (1832) , which also features a roofless ruin, a corpse on a bier, a table around which gang members are playing cards, drinking whiskey from a broken can, and repairing muskets, while 'a solitary dark looking man turned over a large heap of soiled newspapers; selecting and marking such paragraphs as he deemed calculated to excite the bitter feelings of rebel hostility gainst the government in church and state' (pp. 181-2). A haranguing priest, citing 'the great heretic, Cromwell', whips up sectarian animosities against loyal Protestants, until the climactic moment when the new leader steps out from among the assembly: 'He now stood erect among the conspirators; the pallid hue of his cheek succeeded by a hectic flush, and his eye kindled with passionate thought, while the muttered vow of misguided zeal bound his soul to the commission of crimes, from which his gentle soul had hitherto recoiled'(p. 188).

painting. The solemnity of the oath of the Rockites is offset by revelry and drunkenness: the group at the table where the oath is being taken are drinking whiskey from eggshells, while at the far side of the painting, as the *Fraser's* review describes it, 'a boccaugh, or sham cripple, mad with patriotism and pothien, unbuckles his wooden leg, and flourishes his crutch, – he is actively drunk; another leans on him passively ditto, and his face is expressive of a hiccup'. As Svetlana Alpers has argued, the prejudice against Dutch art among proponents of the grand style in history painting derived not only from its democratic sympathies with low life, but also its association with domesticity and the feminine.[31] In this sense, Maclise runs both 'high' and 'low' traditions together, and this transgression of styles is signalled in the painting by the inscription of the feminine in the public space of insurgent nationalism, and the juxtaposition of women (including, remarkably, a nursing mother) alongside images of male virtue and prowess, albeit in its suspect Irish variety. This was going too far for the *Fraser's* reviewer. 'Rockites', he protested, 'were not in the habit of holding their "high solemnities" in ruined abbeys, or of bringing their women and their children with them to their meetings'. It seems, moreover, that both 'women and children' learn fast, for in the left foreground a mother dotes on an infant who is pulling a sword from a scabbard, while in the background at the top of the painting, a young woman is helping an injured Rockite to find refuge in the abbey. In the centre of the painting, a group of keeners lament the dead leader, one 'chanting forth the praises of the deceased in the wild Ullalooh',[32] while another female figure ties a sash on the new Captain's belt.

More than any other departure from propriety, however, it was the eroticism of insurgency, 'the kissing and the courting … going on with the business of the hour', which attracted the attention of the *Fraser's* reviewer: 'All the women', he writes, 'especially the sister who is tying on the sash, and the delicious little minx who is affecting to dread the report of the gun, are most exquisitely depicted' (p. 119). This recalls the pedagogy of the oppressed in Captain Rock's hedge school, as outlined by Thomas Moore, where Ovid's 'Art of Love' was specifically paired with the popular insurgency of the United

31 Svetlana Alpers, 'Art History and its Exclusions: The Example of Dutch Art' in Norma Broude and Mary D. Garrard (eds), *Feminism and Art History: Questioning the Litany* (New York, 1996), p. 195. Putting in a good word for the democratic sympathies of the Flemish school, Lady Morgan noted that 'dead fish and dead game are at least not more offensive objects for familiar contemplation than murdered saints and tortured martyrs' (*The Life and Times of Salvator Rosa*, vol. i, pp. 196-7).

32 In a similar scene in Charlotte Elizabeth's *The Rockite*, a young woman takes up her position by the corpse 'and from that distant corner her suppressed "Ullaloo", the low dirge of death came with an effect, the mysterious wildness of which, little calculated to strike the uncultivated taste of the majority, was yet strongly felt by Driscoll, and not yet lost on the priest' (p. 189).

Irishmen's ballad anthology, *Paddy's Resource*, on the curriculum.[33] The sensuality of the women is so pronounced in Maclise's painting that the *Fraser's* reviewer feels called upon to deny that they are Irish:

> That sunny hair, those blue eyes, that delicately fair complexion, were never yet to be seen, excepting amongst the English of England and the English of Ireland ... the faces of the ladies (for such they be) are as distinguishable from the murky faces of the peasantry as the pure crystal waters of Lake Leman from the dusky current of the Rhone. (p. 119)

It may be that this social elevation is required to explain the ease with which the women occupy public space, but one of its implications is the familiar trope in colonial fantasy whereby the colonised male is deemed to be, at most, the social equivalent of the metropolitan or upper class female. This is, no doubt, intended to diminish both, but it may have the opposite effect of bringing gender and the physicality of the body to bear on colonialism in a way that calls for a total transformation of domestic and political space. By combining public and private spheres into its dissident version of the hidden Ireland, *The Installation of Captain Rock* attests to one of the most important aspects of popular insurgency, the integration of rituals of resistance into the everyday rounds and folk customs of rural life. Agrarian secret societies organised at wakes, weddings and seasonal festivals so that the persistence of folk culture itself, even in its apparently most innocent guise, became charged with political significance. 'Whiteboys', according to Michael Beames, speaking of such societies in general, 'transferred the peasant symbols for "combat and cure" from the stage of communal ritual to the arena of social conflict and its resolution'. Thus, he continues, secret societies did not present themselves to the peasantry as the kind of exotic outcasts conjured up by the romantic imagination, but rather as bearers of rough justice who shared a common language with their victims:

> The experience of the Whiteboy victim, when he was a member of the peasantry, becomes clear: when confronted by his attackers he did not perceive them as a group of bizarrely dressed *banditti*, but as figures he must have seen on countless occasions, season by season, year by year, in the passage of rural life. As such, their significance and their claim to legitimacy cannot have been lost on him.[34]

It is this refusal of the politics of the picturesque, and the external vantage point of the rural poor that accompanies it, which accounts for perhaps the

33 See note 25 above.
34 Michael Beames, *Peasants and Power: The Whiteboy Movements and Their Control in Pre-Famine Ireland* (Brighton, 1983), p. 101.

most disquieting and powerful aspects of Maclise's painting. Notwithstanding its apparent confirmation of some of the main stereotypes of Irish insurgency – that sedition is compounded by inflated rhetoric, superstition, drunkenness and licentiousness – reviewers of the picture were profoundly unsettled by its mode of address, as if somehow all was not as it seemed, and the pictorial form was also undermining this negative image of insurgency: 'I regret that Maclise painted this particular picture', concluded the *Fraser's* reviewer, 'for I am much mistaken he will be taken for a radical, or still worse, a Whig: the fact being that he has never dabbled the least in politics, and has nothing of political feeling, excepting that instinctive disposition to free and gentle Toryism, which is proper to high-minded gentlemen'. The problem here had to do with the fact that the painting lacked one of the key components of the grand style, an underlying unity or singularity of effect which allowed the composition to be taken in at a glance, and which resolved the various contrasts and conflicts in the work. What we are presented with instead, as the *Fraser's* reviewer complained, is as much material 'as would enliven a dozen pictures, and more extravagance than would spoil a score' (p. 119). As a result, there is 'want of unity in the design' derived from an 'admixture of tragedy, comedy and farce' which is difficult enough to resolve in poetry or prose, but almost impossible in the 'mute and motionless' medium of painting. As in the case of the breakdown of the framing narrative in Moore's prose narrative of *Captain Rock*, the absence of an organizing perspective suggests that the subject matter being represented is not under control, particularly from an external vantage point. The formal instability of the work disturbs the composure of the viewer, vitiating the disinterested stance of the ideal spectator:

> In a word, to use a familiar illustration, a calm, cold spectator coming to gaze upon a picture in which the fitful ebullitions of our nature are represented, is pretty much in the situation of a man perfectly sober entering a company excited and flushed with liquor. (p. 119)

The presentation of the scene, in other words, compromises the aesthetic distance of the 'calm, cold spectator', drawing him into the scene and changing his nationality in the process (it is not too difficult to figure out what nationality merits the description of being 'calm, cold' and 'perfectly sober', as against being 'excited and flushed with liquor'). The real offence here is bringing aesthetic transcendence down to earth, and giving a crude local habitation to the disinterested equipoise of art. As the *Fraser's* reviewer again put it, in less polite terms:

> No human being entering the exhibition, unless he be some scoundrel agitator, can have the slightest sympathy [with its subject]. If the visitor

Plate 5 Daniel Maclise, *The Installation of Captain Rock* (detail)

be English, his feelings revolt against the portraiture of those Irish kernes – those rebel ruffians, whose savage deeds, whose atrocious blood-guiltiness he is continually contemplating through the magnifying medium of the lying newspapers. If the visitor, on the contrary, be Anglo-Irish, what are the feelings towards the Rockites? The most intense contempt and hatred commingled – the feeling of the man towards the poisonous reptile: he knows that the Rockites are the most treacherous and cowardly rascals in the wide world, excepting only the agitators by whom they are incited (p. 117).

Clearly, no Irish need apply here for the position of ideal spectator – or at least those Irish from the ranks of the rural poor. It is this unmasking of the political assumptions built into the refinement of the art world which poses the greatest threat to the civilizing designs of imperial culture. Instead of being impartial, the spectator is revealed as a hostile witness, and it is this, perhaps, which accounts for the most incongruous detail in the picture, the scene in the lower right hand corner where a wizened old Terry Alt with a wooden leg is encouraging a young recruit to shoot directly at the beholder (plate 5). The intention here may be to clear a space for the excluded Irish viewer, as if Maclise is insisting that the subjects of a painting have some say at last in their own self-image. This may account for the lack of a controlling vision in the painting, for if, as Cornewall Lewis suggests, artistic form is closely bound up with problems of political articulation, then this is one clear case where aesthetic problems only admit of political solutions.

Maria Edgeworth and the
Aesthetics of Secrecy

WILLA MURPHY

One of Maria Edgeworth's earliest plays – *The Double Disguise* – tells the story of a soldier returning home from war in successive disguises to test the fidelity of his wife. The stealthy husband discovers his wife's true identity by concealing his own. In her preface to *Castle Rackrent*, Edgeworth rehearses this disclosure-through-disguise theme again when she comments that 'a love of truth ... necessarily implies a love of secret[s]' – an assertion that well articulates a fundamental ambivalence in her literary and social project.[1] Again and again, Edgeworth encourages Ireland to adopt Enlightenment ideals of truth, openness, and the transparent light of reason, but mediates these ideals through narratives steeped in falsehood, concealment, stealth and secrecy. At the centre of Edgeworth's novels and tales, from *Castle Rackrent* to *Helen*, lie powerful secrets – secret identity, secret illness, secret genealogy, secret letters, diaries, whispers, gossip and rumours – that on all sides threaten to pull her ideals asunder. The kind of doubleness crudely sketched in *The Double Disguise* takes on a new complexity in her later fiction, equivocating as it does between surveillance and secrecy, enlightenment and obfuscation, revelation and reticence. Edgeworth, in other words, puts secrets in service of moral lessons, but is forever concerned that such dangerous material might tear away from her reformist purpose, and end up participating in the covert culture she means to lay bare. Why does she risk writing tales that might proliferate the sort of secrets she means to dispel?

We might, as some have done, read Edgeworth's simultaneous fascination and frustration with a cryptic Ireland as that of a writer divided between reformist ideals and the real demands of fiction.[2] Gothic secrets feed Edgeworth's narratives – adding flesh and bones to imagination-starved didactic tales. Their persistent presence bespeaks an anxiety that enlightenment ethics, while politically potent, make rather insipid ingredients for a novel. A commitment to the light of reason, in other words, might make for a good schoolhouse, but not a good story. As one of Edgeworth's contemporaries put it, 'chemistry, mechanics, or political economy ... are all excellent things in

1 Maria Edgeworth, *Castle Rackrent* (London, 1992), p. 61.
2 See, for example, Terry Eagleton, *Heathcliff and the Great Hunger* (London, 1995), pp. 161-77.

their way, but vile, cold-hearted trash in a novel'.[3] He attributes all such trash
in Edgeworth's novels to her father. Or again, in Lady Delacourt's words at the
conclusion of *Belinda*, 'The secret of being boring is to tell everything'.[4] The
secret of being a good storyteller, then, is holding back the truth, partially concealing facts even in the moment of their disclosure, refusing to tear any veils
rudely away. In this sense, as Frank Kermode has pointed out, secrecy is
enmeshed in the very nature of literary texts and their interpretation – from
the Book of Exodus to *The X-Files*.[5]

Edgeworth certainly found no scarcity of cloak-and-dagger material as she
cast an artist's eye over Ireland during her lifetime, a lifetime that spanned the
rise of countless conspiratorial movements – including the Defenders, United
Irishmen, Whiteboys, Rightboys, Ribbonmen, and Molly Maguires. These revolutionary and agrarian societies relied on a combination of secrecy and terror
to effect political rebellion. For Ascendancy reformers like the Edgeworths,
Ireland was a land plagued not only with fever and famine, but with an epidemic of falsehood, secrecy, treachery and conspiracy. Nocturnal meetings, ritual oaths, millenarian slogans, coded haircuts and clothing, secret handshakes,
passwords, code-names and cross-dressing, combined with threats of violence
against the ruling class, created an Irish landscape of mystery and terrifying
inscrutability.

It is no secret or surprise that the processes of colonial power generated a
whole culture of concealment in Ireland. When the majority of a population is
excluded from public means of expression and protest, those political energies
move underground, creating a smouldering subterranean culture beneath a
surface of submission and silence. Nineteenth-century Ireland as a whole
might be called a 'secret society' – not in the sense that the majority of Irish
were bound by oath to agrarian movements, and attended nocturnal meetings
to plot the assassination of their landlords, but that secrecy and strategic silence
became mechanisms of survival, and alternative spaces for enacting social and
political power. As W.E.H. Lecky noted, 'Ireland's Catholics learned the lesson
which ... rulers should dread to teach. They became [adept] in the arts of conspiracy and disguise. Secrets known to hundreds were preserved inviolable
from authority'.[6]

For Maria Edgeworth, Ireland is steeped in a threatening secrecy, from
Maynooth Seminary, whose 'closed doors' and 'concealment' represent 'the
dangerous spirit and tendency of Catholicism';[7] to those tenants leagued in

---

3 Quoted in Marilyn Butler, *Maria Edgeworth: A Literary Biography* (Oxford, 1972), p. 271.
4 Maria Edgeworth, *Belinda* (London, 1993), p. 459.
5 Frank Kermode, *The Genesis of Secrecy: On the Interpretation of Narrative* (Cambridge,
   Mass., 1979).
6 W.E.H. Lecky, *A History of Ireland in the Eighteenth Century* (London, 1972), p. 50.
7 Quoted in Michael Hurst, *Maria Edgeworth and the Public Scene* (London, 1969), p. 98.

'secret rebellion' who are 'so secret and cunning, that no proofs could be obtained against them ... [and] who often [give landlords] false clews, to involve them still farther in darkness and error'[8] ; to 'the mass of the [Irish] people' who are 'leagued with the party or interests of the [secret] assassins, so that no information before or after the fact ... can be obtained'.[9] Edgeworth's attitude towards her conspiratorial tenants might be best summed up by the words of the Blind Man to the Fool in Yeats's *On Baile's Strand*: 'a secret is better to you than your dinner'.[10]

This strange society of secrecy and concealment requires close reading by Ascendancy rulers to interpret the silence and darkness, to discover some positive shape in the negative spaces. In an 1831 letter, Edgeworth describes the need to watch constantly, for landlords know not the day nor the hour: 'the apparent present quiet of this country only lulls us treacherously ... [there are] secret societies all over Ireland'.[11] As David Lloyd has pointed out, secret societies like the United Irishmen, Defenders and Ribbonmen act invisibly, communicate without writing, have no visible or permanent leaders but an elaborate system of rotating authority – they are faceless or, in Nancy Curtin's description, 'hydra-headed'.[12] They leave only frustrating negative spaces for powers to interpret, create a gothic text on the Irish landscape, intricately pleated and disguised, in which nothing is as it seems. Government agents were often at a loss as to how to read these negative signs, recognising that a blank space might be interpreted several ways: as one government official reported in the United Irish-infested 1790s, 'that part of the country whence most danger is to be apprehended is apparently most quiet and peaceable'.[13]

A culture of secrecy, Sissela Bok argues, breeds a culture of paranoid over-interpretation – one that reads suspiciously between every line, seeks and suspects plots everywhere, and undertakes constant surveillance.[14] 'The excess of credulity,' Edgeworth writes in *Ennui*, 'when convinced of its error, becomes the extreme of suspicion'.[15] Dublin Castle during this period of unrest was the site of nervous attempts to tabulate and terminate secret societies through a blizzard of dispatches, magistrates' reports, trial minutes, and maps charting the

8 Maria Edgeworth, *Memoirs of Richard Lovell Edgeworth, Esq.*, vol. ii (reprinted Shannon, 1968), pp. 209-10.

9 Quoted in Hurst, *Edgeworth and the Public Scene*, p. 148.

10 W.B. Yeats, *On Baile's Strand*, in John P. Harrington (ed.), *Modern Irish Drama* (London, 1991), p. 15.

11 Quoted in Hurst, *Edgeworth and the Public Scene*, p. 67.

12 David Lloyd, *Anomalous States: Irish Writing and the Post-Colonial Moment* (Dublin, 1993), pp. 125-62; Nancy Curtin, *The United Irishmen: Popular Politics in Ulster and Dublin, 1791-1798* (Oxford, 1994).

13 Quoted in Curtin, *United Irishmen*, p. 68.

14 Sissela Bok, *Secrets: On the Ethics of Concealment and Revelation* (New York, 1984).

15 Maria Edgeworth, *Ennui* (London, 1992), p. 181.

frequency of agrarian unrest county by county. What these documents illustrate is a ruling power's endless legal scrambling to wrap the law around an
amorphous and slippery Irish secret, to produce an official discourse about a
competing unofficial power in order to categorise and control it. They say
something too about the operations of a deeply insecure authority surrounded
on all sides by a secrecy of its own creation – a terrifying secrecy which may
be monstrously beyond the interpretation and control of its makers.

The letters, journals and diaries of Edgeworth's Ascendancy counterparts
bespeak an unhealthy obsession with the surveillance of tenants. William
Parsons, third Earl of Rosse, best known for inventing the world's largest telescope to unlock the secrets of the heavens, was also interested in keeping a
close eye on his mysterious tenants. In his *Letters on the State of Ireland*, he calls
for the creation of a flawless system of surveillance, involving an elaborate lay-
ering of local and central authorities, to keep an eye peeled for secret rebellion.
His recommendations include the creation of a police force 'especially devoted
to the detection of crime'; one with 'an accurate knowledge of locality, and of
the character and habits of almost every individual in the district'; and the
keeping of detailed journals by landlords.[16] Meanwhile, in Co. Wicklow,
Elizabeth Smith, a great fan of the Earl's giant telescope, was busy recording in
her diaries that her tenants, an 'extraordinary slippery people', harbour a 'secret
enmity' towards her and 'require constant watching'.[17]

Like many of their Ascendancy counterparts, the Edgeworths were
involved in developing their own systems of surveillance in an attempt to root
out Ireland's addiction to secrecy and conspiracy. Rumours of a French inva-
sion and United Irish rebellion in 1794 moved Richard Lovell Edgeworth to
perfect the invention of his 'Logograph', and publish an essay entitled 'On the
Art of Swift and Secret Intelligence'. In her *Memoirs* of her father, Maria, who
helped copy down the secret codes for this telegraph, comments that the
'superior advantage of his vocabulary arise[s] from its being undecipherable'
and in 'defiance of detection'.[18]

But for the Edgeworths the Ascendancy's strongest weapon against Irish
secrecy was education. The proper instruction of children and tenants could,
they believed, diffuse Enlightenment ideals throughout Ireland, and turn Irish
hearts of stealth to hearts of truth. The Edgeworth household, as Maria
describes in her *Memoirs* of her father, was a kind of Enlightenment social
experiment, committed to reason, openness and free communication, opposed
to all forms of secrecy and reticence:

16 William Parsons, *Letters on the State of Ireland* (London, 1847), p. 26.
17 Elizabeth Smith, *The Irish Journals of Elizabeth Smith, 1840-1850*, ed. David Thomson and
    Moyra McGusty (Oxford, 1980), 19, 28 October 1845; 13 May 1847.
18 Edgeworth, *Memoirs*, p. 168.

> Some men live with their family, without letting them know their
> affairs. ... This was not my father's way of thinking. – On the contrary,
> not only his wife, but his children knew all his affairs. Whatever business
> he had to do was done in the midst of his family, usually in the com-
> mon sitting room: so that we were intimately acquainted, not only with
> his general principles of conduct, but with the most minute details of
> their every-day application.[19]

So when he was not developing secret telegraphic codes or inventing
machines to climb walls, Mr Edgeworth was compiling with his daughter their
Guide to Practical Education, a kind of twelve-step program for parents who
wanted to become more like the Edgeworths.

Published the year of the United Irish rebellion, the guide shows the marks
of its genesis in the troubled 1790s. Parents are warned that 'some secret inter-
course [might] be carried on between children and servants', a danger 'lessened
by [making certain] arrangements in the house'. These arrangements include
'care in a mother or governess to know exactly where children are, and what
they are doing every hour of the day'; design of a house that 'make[s] it impossible for them to go without detection into any place which we forbid';[20] separate staircases and passageways for servants; and certainty that no passageway
exists between children's and servants' chambers. The guide encourages a constant scrutiny of children's conversations: 'children who are encouraged to
converse about everything ... will naturally tell their mothers if any one talks
to them; ... they will never be the spies of servants, nor should they keep their
secrets'.[21] More often than not in *Practical Education*, 'education' is another
word for surveillance. In the *Memoirs*, Maria Edgeworth praises her father's
constant supervision of his children, which involves keeping 'a register of
observations and facts, relative to his children.' Richard Lovell Edgeworth creates a kind of personal panopticon in his house, keeping 'notes of every circumstance which occurred worth recording.' And, she adds significantly, 'This
he began in the year 1798'.[22]

Another text being written in 1798, and also concerned with discourses of
surveillance and secrecy, was *Castle Rackrent*. Thady Quirk's narrative, with its
first person confessional style, its nods and winks to the reader, its diplomatic
deference to the Editor, might be read as an example of the threatening Irish
discourse of secrecy. His penchant for eavesdropping, his eye for confidential
letters and documents, his tight-lipped posture towards his masters, and his

19 Ibid., p. 15.
20 Richard Lovell Edgeworth and Maria Edgeworth, *Guide to Practical Education* (London,
    1798), p. 201.
21 Edgeworth, *Memoirs*, pp. 184-5.
22 Ibid., p. 185.

gossipy tone towards his readers, all combine to create the kind of Irish voice the Edgeworths came to fear. Notice that Thady witnesses every detail of the downfall of his masters – he is always 'just within hearing distance' of private conversations; or happens to catch a glimpse over his son Jason's shoulder of secret documents – but all the while maintains a strategic silence: 'I never said anything one way or another'; 'I kept myself to myself'; 'I said nothing' is his constant refrain as the Rackrent family self-destructs. Thady, the eagle-eyed, elephant-eared presence, is every landlord's nightmare, whatever his claims to being loyal retainer. For the tale Thady tells, the course of events he silently witnesses, is the strategic take-over of the Rackrent estate by his own son. Wrapped in his great cloak (which, the notes tell us, provides among other things concealment and anonymity to Irish rebels), Thady might be read as not too far removed from those double-dealing tenants who serve their landlords faithfully by day and plot their overthrow by night.

Kathryn Kirkpatrick has recently explored the competing discourses of the text and the glossary of *Castle Rackrent*, the former written by Maria without her father's supervision; the latter written, or at least strongly encouraged and edited by Richard Lovell.[23] Where the original text is generally sympathetic with Thady, the glossary is patronising and suspicious. We might say that the glossary itself acts as a kind of supervisor of a potentially dangerous text, sur-veilling and reining in any perceived complicity with the dispossessed and secretive Irish. Thady's extensive legal knowledge, says the glossary, aligns him with every Irish man, who, 'staking his own wit or cunning against his neigh-bour's property, feels that he has little to lose, and much to gain'.[24]

The glossary aligns clandestine activities not only with the Irish but with women. A gloss on 'the raking pot of tea' disapproves of these 'stealth[y]' women's meetings, 'the joys' of which depend 'on its being made in secret, and at an unseasonable hour', behind a locked door, amidst much 'giggling and scrambling', and involving the exchange of private letters, pocket-books and gossip about men. The gloss adds that the tradition finds its origins among the 'washerwoman and the laundry-maid,' or, as it puts plainly, among 'low life'.[25] What the glossary bespeaks is an anxiety about unsupervised activities, particu-larly among the Irish lower classes and among women.

Interestingly, the writing of *Castle Rackrent* was one activity that went unsupervised by the all-seeing Richard Lovell Edgeworth. And it is this text that is perhaps most complicit with the discourse of secrecy. Maria Edgeworth, despite her reformist rampages against Ireland's furtiveness, knew well the plea-sure and power associated with a good secret. In an 1803 letter to a friend, she

---

23 Kathryn Kirkpatrick, 'Putting Down the Rebellion: Notes and Glosses on *Castle Rackrent*, 1800' in *Éire-Ireland* xxx, no. 1 (1995), pp. 77-90.
24 Edgeworth, *Castle Rackrent*, p. 133.
25 Ibid., p. 136.

describes composing stories in secret as 'one of my greatest delights and strongest motives for writing'. Her favourite stories 'were all written whilst my father was out somewhere or other, on purpose to be read to him on his return'.[26] Edgeworth associates a certain freedom and delight with this secret scrawl, this activity hidden from surveilling eyes, and the succeeding disclosure to her father.

The subtexts of Edgeworth's other novels articulate a similar attraction to the power and pleasure of secrecy, all the while their texts preach against its dangers. *Ennui* is ostensibly a tale about the rewards of truth and the perils of secrecy. When Lord Glenthorn learns the truth about his identity – that his mother Ellinor swapped him with the true Lord Glenthorn when they were infants – he virtuously decides to reverse the secret, giving up his estate and title to the true lord, who has been living the life of a blacksmith. Not unlike Thady Quirk, Ellinor, through her cunning and silence, places her son in a position of property and power, and strips the upper class of its birthright. Nursing the ailing infant lord, she describes her decision to swap the babies:

> I was sitting up in bed, rocking him backwards and forwards this ways: I thought with myself, what a pity it was the young lord should die, and he an only son and heir, and the estate to go out of the family and Lord knows where; … and then I thought how happy it would be for you, if you was in the place of the little lord: and then it came into my head, just like a shot, where would be the harm to change you? … Well, if it was a wicked thought, it was the devil himself put it in my head, to be sure; for, only for him, I should never have had the sense to think of such a thing, for I was always innocent like, and not worldly given.[27]

It might be argued that Ellinor is not so innocent or free of worldly thoughts as she insists. What she recognises in a flash is the power of the secret to change her son's future, and so change history. For an Irish tenant locked into an unjust system, honesty is perhaps not the best policy. This positive power of secrecy – its offer of a liberation from one's 'honest' identity and boundaries – is a power the novel detects and explores. When Glenthorn becomes the target of a tenant conspiracy, he himself becomes adept at the arts of secrecy, writing coded letters, making secret signs, keeping tight-lipped in the presence of his Irish servants. Secrecy actually awakens Glenthorn's faculties, moves him to define himself, cures him of his *ennui*, moving his agent to comment, 'Tis a pity, my Lord … but that there was a conspiracy against you every day of your life, it seems to do you so much good'.[28] Secrecy breathes life into Glenthorn,

26 Quoted in Butler, *Maria Edgeworth*, p. 288.
27 Edgeworth, *Ennui*, pp. 274–5.
28 Ibid., p. 269.

just as it does into Edgeworth's novels themselves. The power of secrecy is not so easily laid to rest by the novel's preaching against it – for in the end the effect of Ellinor's dark secret prevails. Her son, marrying the Glenthorn heiress (a position he could never have hoped to be in without Ellinor's scheming), is restored to his estate; while the true Lord Glenthorn, ruined and miserable, retreats to the forge in which he was raised.

Sissela Bok has argued that secrecy is bound up with identity, with the opacity of human subjects, and can be a source of creative power.[29] Just as the initiation rites of secret societies mean to transform the identity of their members, individual secrets can allow a transcending of one's ordinary boundaries and subjectivity. 'In occupying two places at once,' writes Homi Bhabha, 'the depersonalized, dislocated colonial subject can become an incalculable object, quite literally, difficult to place'.[30] Maria Edgeworth detected this liberating power when she wrote stories in secret; and this same creative power rears its head in her writing – from Harriet Freke in *Belinda* whose secret cross-dressing allows her to participate in the male world of politics and power (she swears that 'it was charming fun to equip herself at night with man's clothes and to sally forth');[31] to Lord Colambre in *The Absentee*, whose disguise allows him to speak and move freely among his tenants and agents, gathering the truth about his estate through a secret identity. The subtext of all these novels is that secrecy empowers and liberates as often, if not more often, than it destroys. What the novels suggests at some subconscious level is, perhaps, that in certain situations it is altogether *reasonable* to be clandestine and secretive. Nineteenth-century Ireland might be one place where survival depends on being reticent and double-dealing, on shifting identity to meet the situation, on telling and keeping secrets. To this extent, the light of reason and the darkness of Irish hearts might not be so far apart as the Edgeworth Enlightenment experiment would like to insist.

So the question I began this essay by asking remains – why all this secrecy in a novelist committed to dispelling it? Edgeworth's obsession with Ireland's culture of concealment may go beyond the desire simply to spin a good yarn. It may more interestingly have to do with her location in that culture – among an Ascendancy power that, as Edmund Burke never tired of pointing out, lacked a *politics* of secrecy. For Burke, as for Foucault, secrecy is indispensable to the operations of power: a ruling class operates most effectively that conceals the violent sources of its power, cloaking them in the pleasing veils of custom and tradition. That power is strongest that achieves a sublime inscrutability, that

29 Bok, *Secrets*, p. 46.
30 Homi Bhabha, 'Remembering Fanon: Self, Psyche and the Colonial Condition' in Patrick Williams and Laura Chrisman (eds), *Colonial Discourse and Post-Colonial Theory: A Reader* (New York, 1994), p. 121.
31 Edgeworth, *Belinda*, p. 293.

ruling class most stable whose violent sources have been worn smooth by the passage of time, naturalised and made part of the very landscape and horizon of our lives. Indeed, Richard Lovell Edgeworth, a great fan of Burke's, recognised too the power invested in custom and tradition: 'in such establishments … there is always to be found a *power*, what the workmen call a *purchase*, of which the skilful legislator can … apply to useful purposes'.[32] In this doctrine of prescription, we might say that Burke writes a politics of secrecy: like the structure of a secret, power maintains itself by an elaborate operation of concealment and revelation, hiding and unfolding, absence and presence. Even the glossary to *Castle Rackrent*, that text so opposed to clandestine activities, admits the power that secrecy has to protect property. The entry on 'fairy-mounts' explains that the sources of these supernatural mounds are actually quite mundane. Really 'artificial caves' constructed near churches, they were used as 'secret granaries, magazines, or places of retreat in times of danger. … The persons who had property concealed there very willingly countenanced every wonderful relation that tended to make these places objects of sacred awe or superstitious terror'.[33] Scratch a gothic tale and you find someone protecting his property from the barbarians. Secrecy, in this sense, becomes a kind of insurance policy for the men of property.

It is just this elaborate veiling of the sources of power in age-old custom and tradition that the Ascendancy lacks – a lack detected by countless writers of that class, not least Edmund Burke, whose condemnation of Ascendancy rule finds its epicentre in this absence. The memory of a violent confiscation of Irish land and lives is too recent for any sublime inscrutability, for any mystifying or seductive veils to be draped around Protestant authority. The unlawful origins of its power and property are too recent to be a secret to anyone – least of all themselves. For here is a power without any secrets, a power exposed, naked and vulnerable to the watchful eyes of its subjects. To discover the nakedness of the prince, says Louis Adrian Montrose, is to demystify the secrets of the state.[34] In Edgeworth's Ireland the prince never had any clothes to begin with. Both ruler and exposed enemy, inspector and inmate, the Ascendancy is in a situation of being inside and outside the operations of power, a supervisor of secrets that is itself an open secret, exposed and surveilled. Edgeworth's Ireland complicates the panopticon model – Foucault's architectural emblem for the operations of power – for it is difficult to know who is watcher and who watched. 'The lower Irish are such acute observers,' Edgeworth comments in her *Memoirs*, 'that there is no deceiving them of the real feelings of

---

32 Edgeworth, *Memoirs*, p. 465.
33 Edgeworth, *Castle Rackrent*, pp. 129-30.
34 Louis Adrian Montrose, 'The Elizabethan Subject and the Spenserian Text' in Patricia Parker and David Quint (eds), *Literary Theory/Renaissance Texts* (Baltimore and London, 1986), p. 328.

their superiors. They know the signs of what passes within, more perfectly than any physiognomist'.[35] The point here is not so much some native Irish gift for clairvoyance but the Ascendancy anxiety over being exposed.

The great secret of the Ascendancy, in other words, is that they have no secret. 'Looking behind the mask of things,' says Foucault, 'one finds not a timeless essential secret, but the secret that they have no essence'.[36] This nothing-behind-the-veil theme crops up again and again in Edgeworth's novels, from Lady Delacourt, whose elaborate secret staircase, secret boudoir, and secret vials all conceal a secret breast cancer that, in fact, doesn't exist. The secret lock on her cabinet is a fitting emblem for this lack: 'How in the devil's name can you expect me to open a secret lock when I do not know the secret?' Lord Delacourt asks his wife. 'Then I will tell you the secret, Lord Delacourt,' she responds, 'that there is no secret at all in the lock'. In the end, Lady Delacourt's great secret is that 'she had no secret to keep'.[37] This lack of any secret among the Ascendancy might help explain the endless fascination with secret birth and genealogy in Edgeworth's novels. Grace Nugent's illegitimate birth in *The Absentee* is shrouded in a mystery involving a ruined convent school girl and a dying soldier. Stories of children who discover they aren't the blood of those claiming to be their parents might be particularly attractive to a class who knew its genealogy only too well. In colonial Ireland there is at once too much secrecy and not enough – too much among the Irish tenants for Ascendancy rulers to unmask; and not enough for the Ascendancy itself to hide behind. To an anxious and exposed Ascendancy, Ireland is at once a deeply opaque and painfully transparent place.

The kind of simultaneous rejection of and attraction to secrecy articulated in Edgeworth's novels, then, might say something about Ascendancy anxieties and desires. They may have detested their tenants' furtiveness; but they were certainly in need of a few good secrets themselves. It is this doubleness that Edgeworth's discourse embodies – desirous of the concealment it claims to detest, proliferating secrets it means to dispel. 'All who are governed by any species of fear,' she writes, 'are disposed to equivocation.'[38] A comment on the sources of Irish reticence and double-dealing, this statement might also be taken as a fitting account of Edgeworth's own precarious project, equivocating as it does between truth and secrecy, revelation and concealment, and spoken by a deeply insecure – and frightened – Ascendancy voice.

35 Edgeworth, *Memoirs*, p. 241.
36 Michel Foucault, 'Nietzsche, Genealogy, History' in Donald F. Bourchard and Sherry Simon (eds), *Language, Counter-Memory, Practice: Selected Essays and Interviews* (Ithaca, 1977), pp. 139–64.
37 Edgeworth, *Belinda*, pp. 266, 298.
38 Edgeworth, *Practical Education*, p. 209.

Ideology and Cultural Production:
Nationalism and the Public Monument in
Mid Nineteenth-Century Ireland

JUDITH HILL

In May 1843 *The Nation* declared:

> The time is coming when, in the streets of Dublin, we will have monu-
> ments to Irish patriots, to Irish soldiers and to Irish statesmen. We now
> have statues to William the Dutchman, to the four Georges – all either
> German by birth or German by feeling – to Nelson, a great admiral, but
> an Englishman; while not a single statue to any of the many celebrated
> Irishmen whom their country should honour adorns a street or a
> square of our beautiful metropolis.

The Nation, a national newspaper, had been set up by members of Young
Ireland seven months previously to help foster a sense of Irish identity in its
readers. It was hoped to appeal to both Catholics and Protestants; to draw
them together under the umbrella of a shared culture. The vision of Dublin
populated by bronze or stone effigies of celebrated Irishmen was part of this
broadly based nationalism; prominent Irishmen of all political allegiances or
religious creeds were eligible. Public depictions of exemplary historic and
political figures would also be a way of demonstrating the culturally unique
character of Ireland, the animating idea of the cultural nationalism of Young
Ireland derived from Thomas Davis. Davis had included such figures – 'Father
Mathew Administering the Pledge in a Munster County', 'The Clare
Election', 'O'Connell's Dublin Corporation Speech' – in the list of subjects he
had advocated for Irish painting in one of his essays.[1] Finally the erection of a
public monument was one of the most direct ways of realising Davis's ambition of putting culture to political use – great figures would become familar,
inspire collective confidence and right action, 'awaken their piety, their pride,
their justice, and their valour ...'[2]

Davis's ambitions for a politicised art were mainly directed towards painting
and songs. He did, however, apply it to one monument in the ballad

---

1 Thomas Davis, *Literary and Historical Essays* (Dublin, 1845), p. 169. His ideas on Irish art
  are discussed in 'National Art', pp. 155-6.
2 Ibid., p.163.

'O'Connell's Statue: Lines to Hogan' which begins 'Chisel the likeness of the Chief' and proceeds to describe the features of O'Connell in terms of Irish history and his imagined involvement, so that he evokes a colossus eloquent of Irish experience. This highly romantic and pointedly nationalist vision can be compared to Thomas Carlyle's cult of great men, explored in a series of lectures given in London in 1840.[3] Emphasising the importance of great men in effecting the course of history – 'They were the leaders of men, these great ones; the modellers, patterns, and in a wide sense creators, of whatsoever the general mass of men contrived to do or to attain' – he concluded that although ordinary men could never aspire to their brilliance and achievement, they could learn from their example. His ideas underpinned the mid nineteenth-century blossoming of the project to erect monuments in Britain to poets, writers, philosophers, politicians, public benefactors and military heroes. Thus when in December 1862 the *Dublin Builder* proclaimed: 'To do honour to the memories of great men is so pre-eminently a national duty ... [When] we see public monuments, we may assume that public benefactors are not forgotten [and we] remember their patriotism with gratitude, and their genius with pride', we not only hear an echo of Thomas Davis but also an awareness of what was being achieved in England.

From 1853 to 1880 some twenty-five statues were erected throughout Ireland, fourteen in Dublin. This represents a modest showing compared to other European countries but in a country which had erected only about sixteen public monuments in the 120 years between 1701 to 1823 it demonstrated a considerable increase in effort. These twenty-seven years from 1853 to 1880, falling between the famine and the land war, also fell between the inspiring and politically unifying influences of Daniel O'Connell and Charles Stewart Parnell. It was a period when the term nationalist was ill-defined. Theodore Hoppen has argued that in borough and county elections national issues were obscured by local concerns, 'drains and cash' rather than 'repeal and reform'.[4] This is corroborated by the experience of men like A. M. Sullivan, John Martin and William Smith O'Brien, Young Irelanders, now with faith in the constitutional route to reform, who failed to attract significant support for various efforts to found nationalist organisations in the late 1850s and 60s. This began to change in the 1870s when the Home Rule movement was established. Another focus for nationalists was the Irish Republican Brotherhood, a secret, oath-bound organisation founded in Dublin in 1858 under James Stephens and committed to a violent overthrow of the existing system. It was a

---

3 Thomas Carlyle, *On Heroes, Hero-Worship and the Heroic in History*, in Alan Shelston (ed.), *Selected Writings of Thomas Carlyle* (London, 1971).

4 See K. Theodore Hoppen, 'National Politics and Local Realities in Mid Nineteenth-Century Ireland' in Art Cosgrove and Donal McCartney (eds), *Studies in Irish History* (Dublin, 1979), pp. 190-227.

relatively small group and, aiming to supplant other forms of nationalist organisation, it contributed to their failure to attract popular support. Together the Catholic Emancipation Act, which had enfranchised the wealthier Catholics, and the Municipal Reform Act of 1840, which had enabled middle class Catholics to secure positions in local government, had given power to a significant group of Catholics. Politicised by O'Connell, they had nevertheless dropped Repeal after the famine but remained faithful to his ambition to advance Irishmen in the modern world – they sought to consolidate Catholic rights with the disestablishment of the Church of Ireland and the establishment of state support for denominational education.[5] Cardinal Cullen, archbishop of Dublin from 1852 to 1878, had organised a hearteningly popular demonstration for a Catholic university in July 1862. Such an issue prioritised Catholics without referring to self-government; an issue avoided by both Cullen and many of his middle-class followers.

For a similar reason this group of Catholics was often to be found behind proposals for nationalist monuments; the O'Connell monument campaign in Dublin was launched two months after the Catholic university demonstration, and when John Gray, Protestant proprietor and editor of the *Freeman's Journal,* the popular organ of moderate, predominantly Catholic opinion, member of Dublin City Council, and the main inspiration behind the Dublin O'Connell monument died in 1875, his statue was erected in Dublin four years later.[6] In Limerick, Maurice Lenihan, local historian, newspaper proprietor and persuasive voice in Limerick Corporation for disestablishment and Catholic education, proposed and pushed through a monument to O'Connell, unveiled in 1857. In Cork, O'Connell was dropped in favour of the Cork 'Apostle of Temperance', Father Mathew, whose monument was organised by both Protestants such as the businessman F.B. Beamish, and Catholics such as the mayor and proprietor of the *Cork Examiner,* John Maguire. In Dublin the more constitutionally ambitious A. M. Sullivan and the Young Irelanders enviously appreciated the unprecedented crowds at the laying of the foundation stone for the O'Connell monument in 1864, but they too adopted monument-building to rally support – a committee dominated by Dillon, Martin and Sullivan was formed on William Smith O'Brien's death in 1864 to erect a monument, and Sullivan vigorously championed a monument to Henry Grattan in 1864 which was unveiled to Home Rule rhetoric in 1876. Patriotic Protestants also formed committees to erect monuments – it was the enthusi-

---

5 These were among the aims of the National Association of Ireland of which John Gray was a prominent member. See R.V. Comerford, 'Conspiring Brotherhoods and Contending Elites, 1857-63' in W.E. Vaughan (ed.), *A New History of Ireland,* vol. v (Oxford, 1989), pp. 415-30.

6 For details about these commissions see Judith Hill, *Irish Public Sculpture: A History* (Dublin, 1998).

asm of Lord Cloncurry and Lord Charlemont that brought a statue of the poet Thomas Moore (the first broadly nationalist statue) to College St, Dublin in 1857; the statue of the viceroy, the Earl of Carlisle, erected in 1870, was claimed to represent a figure who had benefitted Ireland; the equestrian statue of Lord Gough, a highly successful field marshal in the British army, erected in 1880, was justified by his Irish birth; and even a monument to Prince Albert, who had negligible connections with Ireland, could have patriotic overtones, demonstrated in the debate over the site of the monument in 1864. Thus although it was Young Ireland's theories of cultural nationalism that had sent out the call for monuments of Irishmen, it was picked up by separately-formed committees under varying political influences. Their values and power were translated into the subject, sculptural style and positioning of the monuments, the scope of the subscriptions and the character of the dedication ceremonies.

Where they were well represented in council chambers, moderate Catholic nationalists had the pick of the sites. In Dublin, Cork and Limerick they unhesitatingly chose the main axes of central streets and squares, making their monuments the ornaments of late eighteenth and early nineteenth-century Georgian buildings which in all three cases had become the commercial heart of the cities. In Dublin these places also tended to be symbolic – from its place at the foot of Sackville Street the O'Connell monument was within viewing distance of buildings in which O'Connell had been active; the place earmarked for Grattan in College Green 'teems with suggestions of all the chief events of his career' from his student days in Trinity to his speeches in the Irish Parliament.[7]

Because these were places of maximum visibility they were also favoured by other interest groups. In 1855 the mayor of Limerick proposed that the corporation allocate the site at the centre of Richmond Place, a crescent on the main commercial thoroughfare of Newtown Pery, for a monument to Viscount Fitzgibbon, killed at the battle of Balaclava in the Crimean War.[8] This was successfully contested in the council by a group led by Maurice Lenihan, who also waged a vigorous campaign in his newspaper the *Limerick Reporter and Tipperary Vindicator*, and the Fitzgibbon monument was subsequently erected on Wellesley Bridge, then at the edge of the city. In Ennis, Co. Clare, Michael Considine, the secretary of the Trades, was inspired to initiate a monument to O'Connell to counter the proposal by the town commissioners to place cannon from the Crimean War on the site of the old courthouse in Ennis, the place where O'Connell had been elected MP of Clare in 1828.[9]

7 *The Nation*, 15 January 1876.
8 Maurice Lenihan, *Limerick: Its Histories and Antiquities* (1866; reprinted Cork, 1967), p. 513.
9 Ignatius Murphy, 'From Russian Gun to O'Connell Monument', *The Other Clare*, v (April 1981), pp. 45-6.

Considine used his considerable powers of oratory to secure popular support for his project which pressurised the town commissioners to relocate the cannon. A.M. Sullivan also employed oratory and journalism to win the argument for a monument to Grattan in College Green in 1864 against the ambitions of a committee formed to erect a monument to Prince Albert immediately after his death in 1861. At the corporation meetings in February 1864 the argument favoured Albert with moderates like John Gray expressing pride to show loyalty to the queen, and more radical figures like Devitt also expressing unwillingness to show 'disrespect to Her Majesty'; 32 voted in favour of a monument to Albert, 14 against.[10] The fiery rhetoric was left to Sullivan who in the council chamber and at public meetings appealed to Catholic consciences, employing the language of piety: a nationalist should 'kiss the stones of that place and declare them holy, for the national memories they consecrated'.[11] With popular support behind him and with a number of nationalists feeling they had done their imperial duty, the site was secured for Grattan at a corporation meeting in May 1864; with 19 votes in favour of Sullivan's proposal and 11 against, six nationalists had changed sides (although not John Gray), but a considerable number of those who had initially supported the Albert monument had absented themselves, indicating that the claims of loyalty had weakened but not snapped.[12]

The Albert Monument was erected on Leinster Lawn in 1872, near to the Royal Dublin Society and the National Gallery, institutions for the arts and sciences which Albert had promoted during his lifetime, and, as Sullivan remarked, a quiet place, where 'the people of Dublin would be little inclined to interfere'.[13] Two years previously a statue to the Earl of Carlisle had been unveiled in Phoenix Park, another peripheral place with which he was associated. There were conflicting opinions within the corporation and the ultimate power of nationalist public opinion was again demonstrated in the case of the equestrian statue to Lord Gough: an initial request in 1872 for a site on Foster Place was granted by the corporation, the subsequent request in 1878 for a place on the southern side of Carlisle Bridge was also granted, but objections from the O'Connell monument committee and the role of a different corporation department meant that this site was finally refused, and Lord Gough too was consigned to Phoenix Park.[14]

Sculptural style was less a signifier of political allegiance than site. A debate in the *Freeman's Journal* in the early 1860s on the relative merits of classicism

---

10 *The Nation*, 20 February 1864.
11 Ibid.
12 *The Nation*, 7 May 1864.
13 *The Nation*, 5 March 1864.
14 A full account in *Statement of Proceedings Taken to Erect, and to Obtain a Suitable Site for Erecting Thereon, The Gough Equestrian Statue, by John H. Foley, Esq., R.A.*

Plate 1 The Albert Memorial, Leinster Lawn, Dublin; sculptor John Henry Foley, 1872. Prince Albert is flanked by figures symbolising Art, Science, Industry and Agriculture.

and realism in the representation of O'Connell for the national monument, however, did suggest that style might have significance, for whereas a classical figure that would show him 'in calmness and repose … calmly hopeful of his country's rejuvenation'[15] would distance O'Connell from his specific political achievement, 'a living, speaking, acting O'Connell – an O'Connell that will tell of freedom's battles, and how they were won'[16] could have a more overt nationalist message. But the classicism of Limerick's O'Connell of 1857, draped in a toga, presenting him in 'his ever solemn dignity',[17] represented John Hogan's well-developed style, the classicism of which he had tempered for the public monument, dressing O'Connell in contemporary clothes under the toga and executing it in bronze which produces a more variegated surface than marble, the ideal material for classical sculptors but less well adapted to the Irish weather. O'Connell holds the text of the Act of Catholic Emancipation in his left hand, and Catholicism was a prominant theme at the unveiling ceremony where a third of those standing on the platform were priests.[18] The mayor, however, was concerned to diffuse any implication of sectarianism: 'I am well aware that many of my fellow-citizens differed from the late Mr

15 *Freeman's Journal*, 4 November 1863.
16 Ibid., 27 May 1864.
17 Ibid., 15 August 1857.
18 *Limerick Chronicle*, 15 August 1857.

Plate 2 O'Connell Monument, The Crescent, Limerick; sculptor John Henry Foley, 1857. *Plate 3* Earl of Rosse, St John's Mall, Birr; sculptor John Henry Foley, 1876. His scholarly and scientific achievements are represented by the robes of the Chancellor of the University of Dublin, the globe, and the book.

O'Connell in religion and politics, but I am certain that all those who respect talents of the very highest order, public spirit and patriotism will also respect his memory'. So Limerick was presented with a sculpture, in which a timeless ideal was tempered by details which recalled the struggles and achievements of nationalism which, in turn, were diffused by spoken rhetoric.

Similarly conflicting messages were conveyed by John Henry Foley and his contemporaries who matured as sculptors in the 1860s and 70s in a style that had evolved from classicism in Victorian Britain. Here classical idealism, which tried to convey qualities such as nobility and an impression of calm serious-ness, was tempered by the desire to show specific character and the particular details of costume.[19] But, intended to provide an example to the public, the realism was carefully subscribed – it was the characteristics of public duty and private virtue, a sense of vigour, boldness and fairness, that were presented. The overall effect of such figures tended towards the restrained solidity of classi-

19 See Benedict Read, *Victorian Sculpture* (New Haven, 1982).

Plate 4 Oliver Goldsmith, outside Trinity College, Dublin; sculptor John Henry Foley, 1864.

cism, clearly evident in Foley's *O'Connell* in Dublin and his *Earl of Rosse* in
Birr, in Thomas Farrell's *John Gray* and Christopher Moore's *Thomas Moore*.
This priority also influenced the choice of specific details: O'Connell was
noted for wearing a specially-designed green repeal cap at repeal meetings, but
it was his celebrated cloak, not unlike a toga when seen in silhouette against
the sky, that Foley chose as sartorially defining for his Dublin figure; and there
was the priest's cloak for Father Mathew, the robes of the Order of St Patrick
for the Earl of Carlisle, and the robes of the Chancellor of the University of
Dublin for the Earl of Rosse. Foley stood out among his contemporaries for
his ability to model a good facial likeness and to render the details of costume
so that the bronze surface was broken and animated. This can still be seen in
the statues of Oliver Goldsmith and Edmund Burke outside Trinity College.
This detailing, appreciated in the mid nineteenth century as part of the aesthetic, also endowed a public statue with a strong material presence.

Foley accepted commissions from committees of all political persuasions
and applied himself equally to each. But, born and trained in Dublin (although
living and practising in London) he did express an interest in his more nationalist commissions, writing to the Grattan committee that despite overwork 'the
impulse of national feeling [gave him] a deep interest in the subject'.[20] And he
did respond to the requirement for characteristic gestures for these figures with
strong images that, once executed, had the effect of symbols. Thus he presented
Grattan with his arm raised in the expansive and compelling oratorical gesture
for which he was famous, and Father Mathew's downward extending bene-
dicting right hand, his left hand clasping the temperance medal to his heart,
while sentimental, was more expressive of the atmosphere of early nineteenth-
century temperance than the more conventional priestly gesture presented by
Mary Redmond in her statue of Father Mathew erected in O'Connell St in
Dublin in 1891. Thomas Farrell's stone carving of William Smith O'Brien presented a determined figure, arms folded, one leg set purposefully forward; an
image which recalled the fact that O'Brien had led the abortive Young Ireland
rising in 1848, despite the subscription appeal which had emphasised the personal qualities of O'Brien: 'A good son, brother, husband, father, friend, neigh-
bour, citizen'.[21] In each case the rhetoric of the unveiling ceremonies indicated
that the moderate Catholics and reconstructed Young Irelanders were concerned not to alienate those more moderate than themselves, so that the general moral integrity and talents of the figure portrayed and the ideal of unity
were reiterated to diffuse impressions of exclusive Catholic allegiance and
memories of violent fighting. This ideal of unity had become a particularly

20 Letter, Foley to Grattan committee, 8 April, 1869; *The Origin, Progress and Completion of
     the Grattan Statue, Compiled by the Hon. John P. Vereker* (1881), Ms. 1703, Trinity College,
     Dublin.
21 John Morisy, *A Wreath for the O'Brien Statue: Its Origins, Its Inauguration* (Dublin, 1871).

Plate 5 William Smith O'Brien,
O'Connell Street, Dublin; sculptor
Thomas Farrell, 1870. The statue of
Sir John Gray, also by Farrell and
erected in 1879, is visible behind.

forceful theme by 1876 in the hands of Home Rulers when the Grattan statue
was unveiled and much was made of Grattan's credentials as a Protestant orator
who had championed Catholic Emancipation.[22]

Thus, in the hands of Hogan, Foley and Farrell, Ireland gained a number of
portrait statues emitting the civic qualities of statesmanship and control, whose
gestures, clothes and features recalled the events and tenor of Irish history. The
public was invited to read these specific Irish details within a peaceful urban
context. The statues were not unlike their counterparts in England and
Scotland. The same was true of the use of national symbols. Victorian sculptural convention, admitting a screened version of personal character, also admitted
national symbol. Again distinctiveness was conventionalised; the most prevalent
being the use of god and goddess figures to personify virtues and activities. So,
many of the sculptors who entered the competitions for the O'Connell monument in Dublin included representations of Law, Eloquence, Patriotism, Civil
and Religious Liberty, reflecting on the career and reputation of O'Connell.[23]
Similarly, around the base of his design, Foley included four seated winged
classical goddesses – Nike, the goddess of victory – each with attributes to

22 *Irish Times*, 7 January 1876.
23 Two competitions were held in 1864-5. See *Dublin Builder*, 15 February 1865 and 1
    March 1865 for comments on the entries. No one was chosen and Foley was commis-
    sioned.

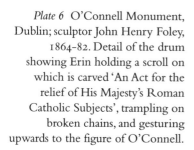

Plate 6 O'Connell Monument, Dublin; sculptor John Henry Foley, 1864-82. Detail of the drum showing Erin holding a scroll on which is carved 'An Act for the relief of His Majesty's Roman Catholic Subjects', trampling on broken chains, and gesturing upwards to the figure of O'Connell.

denote 'the qualities of mind and power exemplified in the career of O'Connell' – Patriotism holding sword and shield; Fidelity carrying a compass with an Irish wolfhound at her feet; Courage strangling a serpent, Eloquence holding a text.[24] Erin, the female personification of Ireland, also appeared in several competition entries,[25] and in Foley's monument she was placed at the front of the drum which rose above the Nike figures and formed a base for the pedestal to support O'Connell. Here, larger than life, at her feet the broken chains of liberty, on her humbly lowered head a crown of shamrocks, she gestures upward to O'Connell. Erin and the wolfhound stand out as the only symbols already used by nationalists in Ireland – by O'Connell in his repeal campaign, the trades on their banners and Young Ireland – to denote Ireland: a drawing depicting the monster meeting at Tara in 1843 published in the *Illustrated London News* showed the outsize banner marking O'Connell's stage decorated with harp, round tower and wolfhound,[26] and O'Connell's Triumph Car, a central part of the procession for the laying of the foundation stone of

24 Foley's presentation to the O'Connell committee was reproduced in *Freeman's Journal*, 14 December 1867.
25 For example, in the Gothic design of Pugin and Ashlin, and in different moods reflecting different periods of Irish history in Joseph Farrell's entry.
26 Illustrated in Gary Owens, 'Hedge Schools of Politics: O'Connell's Monster Meetings', *History Ireland*, ii, no. 1 (Spring 1994), p. 36.

the monument in 1864, was decorated with a figure of Erin, a round tower, an Irish landscape and shamrocks.[27] Even so the bowed figure of Erin owed much to Victorian ideas about the role of women as supporters of male achievement.[28]

The drum, decorated with a frieze in the neo-classical manner, gave Foley the opportunity to illustrate O'Connell's achievements in more detail. He sculpted a dynamic and multi-layered parade of figures to illustrate 'the great theme of [O'Connell's] labours' but which, representing the different classes and professions in Irish society, presents a strong image of its cohesiveness. This was dear to the heart of the moderate Catholic nationalists who appreciated O'Connell for laying down the conditions for social development. This had been articulated by the committee when it assessed the significance of his life: '[His] life was devoted to endeavouring to elevate the country, to give it freedom, commerce, trade, and manufactures, to have its people employed, and happy; and along with that to elevate the mind of the country, and inspire it with something that would lead to great and exalted deeds hereafter'.[29] Along with Foley's reputation as a sculptor, this imagery probably influenced their final decision to commission Foley. Interestingly, and probably reflecting the fact that Foley lived in England, the detailed design of the drum tended to reflect English perceptions of Irish society rather than the social ordering that O'Connell had helped to create. There was the bishop and peasant flanking Erin, reflecting the fact that Ireland was predominantly Catholic and agricultural. But there was no separate figure to represent the trades who had played such an important part in monster meetings and at elections – a figure of a lord mayor stood for municipal authority, commerce and trade, an artisan figure stood with the artist, and there was a poet, historian, lawyer, judge, philosopher and scientist – groups that were small and unrepresentative of mid nineteenth-century Ireland. Only the Albert monument was also decorated with subsidiary figures – four young men representing Art, Science, Industry and Agriculture – although there had been plans to build a fountain at the foot of the John Gray statue embellished with figures of Ireland and patriotism wearing 'the civic crown – the reward of great and generous public services' – the water a specific reference to Gray's persistence in implementing a public water supply for Dublin.[30] There were other examples of distinctively Irish details associated with the monuments, but they tended to be concealed or secondary; the Celtic cross just visible at the back of Father Mathew in Cork, the plan of the substructure of the O'Connell monument in Dublin in the

27 *Freeman's Journal*, 9 August 1864. The Bakers' banner in the 1864 procession depicted Erin with her hands outstretched to a sunburst, and a round tower.
28 Belinda Loftus, *William III and Mother Ireland* (Dundrum, 1990), pp. 57-60.
29 *The Nation*, 4 June 1864.
30 *Freeman's Journal*, 25 June 1879.

form of a high cross laid on its side, the silver trowel with which the mayor ceremonially set the foundation stone in 1864 decorated with Celtic interlace, round tower, Celtic cross, bard and harp and then buried with other 'relics'.

If the political ideology underpinning the monuments was only subtly expressed in stone and bronze, the activities surrounding the projects did put them in one of two camps for contemporaries; those that were financed by public subscription and unveiled to vast crowds, and those financed by the donations of a few and unveiled to a politely clapping audience. Thus the efforts of patriotic Protestants to claim their figures for Ireland were dramatically overshadowed by nationalists – the demonstration that accompanied the laying of the foundation stone for the O'Connell monument in Dublin was the most spectacular seen in Dublin at that date, while the Albert monument, lacking its statue of Prince Albert, was merely viewed by the Duke of Edinburgh in 1872; in 1870 an estimated 20,000 turned out for the unveiling of the statue of Smith O'Brien seven months after the Earl of Carlisle had been unveiled at a private ceremony in Phoenix Park.

There was a strong feeling in England that Ireland after the famine, largely unexplored, and unexplained in literature, was more alien than other foreign countries. It was as though, as Thomas Flanagan has written, 'England had resolutely locked the door against an ugly, insoluble mystery. Ireland itself was locked in with the mystery, a land of incoherences, half-formed ideals, and warring images'.[31] But, on the evidence of the monuments, one important and in many ways heterogeneous group, the moderate Catholic nationalists, had opened the door, stepped a good way over the threshold and was shouting loudly and clearly, in grammatical English. The portrait statues of Irish figures were easily comprehensible to the English and the impression they gave was of a desire for acceptance on largely English terms. The Young Ireland project of the 1840s had been realised with qualifications. With Grattan, Smith O'Brien, O'Connell and John Gray lining the central thoughfare of Dublin, Protestants rubbed shoulders with Catholics. But, their credentials for such public exposure were that they had worked for the rights of the Catholic majority and those who had not had peripheral locations: the rhetoric at the unveiling ceremonies of these 'Catholic nationalists' also evoked unity on Catholic terms. Thomas Davis's request that the portrayal of national figures evoke nationalist emotions was also realised, but in a subdued manner. The distinctive features, gestures and sartorial details were recognisable and, judging by subsequent reproductions, became symbolic. But they were less distinctively Irish than the Celtic crosses erected in Catholic cemeteries by the Fenians to honour the Manchester Martyrs, or the pikemen, Erin figures and Celtic crosses that woud be prevalent at the end of the nineteenth century for the 1798 centenary. The

31 Thomas Flanagan, 'Literature in English, 1801-91', in W.E. Vaughan, *New History of Ireland*, p. 510.

figures could evoke the 'self-denial, justice, beauty, valour, generous life and proud death' for which Davis had hoped, but it would be difficult to distinguish this ideal from the Victorian aim of presenting public honour and private virtue to stimulate emulation. Finally, the statues had the unquestioned political message that Young Ireland required of art, but there was less an implication that Ireland should have a separate, distinctive existence than that Ireland be considered equivalent to England, its pantheon of heroes matching those elsewhere.

Oscar Wilde's Gift and Oxford's 'Coarse Impertinence'

SANDRA F. SIEGEL

I

I must also, for the sake of the good fame and position of the Oxford Union, express a hope that no
other poet or writer of English will ever be subjected to what I feel sure you as well as myself are
conscious of, the coarse impertinence of having a
work officially rejected which has been no less
officially sought for.[1]

The early biographies regard Wilde's gift of his *Poems* to the Oxford Union,
Oxford's undergraduate debating society, as an instance of his inflated sense of
himself. This early view of Wilde's insuppressible, flamboyant, and self-drama-
tizing pursuit of notoriety has persisted across every decade of Anglo-
American criticism. Rodney Shewan, writing in the late 1970s, remarks that
'... Wilde's latest commentator dismisses all of the pre-1886 work as "an exercise in imitation", the productions of that "boyish, carefree plagiarizer"'.[2] A
decade later, in his sustained scholarly study published in 1980, Norbert Kohl
joins Wilde's 'flamboyance' with his 'plagiarism' as twin expressions of one
motive. How familiar Kohl's Wilde is: 'In 1881 ... they [the poems] were printed ... in London. Wilde paid for the publication himself.'[3] This is one sign, for
Kohl, of Wilde's pursuit of notoriety. Kohl does not point out, as he might
have, that in the late nineteenth century publishing one's own work was common practice. Kohl continues: 'The letter that [Wilde] wrote in May 1881, try-

---

1 Oscar Wilde, in a letter to the Librarian of the Oxford Union Society, early November
  1881, as dated by Rupert Hart-Davis (ed.), *More Letters of Oscar Wilde* (Oxford, 1987),
  pp. 36-7.
2 Rodney Shewan, *Oscar Wilde: Art and Egotism* (London, 1977), p. 7. Shewan is referring
  here to Christopher Nassar's *Into the Demon Universe* (New Haven, 1974).
3 Norbert Kohl, *Oscar Wilde: The Works of a Conformist Rebel*, trans. David Henry Wilson
  (Cambridge, 1989), p. 15.

ing to interest the publisher in his juvenilia' concludes with 'the sly confident
claim that "Possibly my name requires no introduction."' Kohl goes on to say
that the success of the book '... appeared to confirm the audacious self-advertisement of its author ...' He cites four brief censorious passages from reviews
published during the summer of 1881. Although he inflects them differently,
he reiterates earlier biographical narratives of those responses: 'Particularly
galling [to Wilde],' Kohl continues, 'was the rejection of a copy of *Poems* that
[he] sent to the library of the Oxford Union ... Normally little attention was
paid to such gifts, and they would certainly not be refused, but on this occasion
there was a veritable explosion. Oliver Elton, who was later to make a name
for himself as a literary historian, was already, at the age of twenty, so well read
as a student that he was able to identify the innumerable allusions in Wilde's
poems to earlier literary works, and he protested vigorously against acceptance
of the volume.' Kohl quotes several lines from Elton's putative remarks, and
concludes: 'As a result, the book was rejected and sent back to the author.'[4] The
pages that follow introduce two stories: one is of the Oxford Union and the
other is of Oscar Wilde. I bring into view considerations about both subjects
which differ from those that Wilde's biographers characteristically emphasize.
These considerations enable us to locate in the encounter between them the
decorous optimism of affability and their refusal to acknowledge their mutual
animosity.

II

Kohl's source for what young Oliver Elton said is Hesketh Pearson's *Oscar
Wilde, His Life and Wit* (1946). This life of Wilde, so richly and memorably
woven with biographical and anecdotal details, has neither a complete bibliography nor any notes.[5] H. Montgomery Hyde, in his *Oscar Wilde* (1975), does
provide notes. From Elton's speech he quotes about twenty lines. For this reference, however, there is no source.[6]

   Richard Ellmann, whose biography was published after Kohl's, cites the
same putative speech that Elton made at the meeting of the Oxford Union.
Ellmann, unlike Pearson, does provide a source. It is a memoir by the poet,
Henry Newbolt, that claims to recall decades later precisely what Elton said in
1881.[7] Yet even in the one source that Ellmann cites, Newbolt himself admon-
ishes his readers: 'The speech was no doubt better than my recollections of it.

---

4   Ibid., p. 15.
5   Hesketh Pearson, *Oscar Wilde: His Life and Wit* (New York, 1946), p. 46.
6   H. Montgomery Hyde, *Oscar Wilde* (New York, 1981), p. 49.
7   Richard Ellmann, *Oscar Wilde* (London, 1987), p. 140.

...'[8] In fact, neither have Kohl, Ellmann, nor any other biographer verified Elton's apocryphal speeches or otherwise looked at the episode as closely as it deserves, nor do we know from any reliable sources what Elton said. A few further observations will illuminate somewhat differently the familiar version of this encounter and its principal players.

At least nine reviews of *Poems* were published in England several months before Wilde presented his gift to the Union, and at least three of these circulated widely. The critical reception was mixed: some reviews did indeed point disdainfully to the various literary echoes and allusions, which in them were cited liberally, and which cast doubt on Wilde's resourcefulness as a poet. These reviews were undoubtedly fresh in the mind of young Oliver Elton, whose erudition Kohl admires and on whose authority, in Kohl's account, the Oxford Union wisely and justifiably rejected Wilde's gift. Other reviews, however, praise Wilde's artfulness and admire his reliance on the traditions that inspire him to seek and, at times, find, his distinctive voice.[9]

Any consideration of the debate that was staged at the meeting – although I will not take up that consideration fully here – must acknowledge that Wilde had been selected only a few years earlier as the recipient of the Newdigate Prize whose Selection Committee read submissions that were signed pseudonymously.

Wilde's 'plagiarism', which some of the reviews abjured and which, at the Oxford Union, was likely to have been rehearsed when the question arose of accepting Wilde's gift, belongs to a considerably wider controversy. That controversy was made familiar by the accusations directed, in the mid-1860s and after, against the young Swinburne; by Chatterton's forgeries; by Macpherson's *Ossian*; and by discussions within the emergent cosmopolitan literary culture of whether art is originary or representational. Obvious examples of such discussions were Arnold, of whom Wilde's opinion was deeply divided, in *The Study of Poetry* and *The Function of Criticism at the Present Time,* and Emerson, of whom his opinion was deeply respectful, in *Quotation and Originality* and *Nature.* There is a great deal more to be said about the currency of the subject of 'plagiarism' and 'originality', a subject to which Wilde would soon turn his attention, first in his fiction and then in his critical essays. That more speculative controversy about the origin of art and the relation of the 'artist' to the artwork he or she produces, a controversy that divided literary opinion and was thought to have practical moral consequences, belongs to a different subject than refiguring, as I wish briefly to do here, Wilde's encounter with Oxford.

8 Henry Newbolt, *My World as in My Time: Memoirs of Henry Newbolt* (London, 1932), pp. 96-7.
9 See, for example, *The Athenaeum*, 23 July 1881, pp. 103-04; *The Dial*, ii, no. 16 (August 1881), pp. 82-5; and *The Academy*, 30 July 1881, p. 85.

III

Rupert Hart-Davis, in *More Letters* (1985), and Richard Ellmann, in his biography (1987), point out that Wilde had been invited by the Librarian to present his book to the Union. Ellmann also points out that after the gift was returned, Wilde received an apology from the Union to which he replied. Nevertheless, for Ellmann, the episode reveals, as it does for Kohl, Wilde's pursuit of notoriety, his dandiacal self-absorption, and his eagerness to promote himself. A little more needs to be said about the episode and about Wilde.

The orchestrated bi-monthly meetings at the Union were preceded by a business meeting during which the Librarian reported on the books he had received. He then moved that the members accept them which, typically, they did. On 11 July 1881, when the Librarian moved that 'Oscar Wilde's *Poems*, presented by the author, be accepted by the Society,' the Minutes record that Oliver Elton opposed the motion. The Minutes record further that four members of the Union rose to speak against and four members spoke in favor of acceptance, although the minutes do not record what was said. It was uncommon at meetings of the Union for debate, greatly anticipated as the principal activity of the meetings, which were convened for topics of which members were duly apprised, to occur during the discussions of items of business. On this occasion, however, Elton, and, perhaps, five other speakers, were poised and prepared to object to the Librarian's motion. Nor do the minutes record what was said when a member from Keble 'asked a question of the Librarian relative to "the discharge of officers of their official duties"'. The minutes do record that '*Questions were asked relative to the Librarian writing to authors to ask them to present their works to the society and the Hon. President and Hon. Librarian replied*' (my emphasis).[10]

It is likely that the interrogation of the Librarian's authority to solicit books revealed certain local animosities, perhaps personal, perhaps political, that the members were conveying to one another and it is unlikely, whatever those animosities and allegiances were, that Wilde himself, who had left Oxford in 1879, played any significant part in the immediate internecine enactments that characterized college life. At the July meeting that voted to return to Wilde the gift he had sent, the consideration of his poems diverted those in attendance from the orderly progression of the programme. Typically, the time allocated for items of business was brief. As the subject of accepting Wilde's gift unexpectedly became the unannounced subject of debate, the Union arrived at the unprecedented decision to refuse Wilde's *Poems*.[11] This undoubtedly prompted the apology to Wilde from the Librarian whose request had set into motion

10   *Minutes of the Oxford Union Society*, 11 July 1881.
11   Hart-Davis, *More Letters*, pp. 36-7.

such untoward behavior on the part of others. Never before had a book been presented that had not been accepted: but in this case, the more indecorous precedent had been established of rejecting a gift that the author had been invited to present.

To the Union's letter of apology, probably in November 1881, Wilde replied that he regretted their decision, his 'chief regret indeed being that there should still be at Oxford such a large number of young men who are ready to accept their own ignorance as an index, and their own conceit a criterion of any imaginative and beautiful work.' In the same letter, he expressed the hope that 'no other poet or writer of English will ever be subjected to what I feel sure you as well as myself are conscious of, the coarse impertinence of having a work officially rejected which has been no less officially sought for.' Two weeks following, at the 17 November meeting of the Union, George Curzon raised once again the question of the behavior of the Union for which, in another letter, Wilde thanked him.[12]

It is worth pausing to notice in the foregoing passage Wilde's innocence and his wishfulness. His innocence permitted him to attribute the behavior of 'such a large number of young men' to their 'conceit' and to their acceptance of their own 'ignorance' – as though the reception of his *Poems* were a simple aesthetic matter. His wishfulness permitted him to imagine that 'ignorance,' rather than knowledge or ill-will, explained the 'coarse impertinence' of the Oxford undergraduates who came only a few years after he left.

Certainly not every undergraduate who voted at the meeting had read Wilde's poems or formed an opinion about them. On the contrary, the debates at the Union that followed the business meeting whose conventions were practiced in this instance, as well, were typically exercises in the ingenuity, wit and rhetorical canniness of those who spoke on controversial subjects: degrees for women, women's suffrage, Home Rule for Ireland, dissolving the monarchy, socialism or free-enterprise, all of these topics – impersonal social issues – the Union considered. It was not only unprecedented to have officially rejected what had been officially sought. Perhaps, more astonishing still, was that when the Union debated upon and then voted to refuse Wilde's gift, it applied the conventions of debate in place for social issues to a collection of poems of a private person. In doing this the Union engaged in yet another odd breach of decorum.[13]

How are we to understand this exchange between Wilde and Oxford, this exchange that Oxford initiated and that Wilde terminated when the Union

12 Ibid., pp. 36-7, as dated, according to Hart-Davis, by the recipient, November 1881.
13 See, for example, David Walter, *The Oxford Union: Playground of Power* (London, 1984), chapter 1 and appendix 8; and Herbert Arthur Morrah, *The Oxford Union: 1823-1923* (London, 1923).

requested a gift of his poems, this exchange which, in turn, provoked Wilde's accusation of Oxford's 'coarse impertinence'?

During his years at Oxford (1874-78) Wilde had not been an active member of the Union. It was the training ground, for the most part, of those who planned to enter the civil service or to pursue a career in politics, neither of which held Wilde's interest. Nevertheless, when he presented his *Poems* to the Library he acknowledged his gratitude to Oxford: in receiving the volume Oxford, by honoring him, would have acknowledged his success. His gift might have consolidated his fragile link to the centre of English literary culture. By refusing the gift, Oxford distanced itself from that association. The offense to Wilde could not have been simple: it was an offense to have had his poems thought unworthy; it was an offense to have had his gift refused; above all, he must have found himself offended by realizing that the conventions of decorum in which Oxford took pride were not observed in dealing with him.

IV

All encounters are a form of exchange: they reveal desires as well as expectations; they confirm or confound what one anticipates; they introduce or foreclose possibilities. Encounters mediate our perceptions of ourselves as well as our perceptions of others. They confirm our sense of who we are. Encounters incline us to test and to revise what we think we know: they confirm possibilities we anticipate or they unfold possibilities that surprise us. Encounters mediated by gifts enjoy a place apart from other exchanges: encounters mediated by gifts express the donor's attachment to the recipient: they express the donor's desire to become or to remain attached; gifts are an expression of being joined, one to the other.

The way in which gift giving joins donor to receiver is perhaps more complicated than at first appears. Though gifts join donor to recipient, this exchange is not exhausted by a single donation and reception. Gifts are presented as gratuitous, yet, at the same time, they incur a debt on the part of the recipient. The donor thus becomes a creditor. Although giving a gift is a generous act, it is as much guided by self interest. Emerson, to whom Mauss, in his remarkable essay on the gift, acknowledged his indebtedness, understood that gifts enrich the giver.

V

If gifts enrich the giver, donors whose gifts are refused are depleted. The circuit of exchange having been broken, the promise of reciprocity is foreclosed. That is one reason for depletion. The second is that a gift is at once an indicator of power and an attempt to preserve it. To refuse a gift renders the donor power-less.

To find oneself powerless when one imagined oneself to be powerful is also the condition of shame, which is the same shame that Wilde must have felt when the Union returned his volume of poems in which he had inscribed: 'To the Oxford Union, My first Volume of Poems'.[14] When his Poems were returned he might have chosen to call Oxford's attention to a half-dozen odd departures from the Union's customary behavior and about which he might have conveyed his displeasure. In the letter he wrote, however, he chose to rep-rimand Oxford for 'coarse impertinence' to which, he wrote, he hopes 'no other poet or writer of English will ever be subjected'.[15] This is a strange inver-sion of a larger encounter that enacted the same cultural logic. That larger encounter is not of a gift given and refused but of a conquest that refused to acknowledge resistance. The one entailed Wilde and Oxford: the other entailed Ireland and England.

Both encounters involve refusal: the one of Oxford's refusal of a gift that ruptured a promising circuit of exchange; the other, of England's conquest of Ireland, that persisted despite successive acts of Irish resistance. When Wilde accused Oxford of 'coarse impertinence,' when accusation replaced the shame he must have felt for having thought himself more worthy in Oxford's eyes than Oxford was prepared to acknowledge, he expressed the same boldness with which, in 1889, eight years later, he reflected on English history: 'Blue-books ... form the record of one of the great tragedies of modern Europe. In them England has written down her indictment against herself and has given the world the history of her shame'.[16]

Here, of course, Wilde invokes England's shame not because England acknowledged the indictment against herself that her own official history records. Wilde invokes England's shame because England fails to acknowledge the discrepancy between the ideology she professes and the ideology she prac-tices. Wilde, writing in 1889, points to England's failure to feel shame. Her shame is her shamelessness. In his earlier encounter at Oxford, Wilde felt shamed although Oxford was impertinent. This larger encounter should have evoked England's shame, yet she felt none.

In 1882, shortly after Oxford returned Wilde's gift, he lectured widely in North America. We are greatly indebted to Robert D. Pepper for his recon-

---

14 I wish to thank Lady Eccles for having made this book available to me, and Princeton University for its services.

15 Hart-Davis, More Letters, pp. 36-7.

16 The Prose of Oscar Wilde (New York, 1916) p. 529. Hereafter, quotations are from this edi-tion. The essay first appeared in the Pall Mall Gazette, above the initials 'O. W.', as a review of J.A. Froude's The Two Chiefs of Dunboy. See Stuart Mason, Oscar Wilde: A Bibliography (London, 1967), p. 160.

struction, with valuable annotations, of Wilde's lecture, 'Irish Poets of the Nineteenth Century', which he delivered in San Francisco on 5 April 1882. It was the last of four lectures that he presented in San Francisco and the penulti-mate of the fifteen lectures that he presented on his California tour.[17] Pepper, like Wilde's early biographers, considers Wilde to be a typically self-absorbed dandy who was indifferent to politics as – according to that elusive construc-tion – dandies are. Rather than consider the lecture, which is decidedly politi-cal in its inflection and decidedly 'Nationalist' in its allegiance, as an expression of Wilde's heartfelt reflections upon Anglo-Irish affairs, Pepper considers the lecture to be an expression of Wilde's attempt to promote himself by appealing to his 'Hibernian' audience. In lecturing on the subject of Irish poetry and poets he was exercising what Pepper attributes to Wilde as his 'considerable talent for self-advertisement'.[18] Although Pepper's reconstruction and annota-tion of 'Irish Poets and Poetry of the Nineteenth Century' brings into view a consideration of Wilde that continues to draw little attention and drew even less when, in 1957, Pepper published his edition, it is interesting that Pepper regards Wilde as 'apolitical'. Accordingly, Pepper subordinates the argument Wilde presents in 'Irish Poets' to what Pepper considers to be Wilde's principal motivation: his desire, by pleasing his audience, to promote – and to indulge – his dandiacal self. Neither before Wilde gave this lecture – nor after – did he ever turn to the subject of Irish poets and poetry nor does Pepper consider Wilde to have made 'any public comments whatever on Irish politics, except for a half-dozen impromptu remarks, mostly to reporters, before and after his West Coast tour'.[19] If Pepper's presumption of Wilde's habitual 'flippancy' inclines him to dismiss the seriousness of his interest in Anglo-Irish affairs, Pepper's presumption that Wilde is not speaking in his own voice – he is speaking, according to Pepper, as an habitual 'plagiarizer'. Pepper considers Wilde's 'Irish Poets' to be largely a reiteration of Arnold's lectures, *The Study of Celtic Literature*. This is not the place to contest Pepper's reading of Arnold, Wilde, and the influence each exerted on the other. What interests me here is that Pepper directs our attention to Wilde's character rather than to his argu-ment.[20]

Pepper's observations about Wilde's public comments on Irish politics are not entirely accurate. In fact, those few excerpts which he provides of Wilde's

---

17 Oscar Wilde, *Irish Poets and Poetry of the Nineteenth Century*, ed. Robert D. Pepper (San Francisco, 1972) p. 45.

18 Ibid., p. 3.

19 Ibid., p. 18.

20 To take up here the complicated issue of plagiarism would require more time than this paper allows. What I wish to call to attention is the way in which the issue of plagiarism serves Pepper as a means of obviating the seriousness of Wilde's political responses. Ibid., 'Introduction'.

'impromptu remarks' suggest more than a casual engagement with the subject. From *Oscar Wilde Discovers America*, Pepper cites the following passage from a 'ten or fifteen minute' speech to a 'huge crowd' of Hibernians in the St Paul Opera House on the occasion of St Patrick's Day: 'When Ireland gains her independence, its schools of art and other educational branches will be revived and Ireland will regain the proud position she once held among the nations of Europe'. In Chicago, on 10 February, he referred to Ireland as 'the Niobe among nations'. In Milwaukee on 5 March, he declared himself 'strongly in sympathy' with Parnell's parliamentary movement for Irish Home Rule. And, for example, upon hearing of the Phoenix Park Murders he said this: 'When liberty comes with hands dabbled in blood it is hard to shake hands with her' but, he added, 'We forget how much England is to blame. She is reaping the fruit of seven centuries of injustice'. Or, speaking of the Land League, of which he had been a member, and which, in 1882, was successful in raising large sums from the Irish in America, he described the League's work as the most 'remarkable agitation that has ever taken place in Ireland, for it has through the influence of America, created a republican feeling in Ireland for the first time'. Perhaps if Pepper had not mistakenly considered 'Irish Poets' and these presumably 'impromptu remarks' to be discontinuous with Wilde's concerns before and after his North American tour of 1882, he might not have dismissed them as readily. It is not, for example, a disinterested, detached, apolitical dandy who, in 1877, in *Saunders' News-Letter*, wrote an impassioned letter of appeal, soliciting support for Henry O'Neill and, again, made a similar appeal, in *The Nation*, a year later. Henry O'Neill was perhaps best known as a portrait painter, as the author of an important political pamphlet, *Ireland for the Irish* (1868), and of *Fine Arts of Civilization*, in which he devotes himself to vindicating the character of the Ancient Irish 'from the errors of other Irish antiquarians, who have described [them] as vile savages'. Wilde praises O'Neill's 'unselfish patriotic devotion to Ireland'.[21]

Or, for instance, in 1889, echoing his mother's noteworthy but greatly neglected pamphlet of 1878 on the emergence of what Jane Elgee called 'the American Irish', Wilde points to the salutary influence – the 'new factor' – that has appeared in the social development of the country. 'To learn the secret of its own strength and of England's weakness, the Celtic intellect has had to cross the Atlantic. At home it had but learned the pathetic weakness of nationality; in a strange land it realized what indomitable forces nationality possesses'.[22]

Nor should we think we are hearing the voice of an indifferent dandy eager for notoriety when, in 1889, Wilde writes: 'If in the last century she [England] tried to govern Ireland with an insolence intensified by race hatred

---

21 See Owen Dudley Edwards, 'Oscar Wilde and Henry O'Neill,' *Irish Book Lover*, i, no. 1 (Spring 1959).
22 *Prose of Oscar Wilde*, p. 530.

and religious prejudice, she has sought to rule her in this century with a stupidity that is aggravated by good intentions'.[23]

VI

We have no reason to conclude from any of Wilde's extant writings that at the end of the decade of the 1880s, when he writes of England's attempt to govern Ireland with 'an insolence intensified by race hatred and religious prejudice' that he was thinking of the 'coarse impertinence' for which, at the beginning of the decade, he had reprimanded Oxford. Yet, once we introduce into view Wilde's reading of Anglo-Irish relations, no extant evidence is required to claim that his affective memory recalled that earlier encounter. Whether the impertinence of Oxford's refusal of his gift or the impertinence of the insolence of England's governance of Ireland, traces of the force of both encounters are imprinted across his life and his work.

Typically, biographies of Wilde turn away from his politics in favor of what they present or project as Wilde's pursuit of notoriety or self-dramatization or other acts that have as their purpose to mask his 'lurid secret'. These readings of his life obscure that larger encounter between Ireland and England. To locate the place of this larger encounter in the psychic economy of Wilde's affective memory – and to see Wilde's place in the economy of that exchange – will enable us to see a different Wilde than the one we have come to know – and a different England, too. When that imaginative adjustment occurs, the politics of Wilde studies as well as the politics of our perception of Wilde will have taken a new turn.

23 Ibid., p. 530.

The Baby and the Bathwater:
Cultural Loss in Nineteenth-Century Ireland

ANGELA BOURKE

This essay examines the process by which the nineteenth-century ideology of rationality, with its linear and colonial thought-patterns, gained ascendancy over a vernacular cognitive system in Ireland, especially after the Famine. It draws on a variety of lives and images from the nineteenth century to illustrate the rich resources of imagination, memory, creativity and communication that were jettisoned when the Irish language and its oral traditions were denigrated and discarded throughout much of the country. It is an attempt to imagine the baby that was thrown out with the bathwater when the old ways were purged. In 1845, when the South American food plant *Solanum tuberosum*, better known by a version of its Taino name, *batata*, succumbed all over Ireland to *Phytophthora infestans*, the potato blight fungus, the result was famine and cultural cataclysm. The huge population of poor, illiterate, mostly Irish-speaking agricultural labourers which had depended for food on the potato was devastated by starvation, disease and emigration, and a rising, English-speaking, middle class quickly moved to occupy the space vacated. The growing social importance of a Maynooth-trained priesthood, drawn mostly from the families of 'strong' tenant farmers, was only one aspect of the cultural change that followed.[1] Life changed for ordinary working people too. The miserable makeshift dwellings in which so many of the destitute poor had lived were swept aside, to be replaced from the 1880s on by the sturdy labourers' cottages provided for by the Labourers (Ireland) Act of 1883. Increased attendance at National Schools meant that literacy levels rose from 47% in 1841 to around 90% in 1911. As vernacular architecture gave way to standardised designs in housing, so oral tradition gave way to print.

The Latin naming of the potato and other plants both native and introduced, and their organisation into families, genera and species as laid down a century earlier by the Swedish botanist Carl von Linné, better known as Linnaeus, typified the literate, scientific, orderly way of thinking fostered by formal education and widely disseminated after the Famine. It found architectural expression in a range of institutional buildings, whose long corridors and

---

1 See Kevin Whelan, 'Pre- and Post-Famine Landscape Change' in Cathal Póirtéir (ed.) *The Great Irish Famine* (Cork and Dublin, 1995), pp. 19-33; James O'Shea, *Priests, Politics and Society in Tipperary (1850-1891)* (Dublin, 1983).

uniform rows of windows still recall the administrative structures they were built to house. Its mastery of the natural world was illustrated and celebrated in the Botanic Gardens in Glasnevin, Dublin, planned in 1789, and greatly expanded in the nineteenth century.

Today the Botanic Gardens include an area where native plants are given their native Irish names, recalling a wealth of lore which was current before the Famine. When that Famine broke out, however, Glasnevin's whole emphasis was on the orderly, Latinate, rationality of the scientific system, the very basis of its existence. Political ideas too were encoded in its layout. Enormous glasshouses built between 1843 and 1876 allowed the Dublin Gardens, like others at Kew and in Belfast, to celebrate the triumphs of colonialism along with those of science, for they sheltered the many species brought back from tropical climates by explorers, and displayed them, duly named and labelled, for the public's edification.

Richard Turner (1798-1881), was the Dublin ironmaster who created the glasshouse ranges of Belfast, Kew and Dublin. He began as a maker of Dublin fanlights, whose basic form recurs in even his most audacious creations.[2] When his curvilinear range at the National Botanic Gardens in Dublin was meticulously restored and reopened to the public in 1995, it was somewhat surprising to see Frank McDonald describe it in the *Irish Times* as 'the most important nineteenth-century building in Ireland'. This was, after all, a home for plants and not for people; but consider what else that century had built! Compared with the convents, orphanages, workhouses, prisons and Catholic chapels that grew up so assertively in the Irish landscape during the nineteenth century, the grand sweep of the curvilinear range has a billowing beauty that is at once exuberant and delicate. Its restoration was a celebration of an Irish craftsman artist's creativity, and of his imaginative and daring solutions to the problems of constructing a transparent building in a rainy climate.[3] Turner's ability to translate the tested techniques of fanlight construction into a third dimension; bending what had been given; making glass, of all materials, appear flexible, stands in sharp contrast to the rigid authoritarianism conveyed by much of his century's architectural legacy in Ireland.[4]

In the area of popular culture in nineteenth-century Ireland, that authoritarianism was expressed in a furious opposition on the part of the institutions of church and state to the uncentralised and unstandardised forms of knowledge and creative endeavour which still endured strongly in rural areas. Poets, storytellers and traditional healers were well known in their own areas, acknowledged as creators, custodians and interpreters of intangible wealth.

2 Jeremy Williams, *A Companion Guide to Architecture in Ireland* (Dublin, 1994), p. 160.
3 Ibid.
4 Maurice Craig, *The Architecture of Ireland: From the Earliest Times to 1880* (London, 1989 [1982]), p. 304.

However they were given short shrift in schools, law-courts, chapels and hospitals. These artists and intellectuals of the vernacular tradition have left no architectural memorial, yet they did create lofty and dazzling three-dimensional constructions, as impressive in their way as Turner's great glasshouses, in which to house information and ideas, new as well as old, and they were adept at guiding their listeners through them.[5]

In the absence of writing, as Walter Ong has reminded us, there is nowhere outside the mind to store information.[6] Oral cultures have therefore developed elaborate verbal art-forms through which to arrange knowledge and ideas in patterns, partly in order to conserve and transmit them with maximum efficiency; partly for the intellectual and aesthetic pleasure of such patterning. Much of what an oral culture has to teach is packaged and conveyed in stories.

By contrast with the Linnaean botany celebrated in Glasnevin, before and after the Famine an Irish ethnobotany of native plants, founded on a combination of practical knowledge and association of ideas, was characteristic of the vernacular tradition and had its most elaborate expression in the Irish language. Although some of its elements were to be found in herbals and other texts, this unsystematised yet detailed knowledge had been transmitted for centuries almost entirely through traditional practices and oral narratives. Some of its stories had been imported from Europe in medieval times and had close connections with medical and religious traditions; others invoked the indigenous 'fairies' or 'good people'[7]

Lus mór is one of several Irish names of the purple foxglove that grows often over a metre high in sheltered places. Printed descriptions of *Digitalis purpurea*, as the Linnaean system calls it, include warnings that all parts of the plant contain glycosides, at once a powerful cardiac medicine and a dangerous poison. In the absence of a formal system of education and accreditation, or of botanic gardens in which to display plants and their properties, vernacular oral tradition stored knowledge about dangerous and useful plants like this one in narrative and ritual practice.[8] The foxglove is widely reputed to have fairy connections, a belief reflected in names like *méaracán sí*, or 'fairy thimble', and made explicit in the following instruction, recorded in Co. Leitrim in 1895 by Leland L. Duncan:

5 See Angela Bourke, 'The Virtual Reality of Irish Fairy Legend' in *Éire-Ireland*, xxxi, no. 1-2 (1996), pp. 7-25.

6 Walter Ong, *Orality and Literacy: The Technologizing of the Word* (London, 1982), p. 39.

7 Nicholas Williams, *Díolaim Luibheanna* (Dublin, 1993); see also Geoffrey Grigson, *The Englishman's Flora* (St Alban's, 1975).

8 Williams, *Díolaim Luibheanna*, pp. 103-8 and *passim*, devotes more space to traditions about *Digitalis purpurea* than to almost any other plant. Lady Gregory collected information about *lus mór*, but glossed it (incorrectly) as mullein. See Lucy McDiarmid and Maureen Waters (eds), *Lady Gregory: Selected Writings* (London, 1995), p. 80.

If you have a cross or peevish child, or one that from being in good health becomes sickly, and you have reason to believe it is a fairy child, the following plan may be tried in order to ascertain whether this is the case. Take lusmore (foxglove) and squeeze the juice out. Give the child three drops on the tongue, and three in each ear. Then place it [the child] at the door of the house on a shovel (on which it should be held by some one), and swing it out of the door on the shovel three times, saying 'If you're a fairy away with you!' If it is a fairy child, it will die; but if not, it will surely begin to mend.[9]

A 'fairy child' meant a changeling substituted for a healthy, attractive human child who had been abducted by fairies. This was a common theme in folk legend; it could be a way of referring to a congenital disability or a failure to thrive,[10] but the legends and the sort of ritual described by Duncan were also often used to discipline or punish children.

Extracts of foxglove were widely used in rural Ireland for medicinal purposes, from what rational medicine considers 'real' conditions, such as heart problems, to 'imaginary' ones like the expulsion of suspected fairy changelings. Fairy belief legend, with its constant theme of ambiguity and danger, could encode both the dangers and the benefits of important plants, drawing attention to them and making them recognisable. Accidents could of course still happen, as they can in a modern pharmacy, and ethnographer Kevin Danaher once witnessed two *banbhs* and twenty-three ducks lying dead in a farmyard, after foxgloves had accidentally been included in their feed.[11] This incident happened in the twentieth century however, when the authority of fairy belief legend had been much undermined.

Practitioners of vernacular botanical and medical knowledge in the nineteenth century walked a narrow path between the cautious respect and gratitude of their neighbours and the vehement opposition of the Catholic clergy. Without the collecting and documenting of oral traditions done by members of the Anglo-Irish gentry, the record today would be much poorer. Lady Gregory collected and published information about herbs and herbal cures around Coole Park, Co. Galway, and gathered many stories about Biddy Early of Feakle, Co. Clare, who used to cure by means of a mysterious bottle.[12]

9 Leland L. Duncan, 'Fairy Beliefs and Other Folklore Notes from County Leitrim' in *Folk-Lore*, vii (1896), p. 163.
10 See Joyce Underwood Munro, 'The Invisible Made Visible: The Fairy Changeling as a Folk Articulation of Failure to Thrive in Infants and Children' in Peter Narváez (ed.), *The Good People: New Fairylore Essays* (New York and London, 1991), pp. 251-83.
11 Williams, *Díolaim Luibheanna*, p. 106.
12 McDiarmid and Waters, *Lady Gregory*, pp. 57-74 ('Biddy Early'); pp. 77-88 ('from "Herbs, Charms and Wise Women"').

Biddy Early was an exact contemporary of Richard Turner, the Dublin ironmaster, although it is unlikely that she ever heard of him, or he of her. She was charged with witchcraft in Ennis in 1865, and many stories are told about her confrontations with priests, usually depicted as officious and self-serving until she outwitted them. She was known to have enigmatic powers and was said to have been seen before dawn riding a white horse – a sign of complicity with the fairies.[13] She was probably the most famous of the 'fairy doctors', described by Sir William Wilde and others, to whom ordinary people resorted when ill or in trouble. According to tradition, she went on curing and prophesying until her death in 1874.

As studies of her continuing fame make clear, Biddy Early was not simply a charlatan or quack, nor were 'herb-doctors' simply amateur botanists. Certainly Biddy Early possessed knowledge of illnesses, as herb-doctors did of plants, but their moral authority had political, social and imaginative dimensions too. Crucially, the paradigms of their knowledge were radically different from those of the dominant culture.[14]

In colonial nineteenth-century Ireland, folklore was fashionable, but only in so far as it could be accommodated within the dominant paradigm. Outside the pages of literary folklore, the storyteller's art became invisible or even, as we shall see in the tragic case of the burning of Bridget Cleary in 1895, came to be regarded almost as a disease: a symptom of lamentable backwardness. Later, in the twentieth century, a newly independent Ireland elevated oral culture to high status when, like other emerging nations in northern Europe, it embarked on the wide-ranging and comprehensive project which still continues, of collecting and cataloguing folklore of all kinds. Rather than counting storytellers among society's artists however, it made them models of conservatism, enlisting them as custodians and symbols of a docile and unchanging peasant culture, in the service of what one scholar has called a 'folk ideology' in Irish politics.[15]

As in the buildings of Richard Turner, which have been celebrated as anticipating present trends in post-modern minimalism, fantasy and technology are linked in oral storytelling.[16] Walter Ong has remarked that narrative cycles are among the roomiest repositories which oral cultures use to store the things

---

13 See Meda Ryan, *Biddy Early, the Wise Woman of Clare* (Cork, 1978), p. 81; Edmund Lenihan, *In Search of Biddy Early* (Cork, 1987), pp. 79-80.

14 Ryan, *Biddy Early*; Lady Gregory, *Visions and Beliefs in the West of Ireland* (Gerrards Cross, 1970); Lenihan, *In Search*.

15 Gearóid Ó Crualaoich, 'The Primacy of Form: A "Folk Ideology" in de Valera's Politics' in J.P. O'Carroll and John A. Murphy (eds), *De Valera and His Times* (Cork, 1986), pp. 47-61.

16 Williams, *Díolaim Luibheanna*, p. 106

they know and wish to remember, including vast amounts of technical information. In Ireland, as in other cultures, storytellers are the interpreters who make the stored materials palatable to the imagination and memory of listeners through imagination and fantasy.[17] As the nineteenth century progressed, however, and literacy levels rose, fantasy was sternly excluded from acceptable discourse. Fairy belief legend, an elaborate system of fictions through which a significant mode of vernacular thinking is articulated, was clearly in opposition to the modes of literacy, and became increasingly associated with poverty and marginality. Although a growing antiquarian interest in its narratives as oral literature led to their publication in numerous collections, its terms of reference were consistently denigrated and repudiated by educated Catholics as they turned towards English literature. Indeed Joep Leerssen has suggested that a literate interest in fairies was almost confined to conservative Protestants.[18] At best, mention of fairies came to be regarded by middle-class nationalists as frivolous, childish or unsophisticated; at worst, it could be sinister, a shibboleth which revealed adherence to discredited ways of thinking.

'When electric light came in,' many Irish country people have said in this century, 'the fairies went away.' The lives of three people born in the second half of the nineteenth century, straddling class, gender and language barriers, illustrate the shift that was completed with rural electrification in the 1940s: away from the vernacular modes of thought that went with the Irish language, and with travelling barefoot through a waterlogged landscape; towards English, and towards literacy, shoes, paved roads and electric lighting. The gains of course were considerable, but so were the losses.

Mary O'Brien, known as 'Sissy', daughter of a strong farmer from Lough Gur in Co. Limerick, was born in 1858. Her memories of girlhood on the 200-acre farm which her father rented from Count de Salis are told in print by Mary Carbery as *The Farm by Lough Gur*. Although this is a second-hand, idealised account, it remains a valuable document of the devoutly Catholic and proudly nationalist rural middle class in post-Famine Ireland. It points to the sharp contrast in education between this class and the labourers and small farmers who shared their religion:

> There were a few small farmers whose land bounded ours who came every Sunday after Mass to hear what was going on in the world from *Freeman's Journal* which my father took in as well as the weekly Limerick paper. Few if any of them could read or write.[19]

---

17 Ong, *Orality and Literacy*, p. 140. See also Angela Bourke, 'Economic Necessity and Escapist Fantasy in Éamon a Búrc's Sea-Stories' (forthcoming).

18 Joep Leerssen, *Remembrance and Imagination* (Cork, 1996), p. 164.

19 Mary Carbery, *The Farm by Lough Gur* (Cork, 1937), p. 27.

The O'Briens spoke English, although many of the poorer people around them – small farmers, labouring people, beggars – still spoke Irish. Unlike most of their poorer neighbours too, they were literate; their whole cultural life centred on the church and on reading. With their mother, Sissy and her sisters read aloud almost every evening: they calculated the total at at least five hundred hours a year, the first hour of each evening devoted to essays, poetry and biography; the second hour to fiction. While Irish-speaking neighbours, and English-speakers too, listened to storytellers tell of the fairies of nearby *Cnoc Áine*, or of the ghostly *Gearóid Iarla*, doomed to gallop around Lough Gur every seven years until the silver shoes on his white horse were worn out, the O'Briens read books written in England. 'Mother enjoyed Maria Edgeworth more than we did', Sissy's account tells us, 'also Jane Austen. We much preferred George Eliot.'[20]

By the age of seventeen, Sissy O'Brien had spent three years at the convent boarding school of the Faithful Companions of Jesus in nearby Bruff, where she learned French, fine needlework and *bonne tenue*, as the FCJ sisters called deportment and etiquette.[21] Returning to the farm, she was shocked at what she now saw as the superstition of the young women employed by her family as house- and dairy-maids:

> The maids did not get into the other world in the way we did who knew more about it. Although they were thankful for holy days and went to Mass, they were really more interested in an old Irish world where fairies, witches and banshees took the place of our angels and saints.[22]

After witnessing the maids' May-eve rituals, when they strewed primroses on the doorstep and took other precautions said to keep the fairies away, Sissy O'Brien lost patience:

> 'Why do you let the maids be so silly?' I asked Mother when they were out of hearing. 'The nuns say we must never miss a chance of curing people of pagan superstition!' 'You can try', Mother said rather coldly; she didn't like me to quote the nuns at her in my 'superior manner'.[23]

This conversation took place about 1875: it illustrates the erosion over one generation of middle-class sympathy for the vernacular tradition, and the part played in that erosion by convent schooling.

20 Ibid., p. 172.
21 Ibid., p. 102.
22 Ibid., p. 158.
23 Ibid., pp. 157-62.

Bridget Cleary, daughter of a labourer in Co. Tipperary, may also have attended a convent school, for the Sisters of Mercy opened a primary school in Drangan, a few miles from her home, about the year of her birth, 1869. She was certainly literate, and was perhaps also taught to sew by nuns, for in her teens she went to Clonmel to serve an apprenticeship as a dressmaker. At the age of twenty-six she was back in her home townland of Ballyvadlea, married to Michael Cleary, a cooper, and living in one of the labourers' cottages recently built by the Cashel Poor Law Guardians.[24]

As skilled artisans, rather than agricultural labourers, the Clearys were not strictly entitled to rent such a cottage, and in fact Bridget's father, Patrick Boland, was the registered tenant. Their occupancy seems to have been the cause of some resentment locally; rumours circulated that the cottage was on the site of a fairy-fort, one of the circular mediaeval earthworks through which fairy narratives are mapped onto the Irish landscape; strange noises had been heard around it before the Clearys moved in.[25] Bridget Cleary was a smartly-dressed and good-looking young woman. As well as working as a dressmaker, she kept hens and sold both eggs and fowl. She appeared successful in all areas of her life, except that she and her husband had no children.

Despite her modern and relatively prosperous way of life, or perhaps because of it, Bridget Cleary was said by some of her neighbours to have an unhealthy acquaintance with another fairy-fort, at Kylenagranagh, about a mile from where she lived, although this may also have been a way of expressing the stigma of her childlessness. People remembered that her mother had known about the properties of herbs, and when she became ill with bronchitis in March 1895, an elderly relative insisted that the fairies were responsible and had spirited her away. Doctor's medicine would not cure her, he said: a herb-doctor must be consulted.

Bridget Cleary's name came to national and international attention a week or so later, when her violent death opened the whole question of Irish people's belief in fairies to general, if muted, discussion. She had been burned to death in her own home by the violent action of her husband, but when the case came to trial, this was presented as the culmination of a process designed to bring her back from the fairies by expelling a changeling left in her place. Instead of being hanged for murder, Michael Cleary was sentenced to twenty years for manslaughter.

The story broke slowly: first, the sick woman was said to have disappeared, and searches were instituted. Then her charred body was discovered in a makeshift grave, and meanwhile rumour took on the contours of oral narrative, producing an elaborate and fantastic story which shocked and fascinated

24 Angela Bourke, 'Reading a Woman's Death: Colonial Text and Oral Tradition in Nineteenth-Century Ireland' in *Feminist Studies*, xxi, no. 3 (Fall 1995), pp. 553-86.
25 Bourke, 'Virtual Reality', and *The Burning of Bridget Cleary* (London, forthcoming).

newspaper readers at home and abroad. One of the first papers to cover the story was the *Clonmel Nationalist*, whose account on Wednesday 20 March 1895 was headed 'Mysterious Disappearance of a Young Woman: The Land of the Banshee and the Fairy':

> What would read as a kin to the fairy romances of ancient times in Erin, is now the topic of all lips in the neighbourhood of Drangan and Cloneen. It appears that a young woman named Cleary, wife of a cooper, living with her father and husband in a labourer's cottage in the townland of Ballyvadlea, took ill a few days ago, was attended by priest and doctor, and believed to have been suffering from some form of nervous malady, she suddenly disappeared on last Friday night, and has not since been heard of. Her friends who were present assert that she had been taken away on a white horse before their eyes, and that she told them when leaving, that on Sunday night they would meet her at a fort on Kylenagranagh hill, where they could, if they had the courage, rescue her. Accordingly, they assembled at the appointed time and place to fight the fairies, but, needless to say, no white horse appeared. It has transpired that her friends discarded the doctor's medicine, and treated her to some fairy quackery. However the woman is missing, and the rational belief is that in the law courts the mystery shall be elucidated. I need not say that the authorities have their own notions of the matter, but I shall reserve further comments until events more clearly develop themselves.

The white horse referred to here recalls the one Biddy Early had been seen to ride one morning in Co. Clare, and the white horse on which *Gearóid Iarla* rides around Lough Gur: a vivid image, and a memorable one on which to hang a story.

Fairy abduction and fairy changelings are a commonplace of the legends told in Irish and English which are still to be heard in many parts of Ireland. They are told more often as tall tales than as factual accounts, but behind any of them the idea may linger that something true is being expressed. They were part of the belief-system of the maids on the O'Briens' farm beside Lough Gur, and underpinned the credibility of practitioners like Biddy Early. They could be used in a variety of ways: as cautions to children or adults against departures from society's norms, as euphemisms for anything from tuberculosis to drunkenness to marital infidelity, or simply as entertainment. They provided narrative maps of the physical and social landscape, marking the boundaries of the known and comprehensible world. They served as charters for action in the routines of daily life, explaining why butter was salted; why lone thorn trees were left undisturbed; why a piece of red flannel was sewn to babies' clothing; why certain places and people were best avoided. They were invoked to account for unusually good or bad luck – and sometimes to account for accidents and acts of violence. We remember that a 'fairy child' could either be one who was ill or disabled, or one who was being punished.

The story told at the time of Bridget Cleary's death, with its detail that the stolen woman could be pulled off her white horse and rescued, bears a striking resemblance to the narrative of the Scottish ballad 'Tam Lin'. Several versions have been collected in Ireland, including one transcribed in Belfast in 1904 from the singing of Ann Carter, an elderly Irish-speaker, originally from Tuam, Co. Galway. Ann Carter called the song 'Lord Robinson's Only Child', and said she had heard it from an old woman in Connemara:

> My name is young Lord Robinson, did you ever hear tell of me?
> I was stolen by the Queen of Fairies when I was a young babie.
> To-morrow will be the first of May, we'll all go out to ride;
> If you come down to Crickmagh, there we will all pass by.
>
> Let the black steed pass you by, secondly the brown;
> When a milk-white steed appears, pull the rider down.
> Then hold me fast and fear me not,
> I'm Lord Robinson's only child.[26]

Like most stories, the one told about Bridget Cleary drew on narratives already known, and believed, or partly believed, by at least some of the people who heard them. Under other circumstances it might have served as euphemism for domestic unhappiness or violence, or as a coded discussion of the issues and personalities involved; but because she died, and because state agencies and means of communication in nineteenth-century Ireland were highly efficient, this vernacular narrative was eventually told far beyond the community where it had been composed and where it could make sense.

Had Bridget Cleary not died of her burns, there might still have been a fairy narrative told about her: she herself might even have constructed it as a way of expressing something about her life. With time however, the story would have become more fictional and less factual as it was assimilated into a pre-existing body of legend. Had the Clearys continued to live in the same area of Co. Tipperary it might have offered an explanation as to why they were more prosperous than their neighbours. Women abducted by the fairies were often said to be infertile on their return, so it would also have drawn attention to the fact that Bridget Cleary had borne no children. Had her body not been discovered it could have provided a reason why her husband was avoided, or an induce-

---

26 Edith Wheeler, 'Irish Versions of Some Old Ballads' in *Journal of the Irish Folk Song Society*, i, no. 2-3 (1904), pp. 47-8 (reprinted 1967). See also Francis James Child, *The English and Scottish Popular Ballads*, 5 vols (New York, 1965 [1882-1898]), vol. i, pp. 335-58 (No. 39).

ment to him to leave the area. This story would eventually have joined other narratives in marking certain places as significant, and at that point the names of the protagonists might have dropped out. Later it might have been told in other communities and assigned to other families, other 'fairy forts'.

Many of the functions of fairy narrative became redundant when Michael Cleary and several of his neighbours were sentenced to spend terms from six months to twenty years in the prisons of Clonmel, Mountjoy and Mary-borough (now Portlaoise). Others became irrelevant when newspapers, rather than oral storytellers, were entrusted with the telling of what had happened. Life was changing, becoming modern, but the peculiar circumstances of this case meant that every aspect of vernacular culture came under grave suspicion. Fairy legend in itself is neutral; a currency, like money, it could be invoked to justify either compassion or cruelty. Even the fairies it depicts are not malevo-lent, but simply amoral, unreliable, not part of 'our' society. When Bridget Cleary died however, instead of being the medium through which ambiva-lence or conflict could be discreetly expressed within oral society, fairy legend was dragged into the public view and ranged with the oral, primitive and 'dark' against the literate and enlightened. Even the wild flowers of the Irish countryside were marshalled into the master narrative of print, and stood accused. Much was made of the remedy prescribed for Bridget Cleary by Denis Geaney, a herb doctor who lived on the slopes of Slievenamon, a few miles from the Clearys. 'Was it lusmore?' witnesses were asked. The answers were inconclusive, but antiquarians and folklorists knew at least that *lus mór* (literally, 'big plant') was much spoken of in folklore of the fairies. Poison was suspected, but a coroner's inquest showed no harm caused by the herbs which were given to Bridget Cleary as she lay ill. Nevertheless, the trial with its atten-dant publicity ensured that middle-class Irish Catholics would distance them-selves even more than before from the ways of oral culture.

The great cultural shifts which followed the Famine in Ireland were felt less in *Gaeltacht* areas than elsewhere. Here, in densely-populated areas of mostly poor land, chiefly along the Atlantic coast and on islands, Irish remained as the language of daily life. The influence of priests and police was less than in other parts of the country; there were no large farms; towns were small, and far apart, and the restless young looked to America rather than to clerical jobs in Ireland for prospects of advancement. Singing and storytelling remained as major out-lets for cultural expression, as well as important vehicles of education, so that when the collectors of the Irish Folklore Commission began work in 1927, they found a rich harvest.

Éamon Liam a Búrc was born in Carna, Co. Galway, in 1866. At fourteen he emigrated to Minnesota with his family, but at seventeen, jumping on and off trains, he lost a leg. His parents brought him back to Connemara, where he lived until his death in 1942.

Éamon Liam became a tailor: a sedentary occupation for which lame boys were often trained (as blind boys were taught music). Like the famous lame 'Tailor Buckley', Tadhg Ó Buachalla, of Gougane Barra, Co. Cork, he also became a storyteller. He could not read or write, but his physical disability did not stop him becoming an expert sailor and fisherman. Like Richard Turner curving fanlights and enlarging them to make conservatories, he moved proficiently in a three-dimensional world, whether of fabric in his tailoring, of wind and water in sailing, or of the imagination. His memory was formidable, but was only one of the pillars which supported his art. He excelled at the long, complex, episodic hero-tales in which various 'King of Ireland's Sons' kill giants and rescue princesses, but also told fairy legends in thoughtful versions that are much longer than usual, full of social and psychological insight as well as technical and topographical detail.

One of his stories, called 'Seoirse Lap and the Fairy Queen' addresses questions of bereavement and grief, natural and premature death, and the conflict a young man may feel between filial obligation and his own sense of adventure.[27] It is full of practical details about the making and selling of nets, yet its plot concerns Seoirse Lap's dealings with a community of fairies who live in the hill beside his house. Led by their queen, they are in the habit of abducting humans who take their fancy, but he manages to outwit them by weaving a net across their exit, sturdily insisting on his right to carry on his trade. The story is told with verve and wit, and recounts how Seoirse travelled through the air with the fairies to adventures far from home, consuming copious amounts of alcohol in the process. The storyteller aims sly digs at city people, their credulity, dependence on money, and standards of hygiene.

Like other tellers of fairy legend, but more than most, Éamon a Búrc plays on the varying degrees of credulity to be found among a complex audience. Details which his audience knows to be truthful are woven together with the frankly preposterous. By telling a story so seductive that no listener would wish to say aloud 'That is a lie!', he subverts his own narrative's claim to authority at the same time as he asserts it, holding out the possibility of access to a club of the adult initiated: like Richard Turner's curved, soaring glasshouses, his elaborate fairy narratives are, after all, designed to be seen through.[28]

In the three-dimensional structures of fairy belief legend, highly-charged and memorable images like that of Biddy Early, *Gearóid Iarla*, or Bridget Cleary emerging from a fairy dwelling on a white horse are the retrieval codes for a whole complex of stored information about land and landscape, community relations, gender roles, medicine, and work in all its aspects: tools, materials and techniques. The storyteller may spend less time at physical work than many of

27 See 'Seoirse Lap agus Baníon na Bruíne' in Peadar Ó Ceannabháin (ed.), *Éamon a Búrc: Scéalta* (Dublin, 1983), pp. 223-38.
28 Bourke, 'Virtual Reality'.

his or her listeners, and may be branded by the unsympathetic as a dealer in mumbo-jumbo, but as Walter Benjamin remarked, 'an orientation toward practical interests is characteristic of many born storytellers.'[29]

That the imaginary structures built in traditional storytelling could accommodate the new as well as the old, and the contemplation of emotional as well as practical problems, we see from the stories Éamon a Búrc told for folklore collector Liam Mac Coisdeala between 1928 and 1942, but a story told as recently as 1976 shows that this art is anything but dead. Its disturbing and unforgettable central image also holds out the intriguing possibility that the baby thrown out with the nineteenth-century bathwater may still be swimming somewhere not far away.

On 16 May 1976, John Henry, of Kilgalligan, Co. Mayo, told some stories in Irish for his friend, folklorist Séamas Ó Catháin. One of them, which lasted only a couple of minutes in the telling, is a version of a well-known legend which belongs to a whole complex of stories about fairy dwellings under the sea.[30] Skilled storytellers in coastal areas, like John Henry and Éamon a Búrc, have always used such narratives to convey to their listeners some idea of the dangers, beauties and mysteries of the sea, and of the skill and wisdom needed by those who venture out in boats.[31]

In this legend, John Henry tells of three men from Portacloy who went fishing for cod in a small boat off Porturlin. He describes the route they took, and the bait and tackle they used – then tells how one of them hooked a live baby up from the sea. His story quickly moves into the realm of the fantastic, as a woman's head appears above the water, scolding the men and demanding the child's return. They hastily throw the baby back, and make for home, barely escaping from a vicious storm that suddenly blows up.

The details John Henry gives of fishing techniques and navigation at sea give his story verisimilitude: they keep the audience listening. In themselves however, they are important cultural wealth, here kept safe by being stored alongside the intensely memorable image of the baby on the fishing line. Like the rhetoricians of the middle ages, or indeed the modern advertising expert, who marks out memory by means of deliberately grotesque or otherwise startling pictures, the finest storytellers know how to select this sort of image.[32]

The baby in John Henry's story underlines the dangers of the sea, and reminds listeners of the separate areas of responsibility and competence allotted to women and to men in traditional society. It expresses some of the unease

29 Walter Benjamin, 'The Storyteller: Reflections on the Works of Nikolai Leskov' in Hannah Arendt (ed.), *Illuminations* (London, 1992 [1973]), p. 86.

30 'Páiste aníos ó Thóin na Farraige / A Child from the Bottom of the Sea' in Séamas Ó Catháin (ed.), *Scéalta Chois Cladaigh / Stories of Sea and Shore* (Dublin, 1983), pp. 54-6.

31 Bourke, 'Economic Necessity'.

32 Frances A. Yates, *The Art of Memory* (London, 1966) pp. 93-113. See also Ong, *Orality and Literacy*, 'The Noetic Role of Heroic 'Heavy' Figures and of the Bizarre', pp. 69-71.

and anxiety caused when these are found to overlap, and also notes, in a wholly non-confrontational, metaphorical way, that crisis pregnancies occur, and that unwanted or unexpected babies do sometimes turn up to change people's lives. That some of these very real babies have been consigned in the past to oblivion in the sea is something we know very well in Ireland at the end of the twentieth century. Following the Kerry Babies case of 1984, innumerable stories came to be told of pregnancies concealed and babies born in ways that showed how inadequate and impoverished was the social ideology of institutions inherited from the nineteenth century.

In terms of imaginative strategies, the baby fished from the sea may represent all that society has chosen to forget. In Brian Friel's play *Translations*, The schoolteacher, Hugh, is given a line from George Steiner when he says 'To remember everything is a kind of madness'. In oral storytelling, however, while much is forgotten, nothing is felt to be irretrievable. Certain kinds of knowledge are consigned to long-term storage, but the storytelling tradition always marks the spot, as fishermen mark their nets and lobster-pots with brightly-coloured buoys. Profoundly ecological in its thinking, the oral tradition recognises recurring connections of kinds to which the linear ideology of the nineteenth century was blind.

Fairy belief legends were a mainstay of popular culture in nineteenth-century Ireland. Their imaginative excess makes it difficult for the literate mind to take them seriously, but it is the essential and beautifully-embroidered padding which has allowed ideas and information to be conveyed without damage and kept safely until they were needed. Walter Benjamin's celebrated essay, 'The Storyteller', points to the differences between artfully-constructed stories and mere information:

> The value of information does not survive the moment in which it was new. It lives only at that moment; it has to surrender to it completely and explain itself without losing any time. A story is different. It does not expend itself. It preserves and concentrates its strength and is capable of releasing it even after a long time.[33]

Artists in various media are working again with the images and ideas of storytelling, and the art of storytelling itself seems set for a comeback, such as traditional music, singing and dancing have already witnessed. In the meantime, in published texts of oral stories and in the precious manuscript archive of the Irish Folklore Collection at the National University of Ireland, Dublin, we have a record of the art by which Éamon a Búrc and others like him guided their listeners through an unseen world inside the hills and beneath the sea, as though they made their own landscape transparent.

33 Benjamin, 'Storyteller', pp. 89-90.

Boccoughs and God's Poor:
Deserving and Undeserving Poor
in Irish Popular Culture

NIALL Ó CIOSÁIN

One of principal issues in the history of ideology in nineteenth-century Ireland has been the scale and character of the social interventions of the state. Compared to contemporary Britain, these were massive and far-reaching, in response to what was seen as acute economic crisis and continuing violence and disorder, most spectacularly manifest in the case of agrarian secret societies. The first half of the century, for example, saw the establishment of a centralised, full-time professional police force and court system, as well as a nationally-organised and funded primary school structure.[1]

In general, studies of these interventions have presented them as acculturating initiatives, attempting to produce change in attitudes and behaviour through a mixture of coercion and persuasion, and producing either massive resistance or massive change. Some studies have gone further, and have examined the reception of these interventions by those whom they affected, and of popular attitudes to those interventions in general. In the area of police and courts, for example, the use of petty sessions courts by the peasantry in Mayo has been discussed by McCabe and the public perception of the police by Griffin.[2]

This paper will consider one aspect of the reception of what was perhaps the most striking change in administration, the introduction of a Poor Law system of workhouses for the destitute, which was established in 1838 following a series of government reports in the previous decade. The Poor Law contrasts with the other administrative innovations in that there had been hardly any provision of that kind before, whereas in the cases of education and law, for example, structures, official or unofficial, predated the large-scale state interventions.[3]

---

1 The classic account is in O. MacDonagh, *Ireland: The Union and Its Aftermath* (London, 1977).

2 D. McCabe, 'Magistrates, Peasants and the Petty Sessions Courts: Mayo 1823-50' in *Cathair na Mart*, v (1985), pp. 45-53; B. Griffin, '"Such Varmint": The Dublin Police and the Public, 1838-1913' in *Irish Studies Review*, no.13 (1995-96), pp. 21-5.

3 Such mechanisms as existed are discussed in D. Dickson, 'In Search of the Old Irish Poor Law' in R. Mitchison and P. Roebuck (eds), *Economy and Society in Scotland and Ireland 1500-1939* (Edinburgh, 1988), pp. 149-59.

The historiography of the Poor Law in Ireland, in common with studies of poor relief mechanisms elsewhere, has been mainly institutional and administrative, an approach dictated by the nature of the source material, the bulk of which consists of administrative records. This is accompanied by discussion of ideological debates within those sections of the élite who were responsible for policy. Some have moved beyond an institutional focus, reconstructing, for example, the lives of some inmates who saw admission to the workhouse as a temporary expedient in a wider repertoire of survival strategies, or looking at the ratepayers who funded the system and at their reluctance or refusal to pay those rates.[4]

Little is known about public attitudes to the introduction of a bureaucratised welfare system, and how this related to popular conceptions of social responsibility and action. Were the ideas on which poor relief was founded shared by any section of the people, were the categories it used widely understood or even translatable into those of a popular culture which was rural and largely Gaelic?

The initial evidence on these issues comes from the report of the inquiry into Irish poverty of 1835. This inquiry, which took a very wide interpretation of poverty and recommended a program of capital investment and training rather than exclusive reliance on a workhouse system, spent two years gathering information at oral hearings. These hearings took place in one parish per barony in 17 counties, and, constitute a rich ethnographic source, both for attitudes and practices. This paper uses principally the reports from the mid-western counties, Roscommon, Galway and Clare, as well as Longford and Cork. The witnesses, whose contributions are given in extensive form, came from all classes. In Kilkee, Co. Clare, for example, they included two landlords, two Catholic priests, an Anglican minister, a doctor, two large farmers, one middling farmer, two small farmers, a cottier with two acres, a labourer, a nailer, a widow 'lately evicted', two beggars 'and several other farmers, labourers and tradesmen'.[5]

In early nineteenth-century Ireland, begging, 'vagrancy' in the language of the report, took place on an enormous scale. Economic crisis and deindustrialisation, producing massive unemployment in both agricultural and textile regions, meant that there was a large number of landless beggars, as well as others whose holdings were insufficient to maintain them throughout the year.[6]

4 H. Burke, *The People and the Poor Law in Nineteenth-Century Ireland* (Dublin, 1987); C. Clear, *The Homeless Young in Nineteenth-Century Ireland* (Galway, 1993); G. O'Brien, 'The New Poor Law in Pre-Famine Ireland: A Case History' in *Irish Economic and Social History*, xii (1985), pp. 33–49.
5 *First Report of His Majesty's Commissioners for Inquiring into the Condition of the Poorer Classes in Ireland*, H.C. 1835, xxxii. All subsequent page references in the text are to this report. There is a brief discussion of the report as an ethnographic source in N. Ó Ciosáin, 'Introduction' in *Poverty before the Famine: County Clare 1835* (Ennis, 1996).
6 T. O'Neill, 'Poverty in Ireland 1815-45' in *Folk-Life*, xi (1973), pp. 22–33.

During the summer months, between the planting and harvesting of the pota-toes, hundreds of thousands of people left their homes to beg. Some of the wealthier witnesses talk of giving to eighty or a hundred beggars every day in the summer, with farmers, cottiers and even the poorest of labourers in employment lodging beggars overnight. The beggars were almost invariably given alms in the form of potatoes rather than money.

How did the attitudes towards poverty and relief held by the less well-off donors compare with official or élite ones? We can begin with one of the dis-tinctions which was fundamental to the official view, that between 'deserving poor', to whom relief should be extended, and the 'undeserving poor', to whom it should not. Those who conducted the inquiry thought that the dis-tinction was not generally made, and that 'indiscriminate almsgiving' exacer-bated the problem of poverty. At first sight, much of the testimony corrobo-rates this, with witnesses declaring that they gave for the grace of God, that 'we do not look into circumstances' before giving, but held to the older Christian idea of charity as benefiting the donor rather than the recipient.

In practice, however, alms were not given without qualification, and many witnesses describe some means of discrimination between beggars. One of the most explicit statements came from Michael Rourke, a labourer in Bally-mahon, Co. Longford:

> I give lodgings to beggars, but would not admit every sort; the means I have of distinguishing is this – I see some of them quarrelling among themselves and blaspheming; many too on fair days get drunk on whiskey. I would not admit such characters into my house ... I am becoming more cautious in giving shelter to beggars ... one of them cut my blanket in two, and took half of it away with her; another stole my wife's cap; and a third stole a knife and fork from me. (p. 563)

Further west, there was a more precisely delineated characterisation of the undeserving poor. This was the figure of the 'boccough', a term used by wit-nesses from Mayo and Roscommon down to west Cork. In Boyle, Co. Roscommon, the testimony was summed up as follows:

> There is a particular class of beggars, called boccoughs, who resort to deceptive means of exciting compassion; they are usually found at fairs and markets, and are the most immoral class among the poor ... Boccough is an Irish word, signifying a beggar who strolls about, affect-ing the appearance of impotence or scrofulous disease. (p. 510)

These beggars were also reported as asking for money, rather than potatoes, and this money was thought to be either hoarded or spent on whiskey.

As a representation, the boccough corresponds to much of the classic image of the undeserving poor in early modern Europe. This was a category which had emerged within the urban cultures of later medieval Europe, partly as the result of poor relief mechanisms in towns and cities coming under pressure from increasing immigration from rural areas, especially in years of agricultural crisis. In adjudicating between claims on relief, urban authorities favoured those who were resident in the towns and saw the newcomers as less deserving of help.[7] A representation of the undeserving poor emerged in the form of a pejorative taxonomy, describing them as constituting different categories of tricksters and frauds. A fourteenth-century municipal statute in Augsburg, for example, forbade entry to five types of beggar: those who pretended to be converted Jews, those who pretended sickness, pilgrims who slept in front of churches, those who claimed to be murderers on the run, and those who wore hoods, presumably monks or pretended monks. Such categorisations developed into a literary genre which constructed more elaborate and ingenious typologies. This literature, which has been extensively discussed by Geremek and Camporesi, reached its height in an Italian work of 1485, *Speculum Cerretanorum,* 'The Mirror of Beggars', which listed 39 categories, including for example '*affarinati*', 'those who beg for flour under the pretence that it is to be made into communion wafers'. Other texts added to this by representing beggars as a fully developed counterculture, with a 'King of Beggars' and a beggars' language, known in English as 'cant'.[8]

The distinction between deserving and undeserving poor remained probably the fundamental distinction in social welfare policy in Europe until the twentieth century, and it underlay many of the developments of the early modern period. From the sixteenth century onwards, for example, when some of the urban poor began to be confined in large institutions, it was often the undeserving who were enclosed, partly because they were considered to be deceitful and dangerous, while many of the deserving continued to be helped at home. 'Indoor' and 'outdoor' relief, therefore, initially corresponded roughly to 'undeserving' and 'deserving'.

These motifs of fraud and counterculture are very much in evidence in descriptions of boccoughs by the witnesses interviewed by the Poor Inquiry. In Kilcreest, Co. Galway, John Griffin, a weaver, told of

> One man who goes about from fair to fair, with his arm bandaged from the elbow down, and though you would think by looking at him that

---

7 S. Woolf, introduction, *The Poor in Western Europe in the Eighteenth and Nineteenth Centuries* (London, 1986); R. Jutte, *Poverty and Deviance in Early Modern Europe* (Cambridge, 1994).

8 B. Geremek, *Truands et Miserables dans l'Europe Moderne (1350-1600)* (Paris, 1980); P. Camporesi, *Il Libro Dei Vagabondi* (Bologna, 1973).

he could scarcely move it, there is not a man in the room can use the two arms better than he. He was one day on the bridge of Ennis, where he had a quarrel with a policeman, to whom he gave a sound drubbing with his crutch and hunted him off the bridge.

Mr Mahon, a farmer, added that

> That man gave his daughter £30 fortune. He is like a king over the others, and people say he has a tribute from each of them. I saw him, at the fair of Kilcreest, take off the bandage in a drunken fit, and defy any man in the fair to try him at the stick. (pp. 478-9)

In Kilkeerin, Co. Roscommon, a stonemason called Gaffney said that

> There is a place near Strokestown, where they assemble every year in immense numbers; at this fair, called the fair of Ballinafad, the beggars are married for a year. The ceremony is performed by joining the hands of the parties over a pair of crutches, and hundreds return to have the rite renewed year after year. (p. 513)

Here the counterculture motif is extended to rites of passage and a suggestion that beggars have their own religion, making use of a convenient pun between a crutch and a cross, a pun which also worked in Irish, since crutches are 'maidí croise', 'cross sticks'.

The word 'bacach', literally 'lame', used in the sense of 'beggar', and with some pejorative overtones, was well-established in nineteenth-century Gaelic culture. 'Deilín na mbacach', 'the beggars' litany' or 'the beggars' rigmarole', a stylised prayer or blessing in return for alms and lodging, was an established oral genre throughout western regions. A song from Co. Waterford, 'Bacach Buí na Léige', 'The Yellow Beggar of the League' was glossed by a twentieth-century editor as follows:

> The beggars in old times in Ireland were a very well organised community, and in each district had something closely resembling a trade union for the purpose of excluding beggars from other districts.[9]

If the witnesses to the Poor Inquiry had an image of the undeserving poor, they also had one of the deserving poor, and a very clear distinction was made between the boccoughs and other beggars. This distinction persisted, to judge

---

9 D. de hÍde, *Amhráin Diadha Chúige Chonnacht* (Dublin, 1906), pp. 288-90; E. Ó Muirgheasa, *Dánta Diadha Uladh* (Dublin, 1936), pp. 380-96; M. Ní Annagáin and S. Clandillon, *Londubh an Chairn* (London, 1927), no. 60.

from a proverb current in Co. Mayo in the early twentieth century, 'ní bacach an fear siúil ach bochtán Dé' ('the wandering man is not a boccough but one of God's poor'). Even a proverb which exhorted charity, in other words, made a clear distinction between types of beggar.[10]

These fundamental categories of official poor relief, along with their representations, were therefore well-established in popular culture in early nineteenth-century Ireland. Differences emerge, however, in the ways in which individual beggars were allotted to these categories. For urban authorities, and later for the state, the undeserving were mobile, usually coming from rural areas into towns, and were not known to those from whom they sought aid. The witnesses to the Poor Inquiry, on the contrary, did not doubt the bona fides of the mobile rural poor, who, they felt, would not undergo the hardship and shame of begging unless they were forced by circumstance. The undeserving, the boccoughs, were often known to the witnesses, and were said to have a fixed abode in a town or village, even though they travelled from fair to fair. Broadly speaking, one might say that these represent almost diametrically opposite ideas of what constituted the two types of beggar. The difference would correspond to that between urban and rural conceptions of the undeserving poor. The attempted substitution of the former for the latter would constitute an ideological counterpart to the way in which the construction of workhouses in the 1830s and 40s represented the extension of urban modes of relief into the countryside.

The existence of a well-defined category of undeserving poor within popular culture and within Gaelic culture implies that the gap between official and popular views was not as complete as the commissioners themselves imagined or as a historian might assume. Whether this category was newly introduced or long-established is difficult to know. It may have been a response to growing numbers of poor and greater demands on charity in the early nineteenth century, but if that were the case, it might be expected to stigmatise the rural food beggars rather than town beggars, since it was the former who were increasing in numbers. Some witnesses in west Co. Cork, moreover, maintained that boccoughs had been more numerous in the past than in the 1820s or 30s.

In this respect, the fact that the undeserving were described by an Irish-language term is inconclusive. It could mean that the Gaelic culture had evolved or adopted the concept of undeserving poor as a category, or it could be that the retention of the term as pejorative after a language shift indicates the stigmatisation of an earlier Irish-language conception of poverty. The fact that the term was used almost exclusively by witnesses in the western, Irish-speaking areas would suggest the former.

There was one influential group in rural Ireland who may well have introduced or reinforced the idea of undeserving poor. This was the Catholic parish

10 T.S. Ó Máille, *Seanfhocla Chonnacht* (Dublin, 1952), p. 81.

clergy who, like the commissioners, were keen to discourage gratuitous relief, and who favoured the establishment of an institutionalised Poor Law system. There was an emblematic story in the testimony of Father Sheehy, parish priest of Kildysert, Co. Clare:

> About six weeks ago a woman, the lower part of whose face was enveloped in a cloth, apparently saturated with a serious discharge, was very successful in collecting alms from the congregation as they came out from mass. In the course of the day I had reason to suspect that she was an imposter, from the rapidity with which she devoured a very abundant dinner, which was given to her by a charitable individual. I had the bandage forcibly removed from her face, and she was found not to labour under any disease whatsoever. As a caution to the bystanders, I pointed out the deceit which had been practiced on them, and I had the greatest difficulty in preventing them laying violent hands upon her. (p. 614)

One of the mistakes this particular beggar made was to beg at the church gates, a practice which was discouraged by clergy of all denominations. In Granard, Co. Longford:

> [beggars] are not permitted to attend the doors or avenues of places of worship. Those who do generally present some disgusting spectacle and are regarded as imposters. (p. 568)

In the case of the Catholic clergy, this was partly because priests were themselves soliciting contributions at mass to fund church poor relief structures or other church expenditure. The most explicit statement came from Michael Comyn, parish priest of Kilkee, Co. Clare:

> Notwithstanding the influx of beggars to this place in the summer, I never saw more than two of them begging at the chapel; this is because I beg myself for the chapel to pay for its building, and the people give to me in preference to them. If I were to stop there would be plenty of them. (p. 625)

The introduction of the Poor Law system, therefore, was not a straightforwardly acculturating process, since one of its most basic categories was shared by most groups in Ireland by the 1830s. The state, moreover, as in the case of the establishment of the national school system a few years earlier, had had its path smoothed by the Catholic church, which by the early nineteenth century was beginning to function as a powerful hegemonic institution, both inside and outside the state structures.

Discourse and Hegemony: Race and Class in the Language of Charity in Nineteenth-Century Dublin[1]

MARGARET PRESTON

Dark as the heathen, in sin they roam;
Their school the wide world, the streets their home;
No voice to warm them, no hand to guide,
How should they know that the Lord hath died?[2]

But, oh! forget not me, an outcast child,
Poor, wretched, homeless, ignorant, and rude;
On whom the eye of mercy ne'er has smiled,
Untaught to fly from ill; or choose the good.[3]

In *Heathcliff and the Great Hunger*, Terry Eagleton cites Gramsci when arguing that hegemony is the '"permanently organized consent" by which modern states exercise their authority'.[4] Britain, says Eagleton, failed in its attempts to establish hegemony in Ireland because it never established this 'permanently organized consent'.[5] While Britain may not have established hegemony

1 I would like to thank Meabh ní Fhuarthain, Kevin O'Neill, Robert Savage, Jim Smith, Mrinalini Sinha, Paula Tirrell, Peter Weiler and Kevin Whelan, who have provided me with a generous amount of their time, advice and critical feedback for this paper. I would also like to thank the Boston College History Department for awarding me the Janet Wilson James Scholarship and the International PEO Sisterhood for the Scholar Award, both of which provided funds toward my travel to Galway where this paper was presented at the 1996 conference of the Society for the Study of Nineteenth-Century Ireland.
2 Miss Macpherson, 'Little London Arabs' in Sarah Davies, *Wanderers Brought Home* (Dublin, 1871), p. 17.
3 Charles Sabine, 'The Outcast's Appeal' in Davies, *Wanderers Brought Home*, p. 24.
4 See Terry Eagleton, *Heathcliff and the Great Hunger: Studies in Irish Culture* (London, 1995), p. 27 and Antonio Gramsci, *Selections from the Prison Notebooks*, ed. and trans. Quintin Hoare and Geoffrey Nowell Smith (New York, 1975).
5 My use of 'Britain' is not to suggest that I do not recognize the Anglo-centric nature of the British nation-state as it operated in Ireland. Indeed, Britain met, on occasion, with similar resistance to the establishment of hegemonic rule in Scotland and Wales. Gramsci says, 'Hegemony is primarily a strategy for the gaining of the active consent of the masses through their self-organization, starting from civil society, and in all the

throughout all of Ireland, this essay will suggest that it did have success in Dublin. To illustrate this success, the language of charity in Victorian Dublin will be examined.[6] This language bolstered Britain's hegemonic control within Dublin by reinforcing the upper classes' desire to create an innocuous working class. Within this discourse, not only the Irish Protestant upper class, but so too the Catholic, described the Dublin poor in the class terminology espoused by the British upper classes. By championing the belief that the Irish poor were morally, intellectually and racially inferior and then attempting to train them to be model employees and loyal subjects, the work of Dublin charities strengthened English rule in Ireland.[7]

When evaluating the language of nineteenth-century Dublin charities, contemporary notions of race and class must be considered.[8] It is difficult to argue that one dominated the other. While most often wealthy charity workers described the poor in class terms, it appears that, at times, conjectures on nineteenth-century racial theories were conflated with those of class. As Gareth Stedman Jones suggests, 'Class [was] a life sentence, as final as any caste system'.[9] Consequently, this suggests that because both upper-class Catholic and

hegemonic apparatuses, from the factory to the school and family.' See Christine Buci-Glucksmann, 'Hegemony and Consent' in Anne Showstack Sassoon (ed.) *Approaches to Gramsci* (London, 1982), p. 119.

6 Women in particular were involved in charity during the nineteenth century. See Maria Luddy, *Women and Philanthropy in Nineteenth-Century Ireland* (Cambridge, 1995); Alison Jordon, *Who Cared? Charity in Victorian and Edwardian Belfast* (Belfast, 1993); Lori Ginzberg, *Women and the Work of Benevolence, Morality, Politics and Class in the Nineteenth-Century United States* (New Haven, 1990); Peter Mandler (ed.), *The Uses of Charity, The Poor on Relief in the Nineteenth-Century Metropolis* (Philadelphia, 1990); Leonore Davidoff and Catherine Hall, *Family Fortunes, Men and Women of the English Middle Class, 1780-1850* (Chicago, 1987) and F.K. Prochaska, *Women and Philanthropy in Nineteenth-Century England* (Oxford, 1980).

7 For a variety of opinions on Ireland, England and race, see Jeffery Richards, 'Ireland, The Empire and Film' in Keith Jeffery (ed.), *Irish Empire? Aspects of Ireland and the British Empire* (Manchester, 1996); Roy Foster, *Paddy and Mr Punch: Connections in Irish and English History* (New York, 1993); Sheridan Gilley, 'English Attitudes to the Irish in England, 1780-1900' in Colin Holmes (ed.), *Immigrants and Minorities in British Society* (London, 1978) and L. Perry Curtis, *Apes and Angels: The Irishman in Victorian Caricature* (Washington, 1971).

8 For discussion of empire and race in the nineteenth century, see Anne McClintock, *Imperial Leather: Race, Gender and Sexuality in the Colonial Contest* (New York, 1995); S.B. Cook, *Imperial Affinities: Nineteenth-Century Analogies and Exchanges Between India and Ireland* (New Delhi, 1993); Vron Ware, *Beyond the Pale* (London, 1992); Paul B. Rich, *Race and Empire in British Politics* (Cambridge, 1986) and Nancy Stepan, *The Idea of Race in Science, Great Britain 1800-1960* (Oxford, 1981).

9 Gareth Stedman Jones, 'Working-Class Culture and Working-Class Politics in London, 1870-1900: Notes on the Remaking of a Working Class' in *Journal of Social History*, vii (1974), p. 493. See also Christine Bolt, *Victorian Attitudes to Race* (London, 1971), p. 188.

Protestant philanthropists accepted and applied British theories of race and class to the Irish poor, they furthered the process of hegemony in Dublin.

Some in the nineteenth-century British anthropological community espoused the idea of a racial hierarchy described as a pyramid in shape. Accordingly, the Anglo-Saxon middle-classes were placed at the top. The less advanced, poorer members of the Anglo-Saxon race came next, followed by the other white races, and finally those of dark skin.[10] Social critics, travel writers and writers of charity pamphlets, among others, accepted and employed these racial theories toward Ireland.[11] In 1860, Charles Kingsley noted during a visit to Sligo,

> I am haunted by the human chimpanzees I saw along that hundred miles of horrible country … to see white chimpanzees is dreadful; if they were black, one would not feel it so much, but their skins, except where tanned by exposure, are as white as ours.[12]

Punch and *The Times* often published editorial cartoons depicting simian-featured Irishmen and women staring up from the newsprint, and *Punch* described the poor Irish as 'the missing link between the gorilla and the Negro'.[13] At times, Dublin charities appeared to accept British theories of racial degeneracy of the poor and apply them. For example, the Dublin Visiting Mission referred to poor Catholic boys as 'wild street Arabs'.[14]

Nineteenth-century theories of class contended that the poor were inferior due to their own immorality, intellectual mediocrity and indolence. They were described as 'dirty, diseased, violent, licentious, thriftless, criminal and political-

---

10 McClintock, *Imperial Leather*, p. 56. She notes that the 'degenerate aristocracy had lapsed from supremacy'. See also Bolt, *Victorian Attitudes*, p. 5.

11 For example of seventeenth-century racial stereotypes, see James Smith, 'Effaced History: Facing the Colonial Contexts of Ben Jonson's *Irish Masque at Court*' in *ELH* (forthcoming). See also Hazel Waters, 'The Great Famine and the Rise of Anti-Irish Racism' in *Race and Class*, xxxvii, no. 1 (1995), pp. 95-108; Fintan O'Toole, 'Going Native: The Irish as Blacks and Indians' in *Études Irlandaises: L'Irland Aujourd'hui* (Autumn 1994), pp. 121-31; Nicholas P. Canny, 'The Ideology of English Colonization: From Ireland to America' in *William and Mary Quarterly*, iv, no. 30 (1973), pp. 575-98; W. R. Jones, 'England Against the Celtic Fringe: A Study in Cultural Stereotypes' in *Journal of World History*, xiii, no. 1 (1971), pp. 154-71 and Edward D. Snyder, 'The Wild Irish: A Study of Some English Satires Against the Irish, Scots and Welsh' in *Modern Philology* (April 1920), pp. 687-725.

12 Charles Kingsley, *His Letters and Memories of His Life*, ed. Frances E. Kingsley (London, 1901), cited in Luke Gibbons, 'Race Against Time: Racial Discourse and Irish History' in *Oxford Literary Review*, xiii, no. 9 (1991), pp. 95-117.

13 *Punch* in 1851, cited in Thomas C. Holt, *The Problem of Freedom: Race, Labor, and Politics in Jamaica and Britain, 1832-1938* (Baltimore, 1994), p. 319.

14 *Dublin Visiting Missions* (1883), p. 5.

ly volatile'.[15] So too, within this language, the upper classes also reveal a deep-seated fear of violent action by the masses.[16] For the wealthy, the moral economy became the yearning for ostentatious deference by the poor in exchange for aid, financial or otherwise.[17] Thus the upper class felt that to achieve the desired result of a mollified working-class population, they should be placed amongst their 'betters,' shown civilized conduct, and provided minimal financial relief.[18] When we look at the language, it appears that many in the upper classes advocated that the working classes be characterized as improveable, yet essentially permanent. It was as though the poor had an impenetrable barrier between themselves and the middle classes, a glass ceiling of class, up to which the poor could approach but through which they could never break. For example, the famous social commentator John Mayhew titled the first chapter of his book *London Labour and the London Poor*, 'Of Wandering Tribes in General'. As Gertrude Himmelfarb notes, 'Mayhew contributed to an image of poverty that made the poor a race apart, uncivilized, unsocialized, less than human'.[19] The upper classes then justified their rule by maintaining that the poor were perpetually children, that is, morally, physically and intellectually inferior, forever needing to be shown the proper way to behave.[20]

15 Jennifer Davis, 'Jennings' Buildings and the Royal Borough: The Construction of the Underclass in Mid-Victorian England' in David Feldman and Gareth Stedman Jones (eds), *Metropolis London: Histories and Representations Since 1800* (New York, 1989), pp. 11-39.

16 See Gareth Stedman Jones, *Outcast London: A Study in the Relationship Between the Classes in Victorian Society* (Oxford, 1971) and Jennifer Davis, 'The London Garroting Panic of 1862: A Moral Panic and the Creation of Criminal Class in Mid-Victorian England' in V.A.C. Gatrell, Bruce Lenman and Geoffrey Parker (eds), *Crime and Law: The Social History of Crime in Western Europe Since 1500* (London, 1980), pp. 190-213.

17 See E.P. Thompson, *Customs in Common* (New York, 1993). Thompson proposes a 'moral economy' in which the poor came to expect 'aid' from the wealthy either through provision of food or other forms of assistance and in return the wealthy expected deference and respect from those they helped. For a discussion of the role of the moral economy in rural charity see Jessica Gerard, 'Lady Bountiful: Women of the Landed Classes and Rural Philanthropy' *Victorian Studies*, xxx (Winter 1987), pp. 183-210.

18 For discussion of social control and charity see Simon Gunn, 'The Ministry, the Middle Class and the "Civilizing Mission" in Manchester, 1850-80' in *Social History*, xxi, no. 1 (January 1996), pp. 22-36; Simon Cordery, 'Friendly Societies and the Discourse of Respectability in Britain, 1825-1875' in *Journal of British Studies*, xxxiv (January 1995), pp. 35-58; Gertrude Himmelfarb, 'Manners into Morals: What the Victorians Knew' in *The American Scholar*, lvii (Spring 1988), pp. 223-32; Gareth Stedman Jones, 'Class Expressions vs. Social Control' in *History Workshop IV* (1978), pp. 163-70 and A.P. Donajgradzki (ed.), *Social Control in Nineteenth-Century Britain* (London, 1977).

19 'The phrase "wandering tribes" was often used at this time to describe the vagrants' (Gertrude Himmelfarb, 'Mayhew's Poor, A Problem of Identity' in *Victorian Studies* [March 1971], p. 320). See also Richard Maxwell, 'Henry Mayhew and the Life of the Streets' in *Journal of British Studies*, xvii, no. 2 (Spring 1978), pp. 87-105.

20 Similarly, Richard Lebow argues that colonizers needed to rationalize their rule over

Caesar Lombroso, the late nineteenth-century criminal anthropologist, provided an example of this view. In his book *The Female Offender,* Lombroso portrayed the poor, criminal female as degenerate. 'Their moral sense is deficient; they are revengeful, jealous, and inclined to vengeances of a refined cruelty'.[21] He further argued, '... women are big children; their evil tendencies are more numerous and more varied than men's but generally remain latent. When these are awakened and excited they produce results proportionally greater ... [T]he criminal woman is consequently a monster'.[22] Lombroso asserted that a poor, criminal woman loses much of her maternal instinct 'because psychologically and anthropologically she belongs more to the male than to the female sex. Her exaggerated sexuality so opposed to maternity would alone suffice to make her a bad mother'.[23] In 1847, Mrs Kate Charlotte Maberly in her pamphlet titled *The Present State of Ireland* advocated education for the poor Irish female while at the same time describing her as 'but one degree removed from a savage state. Ferocious, idle, drunken and revengeful, they are the chief instigation of every outrage, not hesitating, when there is an opportunity, of taking an active part in the disturbance'.[24] Thus the poor woman was a depraved child. Charitable women often characterized their relationship to the impoverished as essentially that of mother to child; and as mothers, Irish charitable women attempted to mould the behavior of the poor, thereby furthering the establishment of British hegemony through class control. In a visit to an Irish Magdalen asylum, Nora O'Mahony makes explicit the indigent woman as child when she quoted the Reverend Mother, head of the asylum, who described the penitents as, '... very good children, real saints most of them'.[25]

Because charities believed the poor to be child-like, they also felt that the poor's moral development was stunted and that they then must be taught virtuous behavior in order to create a better British subject.[26] Social commentators often argued that the poor were more susceptible to sexual and financial temptations.[27] They argued that the conditions in which the poor lived con-

---

the colonized. Therefore when inhuman descriptions became untenable because of Enlightenment thinking and the anti-slave movement, the natives were instead ascribed an inferior human status, often described as 'backward children'. Richard N. Lebow, *White Britain Black Ireland: The Influence of Stereotypes on Colonial Policy* (Philadelphia, 1976), p. 20. See also Bolt, *Victorian Attitudes*, p. 180.

21 Caesar L. Lombroso, *The Female Offender* (London, 1895), p. 151.
22 Ibid.
23 Ibid., p. 153.
24 Mrs Kate Charlotte Maberly, *The Present State of Ireland* (n.p., 1847), p. 28.
25 Nora Tynan O'Mahony, 'In A Magdalen Asylum' in *Irish Monthly*, xxxiv (July 1906), p. 374.
26 See David W. Savage, 'Evangelical Educational Policy in Britain and India, 1857-1860' in the *Journal of Imperial and Commonwealth History*, iii, no. 22 (September 1994), p. 488.
27 As Paul Johnson details, in the nineteenth century, the poor were accused of enrolling

tributed to their immoral behavior. Reformers believed that males and females crammed together in small filthy rooms sleeping four and five to a bed would lead to immorality. So too, poor and ragged clothing failed to keep them decent and could lead to sexual misadventure. In the *Report of the Sanitary Condition of the Labouring Population* the author noted,

> upwards of forty persons sleeping in the same room, married and single, including, of course, children, and several young adult persons of either sex. I have met with instances of a man, his wife, and his wife's sister sleeping in the same bed together. The result of this over-crowding upon morality is palpable and frightful ... by such crowded rooms they were led into temptation.[28]

Social commentator, Henry Worsley, believed that by not separating the sexes at work 'it has proved universally to be prejudicial to morals ... the almost universal absence of chastity and purity among the labouring-class, in our country villages at the present day, it is notorious to every one at all acquainted with them'.[29]

Those described above were persons living in the worst of circumstances. However, within the 'class' of the poor, there was a variety of economic levels. From artisans and shopkeepers to unskilled laborers, the working class was a hierarchy within a hierarchy.[30] However, of the poor who needed state or private aid, there were generally categorized as either deserving or undeserving. Charities often used wonderful phrases to describe those members of the deserving poor. In 1883, the Managing Committee of the Association for the Suppression of Mendicity in Dublin called them the 'unobtrusive classes of the meritorious poor' who were 'praiseworthy [for] desir[ing] to establish a certain

---

their children in life insurance funds and then killing them for insurance money. Paul Johnson, 'Class Law in Victorian England' in *Past and Present*, no. 141 (November 1993), pp. 147-69. See also David Phillips, '"A New Engine of Power and Authority": The Institutionalization of Law-Enforcement in England 1780-1830' in Gatrell, Lenman and Parker (eds), *Crime and Law*, pp. 155-89 and the anonymous 'The Garrett, the Cabin and the Gaol' in *Irish Quarterly Review* (June 1853), p. 311.

28 Cited in 'The Garrett', p. 316.

29 Henry Worsley, *Juvenile Depravity* (London, 1849), pp. 35, 67.

30 Geoffrey Cossick quotes it as three tiered, 'comprised of artisans, the poor and below them 'a class of honest independence with no ties to the general scheme of society', Geoffrey Cossick 'From Gentlemen to the Residuum: Languages of Social Description in Victorian Britain' in Penelope J. Corfield (ed.) *Language, History and Class* (Oxford, 1991), p. 163. See also Olivia Smith, *The Politics of Language 1791-1819* (Oxford, 1984); K.C. Phillipps, *Language and Class in Victorian England* (Oxford, 1984) and Asa Briggs 'The Language of Class in Early Nineteenth-Century England' in M.W. Flinn and T.C. Smout (eds), *Essays in Social History* (Oxford, 1974).

decency of appearance' and in 1835 it called them the 'well-disposed and orderly poor'.[31] Many charities noted in their statement of intent that they helped only those who 'deserved' aid.[32] As St Mary's Industrial Institute noted, it hoped to benefit the 'distressed, but truly deserving portion of the community, viz., the Industrious Poor, will, it is hoped meet with the generous and ready support of a benevolent Public'.[33] The Strangers Friend Society for Visiting and Relieving Distressed Strangers and the Resident Sick Poor stated that

> its benevolent operations are still more extended embracing a most deserving class of the community. It will at once be seen that they are not the noisy importunate beggars, who impede our progress in the streets, hang about our doors, taking every opportunity to exhibit their misery – nor are they those who, with begging letters, fabricated testimonials and well-concerted tales of apparently genuine distress, go about, endeavouring to impose upon the kindness and credulity of the unsuspecting charitable and humane ...[34]

While helping the most deserving, religious conversion was also the goal of a small but vocal Protestant minority in Ireland that desired to save Catholics from hell.[35] Benedict Anderson argues, and this may also be applicable in the case of Ireland, that missionaries actually desired 'to turn "idolaters" not so much into Christians, as into people culturally English, despite their irremediable colour and blood'.[36] The 1883 report of the Dublin Visiting Mission in Connection with the Society for Irish Church Missions, stated that the mission was an 'association for sending Town Missionaries into the back streets and lanes of the city – visiting from room to room – not passing by Protestants but especially seeking out Roman Catholics'.[37] Missionaries described Catholics as idolaters who

31 *Managing Committee of the Association for the Suppression of Mendacity in Dublin* (1833), p. 10; (1834), p. 14, and (1835), p. 11. Certainly names given the poor in general were quite colorful including 'wretched class' or 'neglected persons'. The *Dublin Female Penitentiary* (1814) termed them 'hardened and unworthy' (p. 10) and in 1815 called the women they worked with, 'outcast, degraded, rejected and despised' (p. 9).

32 The *Dublin Providence Home* (1841) clearly noted that it was 'designed for the advantage of *poor females of good character alone*' (p. 5, their italics).

33 Included in the *Second Annual Report of the Ladies Association of Charity of St. Vincent De Paul* (1853), p. 27.

34 *Report of the Strangers Friend Society for Visiting and Relieving Distressed Strangers and the Resident Sick Poor* (1832), p. 4.

35 In Ireland the term 'Souperism' was applied to those persons who exchanged soup for conversion. See Irene Whelan, 'The Stigma of Souperism' in Cathal Póirtéir (ed.), *The Great Irish Famine* (Cork, 1995) and Desmond Bowen, *Souperism: Myth or Reality?* (Cork, 1970).

36 Benedict Anderson, *Imagined Communities* (London, 1983), p. 91. See also, Edward Said, *Orientalism* (New York, 1979).

37 *Dublin Visiting Missions* (1883), p. 3.

blindly threw bog water upon themselves, and who needed to be saved from the clutches of Romanism in order to reach heaven.[38] Thus, besides saving their souls, Irish missionaries may have hoped that conversion would also put Roman Catholics on the road toward becoming loyal subjects to the Empire.

One well-known Dublin proselytizer and member of the Irish Church Missions was Ellen Smyly. In the mid-nineteenth century, Smyly opened the Smyly Orphan Homes which adopted an explicit agenda of prioritizing the acceptance of Roman Catholic children or children of inter-faith marriage, with Protestant children accepted only if room were available. As evinced in a report of one young girl from Smyly's Townsend-street Ragged Schools and Girls Home of 1893, Catholicism is equated with darkness and savagery: '[She] had been a Roman Catholic, but the teaching of the Word was blessed to her soul, and she was steadfast in her determination not to go back to the darkness of Romanism from which she had been delivered'.[39] Sarah Davies, a Dublin philanthropist who worked with Ellen Smyly, noted in her *Wanderers Brought Home* that philanthropists asked of poor Roman Catholic boys, 'Are we to train them in the way which they have begun to walk, the way of ignorance and superstition? Are we to hide from them that light which hitherto has only been exhibited to them in a dark lantern?'[40] Hence one scenario, proposed by Jones, might be that through conversion, 'they could eradicate pernicious customs and dangerous class prejudices from the poor, and to promote acceptance of the moral and political code of their superiors'.[41] Jones also suggests that missionaries were part of the hegemonic process: 'The policeman and the workhouse were not sufficient. The respectable and the well-to-do had to win the "hearts and minds" of the masses to the new moral order and to assert their right to act as its priesthood'.[42]

However, some amongst Dublin's upper-class, Irish Catholic philanthropists did not need to be converted. They adopted the habits, beliefs and language of the British upper classes, thereby establishing themselves as members of that group known as Castle Catholics.[43] The acceptance of nineteenth-century upper-class class ideology comes through explicitly in a number of Dublin's Catholic charities. For example, the [Catholic] Female Penitent Asylum helped

---

38 As wrote the author about some of the converts from Catholicism in the *Report of the Ladies Irish Association* (1887): 'I called on them to join in giving thanks for being taught better things than bowing down to dumb idols, and some to bog water, when, as they believe it to be, blessed by men, falsely called priests of the New Law' (p. 7).

39 *Report of the Townsend-street Ragged Schools and Girls' Home* (Dublin, 1893), p. 6.

40 Davies, *Wanderers*, pp. 74–75.

41 Stedman Jones, 'Working Class Culture,' p. 466. See also Vivien Smyly, 'The Early History of Mrs. Smyly's Homes and Schools' (Dublin, 1976).

42 Stedman Jones, 'Working Class Culture,' p. 466.

43 A term adopted in the late eighteenth century; see Kevin Whelan, *The Tree of Liberty: Radicalism, Catholicism and the Construction of Irish Identity 1760-1830* (Cork, 1996).

young women 'from being the disgrace and scourge of society', training them to wash and mend clothes so that they might become 'ranked among [society's] useful and edifying members'. The Asylum believed that these poor women should work 'to repair the scandal [that they have] given to society'. At the same time the charity encouraged them to petition God for their immortal souls and 'to weep incessantly over their sins, and pray without intermission for their pious benefactors'. These benefactors then received benefits since the 'advantages they confer on society' secured them everlasting blessings.[44]

The House of Protection for Distressed Young Women of Unblemished Character, also a Catholic charity, accepted 'poor young women of unblemished reputation who might be … rendered useful to society'. These women who had been 'reduced to the last degree of danger and distress … by sickness [or] the wickedness of their superiors were … now wandering about in tattered apparel, and seeking in vain for employment'. The charity stated that because they needed the House of Protection's help, these poor women must have already 'waded through the abominations that divided them from our Asylums; or, at least, had renounced their virtuous character and the world, in order to be *entitled to admission*' (their italics). The House of Protection trained needy women as laundresses in hopes of their attaining future employment outside the refuge. Viewing the poor as diseased, the charity describes the 'unhappy women who infest our streets and infect society'. By saving a young woman from the mean streets and providing her with some instruction, the House of Protection '[taught] her to walk to a more perfect way, and thereby render her more dear to God, and more valuable to her employers'. As a more valuable employee, she was also a more loyal subject to the British Empire.[45]

The [Catholic] House of Refuge for Industrious and Distressed Females of Good Character tried to save young women from joining that extensive 'class of misery who were unprotected and reduced to distress'. This charity accepted a young woman only after she 'produc[ed] unquestionable vouchers for the propriety of [her] conduct' and then the charity trained her in washing, mangling (ironing) plain-work and 'other branches of Female Industry until suitable situations [could] be provided for them'. The House attempted to aid in their spiritual enlightenment and 'to impress the duties of religion more deeply in their hearts'.[46] The training of women as laundresses might be considered a metaphor for the spiritual and bodily cleansing of the poor. Possibly the upper classes believed that a clean body and mind would create a benign population of poor persons, more deferent to authority.[47]

44 *Female Penitent Asylum* (Dublin, n.d.), p. 1.
45 *House of Protection for Distressed Young Women of Unblemished Character* (Dublin, n.d.), p. 1.
46 *House of Refuge for Industrious and Distressed Females, of Good Character* (Dublin, 1851), p. 1.
47 See Michel Foucault, *Power/Knowledge: Selected Interviews and Other Writings 1972-77*, ed. Colin Gordon (New York, 1980).

Finally, the annual report for the Committee of the Catholic Ragged Schools discussed many of the poor children it helped, but the charity noted that it had special affection for that class of children who

> through the indolence or vice of their parents, … are thrown on our streets to beg their food … or who, in order to sustain a miserable existence, are compelled to attend those schools opened for their perversion by the enemies of our holy faith.[48]

The charity went on to note that if these children were exposed to the enemy, then they would 'grow up in ignorance, vice and irreligion, and as they approach maturity, are liable to get so inured to crime, so hardened to infamy, as to become pests to society, a disgrace and reproach to their country'.[49] Thus it appears that some upper-class Catholics of Dublin accepted the efforts of British hegemony and worked diligently toward moulding a benign Dublin poor.

Irish Protestant charities, too, discussed the Dublin poor in contemporary class and, as the documentation suggests, racial terms. For example, in one *Report of the Committee of the [Protestant] Dublin Female Penitentiary*, the asylum noted that it was 'for the reception of unfortunate females plunged in sin, but, from conviction, willing to quit the paths of vice, and to whom might be afforded the means of earning a subsistence by honest industry'. When the women found this honest subsistence, they would then no longer be the 'pests of their respective stations in society'. The charity hints at an essentialist notion of class when it noted that it found indigent, Irish women 'herding among the lowest orders of profligate and abandoned characters'.[50] The Penitentiary hoped to save such women from the 'dreadful contamination hardening into the same debased image … and to teach the unhappy and guilty female to remember what she was'.[51] Thus it appears that while trained and given aid, she was *not* to forget the class from whence she came; a state within which her benefactors may have believed that she could be only somewhat improved, but from which she could never be changed.

Within prostitution reform, however, charity workers attempted to erase the penitent's past completely. Linking these two apparently contradictory

48 *Second Annual Report of the Committee of the Catholic Ragged Schools* (Dublin, 1853), pp. 5-6; the enemy were Protestant proselytizers.
49 Ibid., pp. 5-6. What country they are referring to here is, of course a legitimate question and one for a longer paper. If the term country refers solely to Ireland then it identifies nationalistic loyalties and throws ambiguity into my argument. However, if country refers to England, then, I argue, that Irish philanthropists furthered the process of British hegemony in Dublin. Further research on these types of references within both Protestant and Catholic charities must be attempted before drawing any conclusions.
50 *Report [first] of the Committee of the Dublin Female Penitentiary* (1813), p. 7.
51 Ibid., p. 11.

routes of reform appears to be the overwhelming desire by reformers to eradi-
cate penitents' individuality and proscribe their ability to act independently.
Thereby, stripped of her independence, she was more easily disciplined.
Magdalen asylums stifled penitent's identity, calling them by a number ('Mrs
One','Mrs Two', and so on), or if in a religious charity, by the name of a saint.[52]
The Report of the Committee of the [Protestant] Dublin Female Penitentiary explicitly stated that the Penitentiary tried to restrict inmates' autonomy by keeping
them 'secluded from the world ... [and they] should have their thoughts as
much as possible turned from the contemplation of its scenes'.[53] Thus
Magdalen homes (and this was true of many charities) kept the penitents
under a strict regimen of work and reflection.[54] By stifling their singularity,
disciplining them through a strict daily schedule and training them for service-
oriented positions, reformers furthered the rule of the state by attempting to
create a benign population of working-class persons.[55]

   While reformers believed that they could improve the lives of the Dublin
poor, the language of charity indicates that they did not feel that their class status could substantially be changed. Because of their conviction that the poor
were less intelligent, charity workers had limited expectations of the indigent's
ability to learn a skill. Most charities provided training that could qualify persons for a position in the service industries, thereby making them honest,
though certainly keeping them unequal.[56] As Davies emphasized in *Wanderers
Brought Home*, reformers had limited expectations of the mental and physical
capabilities of the poor. For example, orphanages trained boys for 'occupations
suited to their tastes and capacities. They become sailors, soldiers, servants,
tradesmen or teachers'.[57] To be a teacher, however, did not necessarily place
one in a higher class status. As Richard Johnson notes of teachers in the nine-

---

52 Luddy, *Women and Philanthropy*, p. 114.
53 *Report [first] of the Committee of the Dublin Female Penitentiary* (1813), p. 8. The Dublin
   Providence Home was little different as it carefully watched the inmates' 'temper and
   conduct' in order to ascertain in what industry they could be trained; *Dublin Providence
   Home* (1839), p. 4.
54 Anonymous, 'The Magdalens of High Park' in the *Irish Rosary* (April, 1897), pp. 180-1.
   Luddy also notes that the success rates of these asylums are questionable, a fact she
   attributes to their harsh regime and invasive tactics. See Maria Luddy, 'Prostitution and
   Rescue Work in Nineteenth-Century Ireland' in (eds), Cliona Murphy and Maria
   Luddy *Women Surviving* (Dublin, 1989), pp. 51-84.
55 Michel Foucault, *Discipline and Punish: The Birth of the Prison* (New York, 1995), pp. 219,
   192-3.
56 Domestics, however, were often taught to read and write as it was important to their
   position in the home. See *Report of the Female Orphan House* (1881), p. 10; Mona Hearn,
   Below Stairs: Domestic Service Remembered in Dublin and Beyond 1880-1922 (Dublin, 1993)
   and L. Davidoff, 'Mastered for Life, Servant and Wife in Victorian and Edwardian
   England' in *Journal of Social History*, vii (1974), pp. 406-28.
57 Davies, *Wanderers*, pp. 74-5. See *The Report of the Female Orphan House* (1851), p. 10.

teenth century, 'they should be raised but not that far out of their own class'.[58] Many charities advocated that if the poor were 'caught' young, or prostitutes were aided after a 'first fall,'[59] they could more easily be made honest. The General and First Annual Report of the St Joseph's Reformatory School for Catholic Girls stated that the school could save young girls by separating them from the older ones. 'The peculiar training which that most difficult class, criminal children of tender years require, can be fully developed, whilst they are saved from the contamination too often springing from association with those older in years'.[60] Here, too, charity workers attempted to control the behavior of poor children in attempts to mould them into a placid population of persons trained to serve.

Finally, the discourse on philanthropy also provides a glimpse of how society viewed upper-class female philanthropists. While the upper classes considered the characteristics of the poor to be permanent, they also believed that gentlewomen were literally born into their role as 'civilizer'; as Edward Sieveking wrote,

> There are qualities of the heart – tact, gentleness, consideration – qualities that distinguish the true gentlewoman, and the diffusion of which among all classes of women render it so peculiarly desirable that ladies by birth, who feel a vocation ... [should serve the needy].[61]

Using these inherent qualities, said Matthew Hill, gentlewomen could delicately influence and alter the behavior of the poor, thereby making them into honorable, benign members of the lower classes.

> These ladies, in addition to their intelligence, firmness, judgment and kindly disposition ... exercise the potent influence derived from the refined manners and the chastened habit of command which belong to their social position – an influence gently enforcing the prompt obedience of all who have the good fortune to be under their control.[62]

Thus not only were charity women trained to help others, it was this to which they were bred.

58 See Richard Johnson, 'Education, Politics and Social Control in Early Victorian England' in *Past and Present*, xlix (November 1970), p. 113, and *Dublin Providence Home* (1839), p.4.

59 A term used for young prostitutes who were seen to be still redeemable – unlike hardened prostitutes for whom charities felt there was little hope.

60 *General and First Annual Report of St. Joseph's Reformatory School for Catholic Girls* (Dublin, 1862,), n.p.

61 Edward H. Sieveking, 'Thoughts on Nursing' in a paper read at the Annual General Assembly of the Order of St. John of Jerusalem, London, St. John Baptist's Day, 1873.

62 Matthew Davenport Hill, *A Paper on the Irish Convict Prisons* (London, 1857), pp. 22-3.

This essay has suggested that through the language of charity, many members of Dublin's elite, both Protestant and Catholic, accepted the nineteenth-century British ideologies of class. Yet this situation is made more complex by essentialist notions of race which, at times, appeared to be applied to the poor as characteristics of class. The language also suggests that those who saw themselves at the apex of the racial and class pyramid believed that through training, the poor could be made honest though certainly never equal. As the author of the *Social Service Handbook* stated of the Irish poor, 'if properly treated, [the poor] have a fair chance of becoming useful citizens of the state; but who, if not so treated, will in the future, grow up to be an additional burden on the ratepayers'. [63] Thus, by teaching the poor to behave as the upper and middle classes did, Dublin's upper classes attempted to further the establishment of Gramsci's 'permanently organized consent' while Dublin philanthropists endeavored to mould the city's poor into proper, loyal and innocuous subjects of the British Empire.[64]

---

63 J.P. Smyth, *Social Service Handbook Issued by Church of Ireland Social Service Union* (London, 1901), p. 70.
64 Foucault called it a *society of normalization* in which 'the procedures of normalization came to be ever more constantly engaged in the colonization of those of law', *Power/Knowledge*, p. 107 (his italics).

Dependency and Modernization: Perspectives from the Irish Nineteenth Century

THOMAS A. BOYLAN & TERRENCE McDONOUGH

While it would be an exaggeration to say that Ireland played a central role in the development of political economy in the nineteenth century, Ireland's place in the genesis of the contemporary schools of thought in economics is not inconsiderable. Before the famine, classical political economy, based in a utilitarian framework and advocating a policy of *laissez-faire*, was dominant in Ireland both at the level of the academy and in attempts at popular education in economic matters. Indeed, in the work of Longfield and others, Irish political economy in this period anticipated the development of marginalist economic thought.

After the famine, classical political economy in Ireland was largely abandoned and alternative frameworks of thought were sought. This quest led in several directions. Comtist social science was introduced to Ireland by the Statistical and Social Inquiry Society of Ireland. John Kells Ingram and T.E. Cliffe Leslie helped to found an historical school of economics, which inspired modern institutional economics in the tradition of Veblen. Marx included a discussion of Irish agriculture in *Capital* and his views on Ireland along with India have been the initial source of much Marxist writing on Third World and colonial questions.

It is the thesis of this article that recent departures in the analysis of Irish nineteenth-century development (or lack thereof) have interesting antecedents in the contemporary nineteenth-century understanding of the Irish economy, especially in the post-famine period. More specifically we will argue that the different strands of the 'dependency theory' perspective on development can find harbingers in the response of contemporaries to the troubled Irish economy of the last century. In service of this argument, we will undertake a review of the emergence of the several strands of dependency analysis, especially as it was developed and applied in the Latin American context. We will then examine how modern scholars have used these perspectives to understand the economy of the Irish nineteenth century. Finally, we will turn to the nineteenth century itself and examine if these outlooks find corroboration in the work of nineteenth-century observers.

Dependency Theory

The emergence of dependency analysis is of recent origin and its initial development was focused on Latin America. During the course of the 1970s, the domain of application was extended to include most of the underdeveloped world and to the countries of the European periphery. Immanuel Wallerstein's world-system theory represented an historical generalization of dependency analysis. Dependency theory was also extended at an early stage to include not only economics but also the political and cultural domains. These differing domains of dependency were seen as closely interacting, and dependency theory became a critical focus of study for an array of social scientists, including sociologists and political scientists as well as economists. Considerable debate was centred on whether dependency theory could be considered a coherent and well-integrated paradigm for development studies.[1] This interpretation was disputed by Palma, who pointed to the diversity of theoretical perspectives utilized by dependency analyses.[2]

Following Palma, a three-way categorization of dependency studies can be identified: those of the Latin American neo-Marxist tradition (later to include Amin and Wallerstein); the later contributions of members of the Economic Commission for Latin America (ECLA) school; and finally a re-orientation of dependency studies towards the specificity of individual country studies, represented in the work of Cardoso and Faletto.[3] In this section, we do not propose a complete review of the literature. Our more modest aim is to identify the central axes of thought that could be drawn on if we are to appeal to this body of thought in negotiating the history of development and underdevelopment in an Irish context.

The Neo-Marxist Strand

One of the earliest and most interesting contributions to the neo-Marxist school of dependency theory, which also made some of the most ambitious claims for dependency analysis, was provided by Dos Santos in 1969.[4] Dos

---

1   See I. Roxborough (ed.), *Theories of Development* (London, 1979); J. Browett, 'The Newly Industrializing Countries and Radical Theories of Development' in *World Development*, xiii, no. 7 (1985), pp. 789–803.

2   G. Palma, 'Dependency and Development: A Critical Review' in Roxborough, *Theories of Development*.

3   See especially F.H. Cardoso and E. Faletto, *Dependency and Development in Latin America* (Berkeley, 1979).

4   T. Dos Santos, 'The Crisis of Development Theory, and the Problem of Dependence in Latin America' in Henry Bernstein (ed.), *Underdevelopment and Development: The Third World Today* (London, 1973); N. Bukharin, *Imperialism and the World Economy* (New York,

Santos saw dependency theory as the 'periphery-focused' counterpart to the theory of imperialism. It was, he argued, only by 'understanding dependence and conceptualising and studying its mechanisms and its historical force one both expands and reformulates the theory of imperialism.'[5] This theme was central to his overall conceptualization of the complementarity between imperialism and dependency. He argued that:

> Neither Lenin (1917), nor Bukharin (1966) and Rosa Luxemburg (1964) ... nor the few non-Marxist writers like Hobson (1965) ... approached the question of imperialism from the point of view of the dependent countries. Although dependence has its place in the general framework of a theory of imperialism, it also possesses a force of its own which entitles it to a specific place in the general process which is itself influenced by it.[6]

The most widely used neo-Marxist definition of dependency belongs to Dos Santos. He defines dependence as:

> a conditioning situation in which economies of one group of countries are conditioned by the development and expansion of others. A relationship of interdependence between two or more countries or between such countries and the world trading system becomes a dependent relationship when some countries can expand through self-impulsion while others, being in a dependent position, can only expand as a reflection of the expansion of the dominant countries, which may have positive or negative effects on their immediate development.[7]

In the case of Latin America, Dos Santos distinguished three stages or forms of dependence – the mercantile dependence of the colonial era, the financial-industrial dependence that was consolidated at the end of the nineteenth century, and the technological-industrial dependence of the post-war era. This latter phase, which was the primary focus of Dos Santos's analysis, is 'based on multinational corporations which began to invest in industries geared to the internal market'.[8] For Dos Santos, each of these different relations of dependence place fundamental limits on the scope and potential for self-sustaining

1966); V.I. Lenin, *Imperialism the Highest Stage of Capitalism* (London, 1917); R. Luxemburg, *The Accumulation of Capital* (New York, 1963).

5 Dos Santos, 'The Crisis of Development Theory', p. 73.

6 Ibid.

7 Ibid., p. 76.

8 T. Dos Santos, 'The Structure of Dependence' in Livingstone (ed.), *Development Economics and Policy: Readings* (London, 1981).

long-term development of the periphery. Dos Santos suggests that it is possible
to demonstrate that each stage of dependence is reinforced by a necessary
coincidence between dominant local and foreign interests. The only way to
break the circle of dependence is to radically change the internal structure that
reinforces it and to establish popular revolutionary governments which open
the way to socialism.

From the late 1960s and through the 1970s, the analytical work on dependency theory within the neo-Marxist school came to be dominated by the
work of Frank, Amin, and Wallerstein.[9] Their work turned on the existence of
a single world capitalist system which derived its momentum from the development of the capitalist mode of production at the centre and drained the
economic surplus and resources of the periphery. This world system acted
upon and transformed the economies of the periphery with the collaboration
of the local dominant classes. The concept of dependent, or as Amin termed it
'extraverted' development, enabled neo-Marxists to acknowledge that capital
accumulation and output expansion had occurred in the periphery, but
emphasize the distorted and unbalanced character of this process. The contrast
developed here was with the self-sustaining and equitable expansion path,
which it was argued, could be achieved by the pursuit of autarkic socialist
development.

Crotty and O'Malley on the Irish Nineteenth Century

It is curious that the Irish case did not appear sooner in the literature of modern dependency theory. Its proximity and long relationship to Britain and its
subsequent lack of development would seem to make Ireland an obvious candi-
date for the application of dependency analysis. Nevertheless, the application of
dependency theory to the Irish case dates only from 1979 with the publication
of Raymond Crotty's article, recasting his 1966 analysis of Irish agricultural history in dependency terms.[10] We will argue that Crotty's analysis, especially as
expanded by O'Malley,[11] constitutes a rendering of Ireland's nineteenth-century development consistent with the neo-Marxist strand of dependency theory.

9 For useful reviews of this literature, see Charles Barone, *Marxist Thought on Imperialism*
   (Armonk, NY, 1985) and Anthony Brewer, *Marxist Theories of Imperialism: A Critical
   Survey* (London, 1990).
10 Raymond Crotty, *Irish Agricultural Production: Its Volume and Structure* (Cork, 1966), and
   'Capitalist Colonialism and Peripheralization: The Irish Case' in Dudley Seers, Bernard
   Schaffer and Mrja-Liisa Kiljunen (eds), *Underdeveloped Europe: Studies in Core-Periphery
   Relations* (Atlantic Highlands, NJ, 1979).
11 Eoin O'Malley, 'The Decline of Irish Industry in the Nineteenth Century' in *The
   Economic and Social Review*, xiii, no. 1 (1981), pp. 21-42; Eoin O'Malley, *Industry and
   Economic Development: The Challenge for the Latecomer* (Dublin, 1989).

Crotty identifies the relationship between Ireland and Britain as one of capitalist colonialism. We will pass over dealing with the peculiarities of Crotty's definition of capitalism. Crotty starts his argument in 1966 by stating:

> Irish agriculture has been influenced by three factors in particular. The first is the climate of the country; the second is the system of land tenure; and the third is the nature of the demand for its products.[12]

Crotty has little difficulty squaring this earlier analysis with his later espousal of dependency theory. Climate is of course a causal factor in agricultural development, but is essentially an ahistorical background factor in a dynamic analysis. The system of land tenure plays an important role in Crotty's argument, but its role is to magnify the importance of changes in the international market for Irish goods. The insecurity of Irish tenures and short leases make it possible for both peasants and landlords to respond to changes in market prices unencumbered by a great deal of sunk investment and a long term commitment to maintaining family possession of a particular plot of land. The driving factor in changes in Irish agricultural production is prices. The insertion of Ireland into the capitalist market headquartered in Britain determines that these should be international or at least British prices.

Significantly, in line with much recent scholarship, Crotty contends that the colonial relationship to Britain, despite mercantilist restrictions on Irish trade, did not hinder the development of Irish industry in the pre-Industrial Revolution period of manufacture. Indeed, the negative economic consequences of colonialism for Irish development only become evident with the fall in grain prices which followed the end of the Napoleonic Wars.

While Crotty's conception of capitalism dates its advent in Ireland from the sixteenth century, the industrial revolution plays a crucial role in his analysis of the dynamics of Irish agriculture. The rapid expansion of the urban population of Britain and the relaxation of trade restrictions led to an across the board increase in the demand for Irish agricultural production. It is during this period that Irish agriculture is decisively subordinated to the British market. This subordination did not in itself hinder Irish development until the post-Napoleonic crisis.

In Crotty's argument, the reversal of price trends was to have serious and long term consequences for Irish development. The fall in the price of corn was to lead to a contraction of tillage farming and the expansion of pasture. While all farming will tend to be unprofitable in a regime of falling prices, high output farming with high variable costs, that is tillage, will be relatively less profitable than low output pasturage. The solvency of both the landlords

---

12 Crotty, *Irish Agricultural Production*, p. 1.

and the remaining tenants was served by the consolidation of farms and putting them down to grass.

Further, the fall in price was not the same across the board. The prices of cattle and sheep fell less sharply, stabilized sooner, and recovered better than tillage prices. This was due to several factors including improved transportation, more severe competition in corn from the continent, and an increase in British dietary standards. All of these factors were added on top of Ireland's Atlantic climate which in the long term was comparatively more suited to grass than corn.

The expanding population produced by the previous regime of expanding prices and the tenure system made an immediate transition to pasture impossible. Nevertheless, Crotty argues, the rate of growth of population slowed and was stabilizing around the mid-century. This was accomplished by an increase in emigration and a decline in the birth rate. The Great Famine intervened to decisively accelerate a downward trend in population and an upward trend in farm size. Once started these two factors fed on one another. The consolidation of farms made much of the population redundant, raised emigration and lowered the birth rate. A declining supply of rural labour raised wage rates, encouraging pasturage and less use of labour.

This particular pattern of agricultural production was to have important consequences for Irish development. Its extensive character had the consequence of minimizing the rural labor force and consequently any home market for both agricultural products and manufactures that could have been generated from the rural sector. Secondly, the concentration of agricultural production on the export of live cattle minimized the links which could have been built between agriculture and industry, both in the supplying of agricultural inputs and in the processing of agricultural products. In this way the balanced development of the Irish economy was frustrated by its dependent relationship on the British economy.

The pushing of a significant portion of the population off the land is, however, not only a recipe for dislocation and misery in the short-term. It is also an essential condition for the inauguration of capitalist development, providing both a labour force and a potential urban market. Crotty's analysis of the structure of Irish agriculture in the nineteenth century, relying as it does on changes in relative agricultural prices, climate, and systems of land tenure, can at best only partially explain the failure of the Irish economy to industrialize in the nineteenth century. Crotty's 1979 article takes up this issue.

Crotty summarizes the argument in the following way:

> Economic development at the core, involving the progression from cottage to factory production, gave economies of scale both in production and distribution. These scale economies made it profitable to concen-

trate labour and capital intensive production at the core, leaving the periphery to a greater or less extent, dependent on land intensive production. The degree to which this process of peripheralization occurred was exceptional in the case of England and Ireland.[13]

Essentially, Crotty is arguing that competing English imports depressed the demand for similar Irish products. This inevitably raised the unit costs of Irish production preventing Irish industry from effectively competing. The distance to major potential markets in Britain further increased costs. Wage reductions could not compensate because they further lowered demand and hence the scale of production and below a certain level they caused a massive rise in the death rate.

For these reasons, Irish industry failed to flourish despite an almost limitless supply of free labour. As a result, both labour and capital emigrated, contributing to the acceleration of development at the core.

Crotty's account of the factors affecting industry is sketchy. These same themes are taken up in more detail in 1981 by Eoin O'Malley.[14] O'Malley develops in detail the view that Irish industrial development before the Union was reasonably healthy and relatively unaffected by either English restrictions or Irish Parliamentary protections. After the Union, Irish industry survived well until the depression of 1825-6. Prices for cotton and wool textiles fell during the depression and the larger British industries aggressively sought new markets in Ireland. Irish production fell precipitously as woollen production concentrated in Yorkshire and the cotton textile industry centralized around Lancashire and Glasgow. Meanwhile the linen industry concentrated in Belfast, saving the industry for the island, but putting home spinners out of work in Connaught and the remoter parts of Ulster.

This initial crisis was confined to textiles. Milling, brewing, iron-founding, shipbuilding, rope-making, paper and glass-making all expanded. A second industrial crisis emerged with the beginning of the 'Great Depression' in the 1870s. Economies of scale meant that significant advantage had passed to British producers in a number of other industries. Decline set in for Irish iron-founding, paper, bootmaking, rope-making, tanning, milling, and chandling. New industries, like consumer durables, automobiles, and electrical goods located in the south of England near major markets stretching from Birmingham to London.

O'Malley concludes by contending that many of the significant requirements for industrialization were in place in nineteenth-century Ireland including supplies of capital, cheap labour, a basic education system and competent

---

13 Crotty, 'Capitalist Colonialism', p. 226.
14 O'Malley, 'The Decline of Irish Industry'.

entrepreneurs. Nevertheless, Irish industry was unable to overcome the British advantages of large-scale and centralized production close to major markets. O'Malley concludes that 'even given quite favourable local conditions, free market forces can by no means be relied on to generate industrial development, or even to sustain existing employment, in a relatively late-developing economy in close competition with more advanced industrial countries.'[15]

Yoking the arguments of Crotty concerning Irish agriculture and O'Malley concerning Irish industry (this was done in O'Malley's 1989 volume on late industrialization) in the nineteenth century creates a complete analysis in the neo-Marxist dependency tradition. The insertion of the Irish economy into the international capitalist market led to a specialization in agriculture and a particular kind of agriculture which was inimical to further development through lack of spin-offs and the generation of a shrinking domestic market. Ireland in the nineteenth century was deindustrialized through cheaper competition with the British mainland. A number of subsequent treatments of Ireland and dependency theory have appeared since, including extended treatment of development questions in the context of the Irish Republic, but the outlines of the argument in regard to the Irish nineteenth century have remained similar. Ireland could be cited as one example of the development of underdevelopment.[16]

Marx and Engels on Ireland

Significantly, searching for the antecedents of dependency theory in the work of Marx and Engels takes us directly to their writings on Ireland. Engels first wrote about the Irish in his *Condition of the Working Class in England* in 1844, describing conditions in the Irish immigrant districts of Manchester.[17] Engels became intimately involved with Mary Burns, an Irish immigrant, who introduced him to the working class movement in Manchester and to Irish political questions. He toured Ireland with her in 1856. He corresponded with Marx frequently on Irish questions and undertook to write a history of Ireland which he never completed. It was Engels who described Ireland as 'England's first colony.'[18]

---

15 Ibid. p. 41.
16 See especially Jim MacLaughlin, *Ireland: The Emigrant Nursery and the World Economy* (Cork, 1994); Ronnie Munck, *The Irish Economy* (London, 1993); Denis O'Hearn, 'The Irish Case of Dependency: An Exception to the Exceptions' in *American Sociological Review*, liv (August 1989), pp. 578-96; John Kurt Jacobsen, *Chasing Progress in the Irish Republic: Ideology, Democracy and Dependent Development* (Cambridge, 1994).
17 See Karl Marx and Frederick Engels, *Ireland and the Irish Question* (New York, 1972), pp 37-43.
18 Ibid., p. 83.

In addition to closely following Irish political developments, Marx devoted a section of *Capital* to analyzing contemporary events in Irish agriculture.[19] Marx saw the consolidation of farms in Ireland as a further example of the accumulation of capital in agriculture. Marx located events in Ireland within the context of the British economy as a whole, arguing succinctly that 'Ireland is at present merely an agricultural district of England which happens to be divided by a wide stretch of water from the country for which it provides corn, wool, cattle and industrial and military recruits.'[20] Towards the end of this section of *Capital*, Marx observes presciently that Ireland's 'depopulation must go still further, in order that she may fulfil her true destiny, to be an English sheepwalk and cattle pasture.'[21]

Elsewhere Marx attributes these developments to the repeal of the Corn Laws and the consequent drop in corn prices combined with the opposite movement of the prices of cattle and wool. Those displaced by the increase in pasture were bound for the emigrant ship. Marx attributes the lack of opportunity for industrial employment to the opening of the Irish market to English industrial competition: 'The Union which overthrew the protective tariffs established by the Irish Parliament, destroyed all industrial life in Ireland ...'[22]

These remarks on Ireland are notable in that they stand in contrast to Marx's more general view that trade, even though creating often violent dislocation, should bring with it the implanting of capitalist social relations and subsequent development. Marx's views on Ireland form a substantial part of the base in Marx's work for the later dependency view that exposure to the world capitalist market, far from bringing progress in its train, sponsored the development of underdevelopment.

Other Strands of Dependency

The development of the concept of dependency was not confined to its Marxist adherents. Members of the Economic Commission for Latin America (ECLA) school were reformulating their thinking along dependency lines. The motivating factor was the dramatic slowdown in economic growth in Latin America in the early 1960s along with a series of undesirable consequences of that growth which had occurred. Writers such as Furtado and Sunkel, leading members of the ECLA structuralist school, attempted to explain the undesirable consequences of the import-substituting industrialization which the ECLA had earlier recommended for the Latin American economies. Furtado

19 Ibid., pp. 99-116.
20 Ibid., p. 105.
21 Ibid., p. 115.
22 Ibid., p. 148.

emphasized cultural dependence, while Sunkel focused on dependence on foreign investment.

Writing in 1973, Furtado suggested an explanatory framework which identified cultural dependence as a critical causal factor in generating underdevelopment.[23] His thesis is centred on the transfer of technical progress from the developed world to the underdeveloped world, thereby facilitating spectacular increases in labour productivity in the periphery. Of the resulting surplus, some will be externally appropriated, but a portion will remain in the domestic economy. It is this latter portion to which Furtado directs his analytical attention, more particularly to the manner of its disposition. For Furtado,

> The surplus remaining in the country was basically used to finance a rapid diversification of the consumption habits of the ruling classes through the imports of new products. It was this particular use of the additional surplus that gave rise to the social formations that we now identify as underdeveloped economies.[24]

For Furtado, the central informing idea of this thesis is that 'consumption dependence' militated against capital investment by lowering the propensity to save. Given the continued expansion of new consumer goods from the centre, there is increasing pressure from elite domestic groups to raise their incomes and consumption. This is accomplished through an expanded volume of traditional exports and/or increasing the rate of exploitation of labour, thereby increasing the income inequalities within the economy. The interaction of external and internal processes, conjoined with what Nurkse had earlier termed the international demonstration effect, were for Furtado major inhibiting factors of long-term development in the periphery.

A similar pessimism is also contained in the work of Sunkel.[25] For Sunkel, the key influence is investment by the transnational corporation and the mainly negative impact of the ensuing linkages. Due to the influence of transnational capitalism, national autonomy is undermined and with it the capacity for self-sustaining development. While Sunkel is prepared to concede that transnational corporations can and do promote industrialization in the periphery, this growth will always be limited and based on technological dependence and backwardness relative to the metropolitan centres. Simultaneously, Sunkel argues that transnational capitalism reduces the capacity of indigenous accumulation to overcome the circle of backwardness, both through the generation

23 C. Furtado, 'Underdevelopment and Dependence: The Fundamental Connections', Seminar Paper, Centre of Latin American Studies, Cambridge University (1973).
24 Ibid., p. 2.
25 O. Sunkel, 'Transnational Capitalism and National Disintegration in Latin America' in *Economic and Social Studies*, xxii, no. 1 (1973), pp. 132-76.

of net capital outflows and through the promotion of consumerism, with the latter lowering the national savings rate. While Sunkel documents and analyzes an array of negative impacts arising from the presence of transnational corporations in the periphery, he offers no policy solutions in either the economic or political domains.

The later ECLA writers concentrated on the salient characteristics and mechanisms which operated within the periphery. This was in contrast to their contemporaries in the neo-Marxist school, whose aim was the more ambitious project of theorizing the evolution of the world capitalist system as a whole. What Palma identifies as the third approach to dependency studies carries this approach further in emphasizing the diversity of conditions in the periphery and the consequent diversity of dependent relations.

This approach is based on the work of Cardoso and Faletto.[26] While it shares much in common with the two other approaches already discussed, it differs in its relative and strategic emphasis. This third approach gives greater emphasis to the possibility for internal generation of change. For Cardoso and Faletto a basic assumption underlying their analysis is that social structures are not immutable:

> It is necessary to recognise from the beginning that social structures are the product of man's collective behaviour. Therefore, although enduring, social structures can be, and in fact are, continuously transformed by social movements. Consequently, our approach ... emphasises not just the structural conditioning of social life, but also the historical transformation of structures by conflict, social movements, and class struggles.[27]

They are concerned with contemporary dependence and they note that new forms of dependency will in turn give rise to new social and political adaptations and reactions inside the dependent countries.[28] They devote considerable energy to analyzing the complexities of the social divisions these adaptations generate and identifying who are the direct and indirect beneficiaries of dependent development. Consequently, their view of the internal domestic lines of social class division is more nuanced and complex than that provided by either the neo-Marxists or the ECLA school.

For Cardoso and Faletto, the diversity of conditions prevailing within the periphery in the economic, social and political domains renders it impossible to generalize with respect to either the impact of dependency relations or the

26 Cardoso and Faletto, *Dependency and Development*.
27 Ibid. p. x.
28 F.H. Cardoso, 'Dependency and Development in Latin America' in *New Left Review*, lxxiv (1974), pp. 83-95.

conditions pertaining to their continuation. Peripheral economies are not monolithic or homogenous. On the contrary, the diversified morphology that constitutes the underdeveloped world, be it in resource endowment, timing of integration into the international system, or the level of economic development, militates against generalization. Central to this analysis is the balance of political forces in individual countries of the periphery. In contrast to the neo-Marxist position, Cardoso and Faletto insist on the specificity of individual countries with respect to historical trajectories and by implication to capacities to negotiate their particular relations of dependency.

A Modern Institutional Account

An analysis of the Irish nineteenth century which is broadly similar to the Cardoso and Faletto approach can be found in Lars Mjoset's recent work for the National Economic and Social Council (NESC).[29] Mjoset grants the salience of the Crotty-O'Malley argument that much of the character of the Irish nineteenth-century economy can be explained by its insertion into the British and beyond this into the wider international capitalist economy. Mjoset places special emphasis on Crotty's observation that the Irish economy increasingly specialized in extensive agriculture, specifically the export of live cattle. Mjoset accepts that this development is particularly important in encouraging emigration, inhibiting the growth of domestic demand, and discouraging linkages between the agricultural and industrial sectors. Like Cardoso and Faletto, however, Mjoset allows for an element of social choice in the manner of adjustment to immutable external realities.

Referring to the Swiss success in deepening its industrialization during the nineteenth century under a regime of open trade, Mjoset contends that the Irish experience of deindustrialization was not inevitable. Mjoset argues strongly that a sole reliance on external factors as explanation is bound to be inadequate and that a complete explanation must also refer to the specific internal features of the society in question. With regard to Ireland, he contends:

> Certainly, British rule cannot be made fully responsible for these economic adjustments by the middle classes with respect to price developments and British reforms. Their adjustments were determined by class interests under the constraints of Irish geo-climactic conditions. We need to look at the internal structures which evolved, internal features which are displaced by explanations which refer to English oppression.

29 Lars Mjoset, *The Irish Economy in a Comparative Institutional Perspective* (Dublin, 1993).

After all, British control gradually receded, and social structures specific to Ireland evolved in that process.[30]

Among these specifically Irish social structures, Mjoset identifies the character of nationalist mobilization and land reform, the influence of the Catholic Church, and the paternalistic family structure.

The famine at mid-century swept away the poorer classes on the Irish landscape, small holders, cottiers, and landless labourers. This demographic change was preserved and intensified through continuing emigration. The departure of the less well-off left behind a more homogenous group of middle-class tenant farmers, who in agitating for land reform and national independence rejected further redistribution or nationalization of land. Mjoset agrees with Lee that this created a conservative 'possessor' mentality which spread throughout Irish society.

The role of the Catholic Church in providing a rallying point for Irish national identity led to its entrenchment at the centre of Irish life. As other societies became increasingly secular, Ireland underwent a 'devotional revolution' in the aftermath of the famine. The authoritarian and bureaucratic nature of the Church reinforced conservative tendencies within the emerging nation. The practice of impartible inheritance which developed after the famine reinforced the culture of emigration for non-inheriting sons and daughters, and led to an authoritarian, essentially conservative family structure.

Mjoset lays great stress on all of these factors in creating a deficient or non-existent national system of innovation within Ireland. In the spirit of Cardoso and Faletto's integration of internal factors in dependency analysis, Mjoset argues that the peculiar character of Irish social institutions are important in conditioning the particular response of the Irish economy to its dependent relationship to British capitalism in the nineteenth century. Mjoset further holds out the hope that the reform of Ireland's national system of innovation can alter the trajectory of the country's future development.

Institutionalist Forerunners

As with the neo-Marxist dependency perspective, forerunners of Mjoset's analysis can be located within the Irish nineteenth century itself. These antecedents can be found in three interrelated developments. The first is the introduction of Comtist social science to Ireland. The second is the emergence of the British school of historical economics in Ireland. Finally, the academic recovery of the Brehon Law tradition under the influence of Sir Henry

30 Ibid., p. 241.

Maine's historical jurisprudence was utilized to justify the necessity of sweep-
ing land reform in Ireland.

Comtist sociology as a system was enthusiastically introduced to Ireland by
John Kells Ingram. Ingram held that political economy could not be isolated
from other branches of social science. Indeed, economics must be considered a
subordinate branch of the more inclusive science of sociology and could only
be understood with reference to society as a whole. This understanding of the
economy was bound to accord more importance to the differing political and
cultural institutions of various times and places. Comte's sociology was historicist in that in common with other strands of thought at this time it held that
explanation of social phenomena rested in historical development.

One the one hand, Comte's system was positivist in that it held that all
social phenomena were data from which a comprehensive science of history
could inductively be built. On the other hand, Comtists held that the object of
an improved understanding must be an improvement in the moral basis of
society. Comte went so far as to establish an alternative religion of 'humanity.'
All of these aspects of Comte's thought were vigorously propounded by
Ingram. The positivist methodology was pursued in practice by the newly
founded Statistical and Social Inquiry Society of Ireland.[31]

The second post-famine development in Irish social science is the birth of
the British historical school of economics. Irish economists had a dispropor-
tionate influence in the formation of this school. Ingram was a prominent proponent and published the only full-scale treatment of the history of economic
thought from the historical point of view.[32] Even more influential was T.E.
Cliffe Leslie. Leslie began what has been called the English Methodenstreit in a
series of articles in the 1870s. Leslie argued against what he considered to be an
overly abstract deductivism in classical political economy. He contended
instead that economic understanding must advance through the inductive
consideration of the specific character of particular economies. Like the later
dependency theorists, Leslie resisted the temptation to construct universal gen-
eralizations about what must remain individual situations. Influenced by the
work of Sir Henry Maine, Leslie believed that explanation must rest with the
historical development of particular times and places.[33]

---

31 See John K. Ingram, 'The Present Position and Prospects of Political Economy' in R.L.
    Smyth (ed.), *Essays in Economic Method* (London, 1962); Robert B. Ekelund, 'A British
    Rejection of Economic Orthodoxy' in *Southwestern Social Science Quarterly*, xlvii (1966),
    pp. 172–80.
32 John K. Ingram, *A History of Political Economy* (Edinburgh, 1888).
33 Gerard M. Koot, 'T.E. Cliffe Leslie, 'Irish Social Reform, and the Origins of the English
    Historical School of Economics' in *History of Political Economy*, vii, no. 3 (1975), pp. 312–
    36; Gregory C.G. Moore, 'T.E. Cliffe Leslie and the English Methodenstreit' in *Journal of
    the History of Economic Thought*, xvii (Spring 1995) pp. 57–77.

Like Cardoso and Faletto, the English historical economists in Ireland saw their approach as consistent with social reform. Ingram saw his project as 'describing objectively existing economic relations, not as immutable necessities, but as products of a gradual historical past, and susceptible of gradual modification in the future …'[34] Leslie's conviction of the inadmissability of universal principles led him to reject the English land ownership pattern as the solution to Ireland's agricultural ills. Instead, he fervently supported peasant proprietorship.

The third current to emerge in Ireland in the post-famine period was the application of the historical jurisprudence of Sir Henry Maine to the study of the Celtic Brehon Law tradition. Maine argued that social norms were the result of a long historical and evolutionary process. No programme, however advanced, could succeed if it found itself at variance with prevailing, historically established custom. In societies less advanced than Victorian Britain, the customary was to be given more weight than the contractual.

The Irish application of these principles found expression in the publication of *The Ancient Laws and Institutes of Ireland* in six volumes by the Brehon law commission. Work on the first four volumes was begun by Eugene O'Curry and John O'Donovan. Following their deaths, the work was taken up by W.N. Hancock and A.G. Richey, professors of political economy and jurisprudence at Trinity College. Inspired by Maine's approach, Hancock and Richey reconstructed the character of early Irish society, finding it based on kinship and status, and, crucially, joint ownership of property. The contemporary social organization of Ireland was in their view closer to this earlier Celtic order than to present day English society. This observation led them to defend the customary rights of the Irish tenantry and to support the institution of peasant proprietorship. Both were influential in the passage of subsequent land legislation.[35]

Critics of Dependency: Nineteenth and Twentieth Centuries

The major critique of the dependency approach is that it lends too much weight to forces external to the local economy. A more comprehensive explanation, critics contend, would involve a much greater emphasis on structures and institutions at the local level which condition growth and development. Modernization theory represents a simplistic version of this kind of critique. Modernization theory is in many ways the inverse of the dependency argu-

---

34 Quoted in A.W. Coats, 'The Historist Reaction in English Political Economy 1870-1890' in *Economica* (May 1954), p. 149.

35 See Clive Dewey, 'Celtic Agrarian Legislation and the Celtic Revival: Historicist Implications of Gladstone's Irish and Scottish Land Acts 1870-1886' in *Past and Present*, lxiv (August 1974), pp. 30-70.

ment. While dependency theory argues that exposure to the world market tends to lead to the development of underdevelopment, modernization theory contends that only integration into the world market can lead to growth and development. This integration can most effectively take place with the creation of 'modern' institutions, values, outlooks, and norms of behaviour. Failure to modernize in this way retards the full development of the markets and leads to economic inefficiency.

Much conventional Irish historiography of the nineteenth century implicitly or explicitly shares this view.[36] Modernization theory has strong parallels with the classical political economy perspective which dominated Irish academic thought in the first half of the nineteenth century. An education in liberal principles and an extension of the unfettered market were held to be the solution to the problems faced by the Irish economy.[37]

This approach, both in its nineteenth and twentieth-century versions, fails at least partially because it has been tried and did not work. While the dependency approach may be criticized for lending insufficient weight to domestic factors in explaining underdevelopment, it does demonstrate that an uncritical embrace of liberal market institutions is unlikely to be effective. In positing modernity as a uniform goal towards which all successful development in all places tends, modernization theory ultimately also ignores the specificity of local conditions.

The 'modes of production' school also criticizes the weight given to external explanation in dependency theory, this time from a Marxist perspective. This school argues that metropolitan-style development is a phenomenon of the capitalist mode of production. The failure of peripheral areas to develop is due to the persistence and dominance of precapitalist modes of production which lack the accumulative dynamic of capitalism. The 'modes of production' school contends that articulation with the imperial capitalist economy tends to reinforce these precapitalist modes, at least initially.[38] This kind of analysis applied to the Irish nineteenth century is taken up currently in the work of Slater and McDonough.[39] They argue that much of the character of the Irish economy in this period is explained by the persistence of feudalism into quite late in the nineteenth century.

As with the other schools of thought, antecedents can be found in the nineteenth century. While in the first volume of *Capital,* Marx predicted the

36 See for example, Joseph Lee, *The Modernization of Irish Society, 1848-1918* (Dublin, 1989).

37 See Thomas A. Boylan and Timothy P. Foley, *Political Economy and Colonial Ireland* (London, 1992).

38 For a useful discussion of this perspective, see Brewer, *Marxist Theories*, pp. 225-59.

39 Eamonn Slater and Terrence McDonough, 'Bulwark of Landlordism and Capitalism: The Dynamics of Feudalism in Nineteenth-Century Ireland' in *Research in Political Economy*, xiv (1994).

establishment of capitalist relations in Irish agriculture, he seems to call this conclusion into question in volume three, probably written five years later in 1870. In an analysis of capitalist rent, Marx contends that in Ireland ground rent only 'formally exists, without the capitalist mode of production itself.'[40] He then goes on to analyze the continued exploitation of tenants by landlords. Comments by Engels in correspondence in 1888 and 1890 echo these observations, with Engels contending that Ireland has yet to 'pass from semi-feudal conditions to capitalist conditions'.[41]

While this paper has centrally concerned itself with the dependency school, it is interesting to note, in conclusion, that all the major modern approaches to analyzing the political economy of Ireland in the nineteenth century can find strong antecedents among nineteenth-century social scientists.

---

40 Marx and Engels, *Ireland and the Irish Question*, p. 117.
41 Ibid. p. 343.

Nassau Senior, the *Edinburgh Review* and Ireland, 1843-49

PETER GRAY

I

Despite the best efforts of Irish revisionists to exorcise any trace of emotiveness from historical writing, the recent academic literature on the Great Famine of 1845-50 has retained a dramatis personae of numerous villains alongside a few humanitarian heroes. The purpose of this essay is to consider the political role of one individual who is generally classified amongst the villains. Nassau Senior was, in the opinion of the economic historian Cormac Ó Gráda, a master of distortion, an inhumane cynic on the '"hard left" of radical Whigdom' who lacked even the honesty to admit his 'back-room role' in designing Whig relief 'experiments'.[1] In her recent history of the Famine, Christine Kinealy also denounces Senior (alongside Harriet Martineau) as a champion of the 'prevailing dogma' that determined the grossly inadequate relief policy of 1846-50.[2] Without seeking to defend Senior's record in these catastrophic years, it strikes me that both these judgements are demonstrably inaccurate, and based on misunderstandings of Senior's ideas and political influence in the 1840s.

This confusion is understandable. Senior was indeed one of the leading 'classical' economic theorists of his day, with personal connections at the top table of Whig society. His writings on Ireland in the 1840s – expressing explicit policy prescriptions as well as economic analysis – appeared in the *Edinburgh Review*, often seen as the 'house magazine' of the Whig party, and were taken extremely seriously by interested observers. Moreover, his creative influence on social policy-making in the 1830s, particularly as regards the English poor-law reform act of 1834, has long been undisputed.[3] Given the need most historians feel to explain in ideological terms the failure of British response to the Great Irish Famine – arguably the worst peacetime social cata-

---

1 Cormac Ó Gráda, *Ireland before and after the Famine* (Manchester, 1988), pp. 112-13.
2 Christine Kinealy, *This Great Calamity: The Irish Famine 1845-52* (Dublin, 1994), p. 355.
3 Although recent research has emphasized that Senior was by no means the sole author of the bill, and that influences other than classical economics and Benthamism were involved, see Peter Mandler, 'Tories and Paupers: Christian Political Economy and the Making of the New Poor Law' in *Historical Journal*, xxxiii (1990), pp. 81-103.

strophe in any European state in the last two centuries – the temptation to blame the 'classical political economy' represented by Senior is powerful. The flaw lies in the tendency to oversimplify the complex web of ideas and motivations underlying this policy, and in particular to ignore the frequently bitter and personalized disputes within governing circles over how to deal with the Irish crisis. In his 'new economic history' of Ireland, Ó Gráda writes that he knows of no way of measuring the role of Senior's writings in constraining relief.[4] This may be overly pessimistic: close political analysis of private correspondence as well as public commentary may serve as a suitable (if admittedly inexact and non-quantitative) method of analysis.

For a 'Whig', Senior was a late addition to the *Edinburgh Review* stable of essayists and critics; indeed his economic writings had been the subject of considerable criticism in that review in the 1830s.[5] He was first approached by the editor Macvey Napier in May 1841,[6] and became a regular contributor on a range of topics for the next eight years. The 'innately conservative' Napier, who edited the *Edinburgh* from 1829 until his death in 1847,[7] was anxious to see off the challenge posed by the new monthly periodicals and to consolidate the journal as the agreed voice of a Whig party now endangered by Conservative revival. Napier was aware that Senior had by 1841 established a formidable name for himself in the public sphere, and appeared a useful recruit.

As the first Drummond Professor of Political Economy at Oxford in 1825-30 (a post he held again in 1847-52), Senior had developed a more 'optimistic' strand of classical economic theory that questioned the rigidity of Ricardo's law of diminishing returns and the universal applicability of Malthus's theory of population. Yet he declared himself wary of applying the theory of economical 'science' directly to policy. In his *Outline of Political Economy* (1836) he warned his readers explicitly that while the subject of political economy was the nature, production and distribution of wealth, legislation had a different purpose: the promotion of human welfare. Knowledge of economic principles was vital for the legislator, but was of itself insufficient as it comprised only a partial explanation for human behaviour and motivations. While there was an 'art of government', there could be no 'art of economics' – at least at its present state of development.[8]

Senior's espousal of this apparently self-denying position (one which some contemporary economists, such as McCulloch would have rejected), may have

4 Cormac Ó Gráda, *Ireland: A New Economic History 1780-1939* (Oxford, 1994), p. 192.
5 [Herman Merivale], 'Senior on Political Economy', in *Edinburgh Review*, lxvi (October 1837), pp. 73-102.
6 Senior to Napier, 12 May 1841, Nassau Senior Papers, National Library of Wales, Aberystwyth, C283.
7 Joanne Shattock, *Politics and the Reviewers: The 'Edinburgh' and the 'Quarterly' in the Early Victorian Age* (Leicester, 1989), p. 25.
8 Marian Bowley, *Nassau Senior and Classical Economics* (London, 1937), pp. 254-5, 263-6.

come about in consequence of his initial forays into social questions, as a commissioner of inquiry into the English poor laws in 1832-34, and as a semi-official investigator into the law of combinations in 1830 and into Irish poverty in 1831. It is clear, however, that he meant such limitations to apply to the discipline rather than to himself; his own discussions of social questions, he wrote in 1847, had been undertaken as a moralist or statesman.[9] There was an element of disingenuousness here: lacking a parliamentary seat,[10] and having access to policy-making mainly through aristocratic patronage, he must have been aware that his influence was primarily due to his ability to articulate a political language that drew its power from a widespread public assumption of the omniscience of economic doctrine.

Although usually referred to as a Whig, in fact Senior's politics were more personal than partisan. He moved freely amongst a broad range of liberal politicians, Tory as well as Whig and Radical. Like his former teacher and close personal friend, Richard Whately, he favoured the idea of a centrist reforming liberal administration excluding the extremes of both traditions.[11] This did not conflict with his position from around 1830 as a member of Lord Lansdowne's Bowood circle of advisors and protégés. This was the social centre of what Peter Mandler has termed the 'moderate liberal' wing of the Whig-liberal party, which drew on Lansdowne's Shelburnite or non-Foxite tradition of whiggery, and which emphasized commercial and financial reforms along the lines of orthodox political economy. Lansdowne's other associates included Whately and Thomas Spring Rice (later Lord Monteagle), and the group tended to work closely within the party with the former Canningites Palmerston and Melbourne.[12]

Although triumphant over English poor law reform in 1834, the political limitations of the Senior-Bowood nexus were evident by 1836. Ireland had interested Senior since his first visit there in 1819, when he had become convinced that Ireland's evils were founded on the economic consequences of absenteeism and the Protestant Ascendancy.[13] By 1831 he was considered sufficiently expert on the subject to be asked to investigate semi-officially the question of the relief of Irish poverty. Senior's response was virtually identical to the official report on Irish social conditions prepared in 1836 by Richard

9   Ibid., p. 264.
10 Senior was urged to stand for Oxford in 1837, but declined on the grounds of expense, his lack of oratorical skills, and the unlikelihood of success in a predominantly Tory seat, Howick to Senior, 15 June, Senior to Howick, 15 June 1837, Senior Papers, C122, C123.
11 Whately to Senior, 2 January 1845, in E. Jane Whately (ed.), *Life and Correspondence of Richard Whately* 2 vols (London, 1866), vol. ii, pp. 76-7.
12 Peter Mandler, *Aristocratic Government in the Age of Reform: Whigs and Liberals 1830-1852* (Oxford, 1990), pp. 102-4.
13 S. Leon Levy, *Nassau W. Senior 1790-1864* (Newton Abbot, 1970), pp. 218-19.

Whately, now Anglican Archbishop of Dublin, which was generally endorsed by his former student. Granting a right to poor relief to the able-bodied poor in Ireland was ruled inadmissable, but the advocates of classical economics recognized that Ireland was to some extent an exceptional case, destined to follow a different path to development to the English norm, and thus requiring different measures. Pure *laissez-faire* was inappropriate, but the problem was to find ways of stimulating the economy that would not contribute to the causes of stagnation by inhibiting exertion. Education was one field evidently suited to intervention, as Senior identified the existing state of Irish society as being suffused with ignorance, expressed in the people's systematic opposition to the law and apparent incompetence in their daily occupations. Whately and Senior demanded the expansion of the (theoretically non-denominational) national school system established in Ireland in 1831.[14] More innovatory was their call for transitional aid in the form of state-sponsored remunerative public works, such as the construction of roads, canals, railways and harbours, and granting assistance to landlords for drainage and waste-land reclamation.[15] The 1836 Whately report argued that if combined with state-sponsored assisted emigration, such measures could bring about a reversal in Ireland's fortunes. Conversely, any extension to Ireland of a poor law granting a right to relief to the able-bodied, would be disastrous to the country. Senior argued that given Ireland's poverty, the principle of less-eligibility entrenched in the workhouse test would not be workable, and the consequences would be worse than in pre-1834 England.[16]

For various reasons, the Senior-Whately plan of 1836 was rejected by the Whig cabinet, and an amended form of the English poor law, granting able-bodied relief within the workhouse at the discretion of the guardians, was extended to Ireland in 1838, despite their angry protestations.[17] Two things are evident from this debacle: firstly that the brand of economic orthodoxy represented by Senior was far from being an obsessive advocate of *laissez-faire* for Ireland, and secondly that there were other tendencies in Whig-liberalism pre-

---

14 For the economic agenda underlying Whately's education programme in Ireland, see Thomas A. Boylan and Timothy P. Foley, *Political Economy and Colonial Ireland* (London, 1992), pp. 67-99.

15 Nassau W. Senior, *A Letter to Lord Howick on a Legal Provision for the Irish Poor* (London, 1831), p. 45.

16 *Third Report of the Commission for Inquiring into the Condition of the Poorer Classes in Ireland*, Parliamentary Papers 1836 (35) xxx, p. 1; *Letter from Nassau W. Senior, esq., to H.M. Principal Secretary of State for the Home Dept., on the Third Report from the Commissioners for Inquiry into the Condition of the Poor in Ireland, Dated 14th April 1836*, Parl. Papers 1837 (90) li, 241. Senior's paper made certain criticisms of the details of the Whately report, but endorsed its principal recommendations.

17 Whately was still furious in 1843 at the 'trickery' by which the bill was passed, Whately to Senior, 29 September 1843, Senior Papers, C628.

pared to spurn orthodox opinion and antagonize its leading proponants. This divergence would become clearer in the 1840s.

II

Senior's first *Edinburgh* contribution on Ireland was a focused and cautious piece on mendicancy published in April 1843.[18] In this he acknowledged the 1838 Poor Law as an established fact (albeit still in the experimental stage), but argued that the omission of clauses outlawing mendicancy had removed any hope that it might initiate the reform of Irish character. The article had little immediate impact, but was to provide the justification for an Irish Vagrancy Act passed in 1847 – itself a pet project of Lord Lansdowne.[19]

Senior returned to the Irish question more generally later that year. The choice of topic was obvious: from May 1843 the island had been convulsed by a series of mass 'monster meetings' organized by Daniel O'Connell's movement for Repeal of the Union. Such was the momentum generated by the campaign, and its ability to absorb pent-up agrarian grievances, that many contemporaries feared that social revolution or civil war would break out. Always favourable towards Irish reformism, the Whig leader Lord John Russell joined Irish liberals in attacking the inaction of the Conservative government and demanding positive Irish measures. His aim was unambiguous – to wean O'Connell back to the reformist 'Justice to Ireland' political strategy of the later 1830s, while simultaneously reviving Whig morale on a traditional Foxite issue.

Yet Russell's party was united only by opposition to Peel's government. Consensus on economic measures was unlikely, so it was probable that agreement on 'healing measures' for Ireland would be confined initially to questions of the established church and Catholic rights. The party leaders were able to achieve a degree of cohesion through their mutual endorsement of Nassau Senior's article in the January 1844 number of the *Edinburgh Review*.[20]

The initiative for the article came from Senior and Lansdowne, who agreed that a statement of Whig-liberal measures was expedient at a time when Irish agitation was 'making the whole empire shake'. From the beginning the article had a political purpose, as Senior was persuaded that Peel's ministry could be destabilized by the Irish question.[21] Senior had already a clear idea of what was

18 [Nassau Senior], 'Mendicancy in Ireland', in *Edinburgh Review*, lxxvii (April 1843), pp. 391-411.

19 Lansdowne to Russell, n.d. (February 1847), Russell Papers, Public Record Office, Kew, PRO 30/22/6B, fols 13-14.

20 [Nassau Senior], 'Ireland', in *Edinburgh Review*, lxxix (January 1844), pp. 189-266.

21 Senior to Napier, 5 June 1843, Macvey Napier Papers, British Library, London, Add. MSS 34,623, fols. 589-91.

required in Ireland; his starting points were the remodelling of the established church, a provision for the Catholic clergy from an imperial fund, the improvement of national education, and the abolition of the lord lieutenancy.[22] The article was from the outset a Bowood project. Monteagle, Whately and Lord Hatherton (Irish chief secretary 1833-34) read the early drafts, and Lansdowne gave it his imprimatur.[23] Monteagle, who was then the *Edinburgh's* chief commentator on economic policy, had some reservations about the final draft, fearing that Senior's lack of local knowledge had led him to be somewhat rash in his language and to exaggerate his criticism of the Catholic church, and regretting that he omitted to deal with the poor law and land tenure issues. However, some of Monteagle's suggestions were adopted, and he was always in agreement with the main points and principles.[24] Since 1836 the moderate agenda had shifted away from developmental intervention towards the promotion of agencies of social control and economic stimulation – reflecting both the limited revival of Irish commercial agriculture from the mid-1830s, and the railway speculation boom in Ireland that had shadowed that of Great Britain. For moderate liberals the central problem in Ireland was not the structural inequalities of the land system, but the privileges of the established church and the absence of state control over the Catholic clergy.

Macvey Napier was anxious to assert his journal's position as the official mouthpiece of the party, and rebuked Senior's suggestion that a 'mixed government' might implement his recommendations. In late November and early December, copies of the manuscript were circulated to other party leaders for their comments. Russell took a keen interest in the paper, believing it 'able, calm and judicious'; but his detailed objections reveal the disparity of perspective lying behind the superficial consensus. Senior argued that Catholic endowment was necessary to separate the clergy from the unruly masses and the 'revolutionary' party. This was argued from first principles with rigorous logic:

> 1. I trace the physical evils of Ireland to the concurrent want of capital and of small proprietors. I trace the want of capital to insecurity, ignorance and indolence; and both of these to insecurity. 2. I trace insecurity to the hatred of the law. I say that the law cannot be popular till the institutions of Ireland are just, and justice requires the two churches be put on equality. Therefore the Catholic priests must be paid.[25]

22 The first two of these had been raised regularly in Senior's previous writings, see *Letter to Lord Howick*, pp. 66-78, 'Letter … on the Third Report from the Commissioners', p. 12, Nassau Senior, *On National Property* (1835).

23 Senior to Napier, 2 June, Hatherton to Senior, 4 July, Whately to Senior, 29 September 1843, Lansdowne to Senior, October 1843; Senior Papers, C305, C139, C628, C204.

24 Monteagle to Napier, 7 December 1843, Monteagle Papers, National Library of Ireland, Dublin, MS 13,394/4.

25 Senior to Napier, 14 November 1843, Napier Papers, Add MSS 34,624, fols 216-17.

Russell's defence of the Whig government's record in 1835-41 – when he had postponed endowment on finding the Catholic prelates averse to it – and the tone of his comments on future policy, expressed a different priority: 'Unless the feelings of the Irish people, their national pride and ambition are satisfied, it is useless to propose stipends for their clergy or outlay of money. They will consider such offers as bribes to church them'.[26] Senior amended his draft to take account of some of these cavils, but Russell did not press them. He told Napier: 'I must repeat that although a general concurrence of views between the *Edinburgh Review*, and the bulk of the Whig party is very desirable, it would injure both the party and the *Review*, if the writers in the *Review* were checked in their general observations, or the party bound to enforce practically all that is speculatively beneficial'.[27]

For Russell and his circle, the *Edinburgh Review* article was of value as a reformist manifesto that was broadly acceptable to most elements of the party, but their commitment did not extend to the ideological premises from which Senior and Lansdowne drew their version of 'justice to Ireland'. For Senior the moral evils of Ireland – the absence of the structural and internalized instruments of 'civilization' central to classical theory – were at the root of the physical ones. Consequently, Catholic endowment was the primary instrumental measure required to further the desired end of economic development along orthodox lines. Senior believed it worthwhile to conciliate only the clergy and the gentry, for O'Connell and his 'revolutionary party' were beyond the pale. Indeed in his earlier drafts Senior had included a character sketch denigrating the Irish leader as intellectually shallow, morally dishonest and (worst of all) inadmissible to good society.[28]

The 1843 events led Senior to go beyond his original intention and address (in passing) the land question in his paper. 'Fixity of tenure' he denounced as the desire of the social revolutionaries in the repeal movement to confiscate the property of Ireland. In his description of the material evils of Ireland he was, however, prepared to modify the orthodox theory so far as to admit that 'want of small proprietors' might be a problem of equal weight to 'want of capital'. A society could succeed if supplied with one and not the other, but his strong preference remained for an adequate supply of capital and a tripartite division of labour. Peasant societies lacked middle classes and hence were deficient in civilization, and were less likely to facilitate high labour productivity and a rapid accumulation of wealth. The achievement of social harmony under such a system required considerable capital investment, but this would be forthcoming from England once the principal moral evil of insecurity was

26 Russell to Napier, 14 November 1843, ibid., fols 255-6.
27 Russell to Napier, 9 December 1843, ibid., fols 719-20.
28 Nassau W. Senior, *Journals, Conversations and Essays Relating to Ireland*, 2 vols (London, 1868), vol. i, p. 139.

removed. Senior did not rule out the desirability of 'small proprietors', but these were subsidiary to his main arguments, and bourgeois rather than peasant ownership was implied.[29] He believed that the solution to Irish social conflict lay in the harmonization of interests inherent in a fully capitalized large-farm society – turning the land from a source of subsistence into a 'machine for the investment of capital'.[30] The existing land law was largely satisfactory, and the problem lay in the ignorance and resistance to the law that characterized Irish rural society. While 'justice to Ireland' represented for Foxites such as Russell a positive response to the articulated grievances of Ireland, Bowood was more interested in finding mechanisms to persuade the Irish to accept the justice of anglicized social and economic relationships. Peel's cautious steps towards implementing the sort of agenda Senior had in mind, most noticeably in the augmented grant to Maynooth in 1845, further persuaded the moderates of the desirability of some form of 'mixed government'. Despite Senior's advocacy, Catholic endowment was to have a low place in Russell's agenda in government until he turned to it in desperation for a 'comprehensive measure' in 1848. By then, as Whately feared, it was too late.[31]

III

The Whigs returned to power in July 1846, just as a second, and nearly total, failure of the potato crop threw Ireland into a deepening famine crisis. Whereas opposition had allowed party leaders to fudge their differences, the imperative question of famine relief forced open the fault lines of the new government. There was a general consensus that relief policy should also promote a rural transition that involved the commercialization of agriculture, righting the perceived capital-labour imbalance, and accelerating a tripartite division of labour in the countryside, but sharp divisions emerged on the relative weight of relief and reconstruction, and on the strategies necessary for both.

In the confusion following the unexpected second potato failure, Charles Trevelyan, the Assistant Secretary to the Treasury, emerged as the key policy-

---

29 [Senior], 'Ireland', pp. 190-7, 241-2. The reference to small proprietors appears to have been inserted in response to the Foxite former Lord Lieutenant Lord Fortescue's pressing of the subject, Fortescue to Senior, 17 November, Senior to Fortescue, 24 November 1843, Fortescue Papers, Devon County Record Office, Exeter, 1262M/FC99.

30 Senior, 'Letter ... on the Third Report from the Commissioners', p. 5.

31 Whately to Senior, 4 September 1847, Senior Papers, C669. For the endowment proposals of 1848-9, see Donal A. Kerr, *'A Nation of Beggars'? Priests, People and Politics in Famine Ireland 1846-1852* (Oxford, 1994), pp. 166-95.

maker. Overhauling the public works relief set up by Peel in the previous sea-
son, and introducing the 'labour rate' principle to make Irish property more
responsible for the relief of Irish poverty. In seeking to transform the public
works into a penal mechanism to oblige Irish peasants to exert themselves and
Irish landlords to undertake their 'moral duties', Trevelyan had the energetic
support of Charles Wood, the new Chancellor of the Exchequer and Earl
Grey, the colonial secretary. All shared a 'moralist' agenda which held the moral
failings of the people rather than environmental factors responsible for Irish
distress, and which used providentialist ideas to lend divine sanction to their
policy prescriptions. They differed most sharply from Senior in adhering to a
labour theory of value and in denying that the wages-fund in Ireland was
rigidly fixed. Ireland, in their view, required not so much imported capital, as
the will to create wealth from abundant latent resources. The moralists were
conscious that the bulk of British middle-class opinion, spurred on by the liberal press, supported a more retributive policy against Irish landlordism and in
particular the extension to Ireland of the outdoor relief clauses and local
responsibility in the English poor law.[32]

Moderate liberals held views antithetical to such moralist dogmatics, and in
general regarded the Irish situation in a coolly secular light. After suffering a
rebuff in the cabinet on the terms of the August 1846 poor employment
('labour rate') bill, the moderates put their energies into resisting any further
moves towards an extension of the poor law. Nassau Senior articulated their
fears in an *Edinburgh Review* article of October 1846, which was again produced in collaboration with Lansdowne and Monteagle.[33] All were in a state of
'utmost anxiety' about the intentions of the cabinet regarding the poor law.
The article was directed ostensibly against the radical economist George
Poulett Scrope's 'anarchical' proposals for extending the Irish poor law,[34] but it
was also implicitly critical of moralist assumptions. Senior was anxious to
defend the record of Irish landlords against the assaults of British radicals and
the press. He assailed moralist and radical assumptions of an unlimited Irish
wages-fund, and insisted that landlords should not be compelled to bear the
burdens of relief unaided. Although he rejected Malthusian pessimism for such
a 'civilized society' as England, where labourers were intelligent enough to

32 See Peter Gray, 'Ideology and the Famine', in Cathal Póirtéir (ed.), *The Great Irish
    Famine* (Cork, 1995), pp. 86-103.
33 [Nassau Senior], 'Proposals for Extending the Irish Poor Law', in *Edinburgh Review,*
    lxxxiv (October 1846), pp. 267-314; Lansdowne to Napier, 3 July, Senior to Napier, 5
    August 1846, Napier Papers, Add MSS 34,626, fols 268-9, 330-3.
34 George Poulett Scrope, *Letters to the Right Hon. Lord John Russell, on the Expediency of
    Enlarging the Irish Poor Law* (London, 1846). The anti-Malthusian Scrope claimed that
    not only could Irish landowners afford a comprehensive relief system, but that 'it is
    notorious that Ireland possesses the means within herself of maintaining and employing
    twice or four times the number of her existing population'.

choose a higher standard of living over the proclivity to reproduce, the same could not necessarily be said of a 'backward' country like Ireland. Faced with the imminence of social collapse, Senior now abandoned his previous interventionist leanings and embraced a ruthless *laissez-faire* line:

> The labouring poor of every country is condemned by nature to a life, which is one struggle against want … Hunger and cold are the punishments by which she represses improvidence and sloth. If we remove these punishments, we must substitute other means of repression. The pauper by some other means must sacrifice his immunity from the ordinary obligations of life … his situation must be rendered less eligible than that of the independent labourer.[35]

As less eligibility was impossible in Ireland, the poor had to be left to their own devices. At the same time, the extraction of rent and the increase of landlord powers *vis-à-vis* their tenants were vital there if what now appeared an excessive population was not to rise further out of control. Previous British misgovernment and the inappropriate extension of English constitutional liberties to Ireland had brought about the present crisis; evictions and greater coercive powers were vital if equilibrium was to be restored.

Senior's strictures were also directed at the Prime Minister, who was suspected of being both a weak link in the chain against extending the poor law and of harbouring heterodox opinions on Irish land reform and poor relief.[36] Russell's antagonism towards Irish landlordism was well known, and his continuing yearning for unspecified 'comprehensive measures' of Irish reform a constant worry to orthodox opinion. The prime minister's suggestion in late 1847 that a form of Ulster tenant-right be legalized throughout Ireland provoked paroxysms of anger.

In the short term Senior's initiative was successful, insofar as Russell declared his unwillingness to extend the poor law in September 1846. Yet the impact was only partial and temporary, and the Prime Minister also stated his dislike of the illiberal tone of the article – the first five pages of which seemed, in his mind, to 'contradict all of what Whigs have maintained from 1796 to 1846'.[37] More importantly, Senior's suggestions as to alternative relief measures – he now rejected public relief works as counter-productive – amounted to little more than limited government grants in aid of local charitable subscriptions, and were clearly inadequate to the imperative of saving

35 [Senior], 'Proposals', p. 303.
36 Senior to Napier, 14, 21, 22 August 1846, Napier Papers, Add MSS 34,626, fols 347-8, 364-5, 368-9.
37 Russell to Napier, 8 September 1846, Napier Papers, Add MSS 34,626, fols 404-5.

life in Ireland which had been declared by Russell and his Lord Lieutenant Bessborough.[38]

Senior was thus a late convert to a policy of *laissez-faire* in Ireland, and embraced it only in response to what he regarded as the demoralizing and socially destructive forms of intervention adopted by Russell's ministry. In the following six months, the unremitting pressure of Irish distress would lead to a series of measures being passed against the expressed opposition of the Bowood group: first the temporary relief (or soup kitchens) act of February 1847, followed by the poor law extension act of June 1847, which embodied many of the clauses against which Senior had written. Only the admission of the fateful quarter-acre clause amendment in the poor law act prevented resignations from the cabinet.

The history of relief policy-making during the Great Famine demonstrates not the dominance of Senior and orthodox political economy, but their marginalization. During the poor law debates, Whately, Monteagle and Senior issued jeremiads against the bill from the sidelines, and Lansdowne kept an uneasy silence in the cabinet. Senior was by now convinced that the potato failure had left Ireland over-populated by a redundant mass of two million people, who could not be 'safely' relieved from famine; he confided to Whately that he would 'rather encounter all the miseries that will follow the rejection of this bill to those I anticipate from its passing'.[39] On this question, however, the running was made by Wood and Trevelyan, strongly backed by middle-class radicalism. Only when both these elements combined to stymie Irish proposals for state intervention in the international food trade, or Russell's proposals for land reform, did orthodoxy make itself felt. Its achievement was essentially negative – blocking remedial experimentation in alliance with other elements within the wider liberal bloc.

Even the *Edinburgh Review* seemed to acknowledge the ascendancy of moralist dogma by publishing in its January 1848 number Charles Trevelyan's apologia for the Treasury's policy, later published separately as *The Irish Crisis*. This diatribe declared the potato disease to be part of God's plan for Irish reconstruction, defended the rigid imposition of the extended poor law and advocated self-exertion by all classes as the means to unleash the potentially unlimited resources of Ireland.[40] The *Edinburgh's* new editor, William Empson, was unhappy with Trevelyan's blithe dismissal of Malthusian doctrine, but failed to persuade the author to adopt a more 'orthodox' tone.[41]

38 *Hansard's Parliamentary Debates*, 3rd ser., lxxxviii, pp. 777–8 (17 August 1846: Russell).
39 Senior to (Whately), 20 April 1847, Monteagle Papers, MS 13,397/10.
40 [Charles Trevelyan], 'The Irish Crisis', in *Edinburgh Review*, lxxxvii (January 1848), pp. 229–320.
41 Empson to Trevelyan, October 1847, Treasury Papers, Public Record Office, Kew, T64/367A/2. Empson had been a colleague of Malthus at Haileybury in the 1820s.

IV

Trevelyan's arrogant treatment of the *Edinburgh* editorial staff,[42] and the grow-ing awareness that famine conditions had not ended with the harvest of 1847, led the review to return to the safer hands of Senior in late 1848. Senior had travelled in the north west of Ireland in September of that year in the compa-ny of his brother Edward, a poor law inspector, and was eager to bring to a wider audience the observations he had already expressed privately to Lansdowne.[43] Everything he had seen there (admittedly mostly in Donegal, by no means the most distressed county in Ireland in 1848) had convinced him that his warnings about the counter-productive effects of the poor law had been more than justified.[44] In extending an English institution to a more back-ward society, the government had created 'a gigantic engine of confiscation and demoralization'. Such was the polemical slant of the third article, pub-lished in January 1849, that he denied that famine, in the sense of a physical catastrophe, was still continuing – all distress was now solely attributable to the malign working of the poor law. Senior was more blunt than most moderates in asserting the absolute character of Irish over-population and insisting on the necessity of diminishing the number of people by any means. Like the Conservative leader Lord Stanley, but unlike Monteagle, he ruled out any extensive state emigration scheme as too expensive to be practicable. The implication was clear: in the absence of voluntary emigration, mass starvation was inevitable. Any hope for the future lay in amending the poor law and strengthening the rights of property. In an almost parodic return to his more 'optimistic' views of five years previously, he added that Catholic endowment (now in practice a dead duck) might help sugar the pill.[45]

Senior's last piece on Ireland for the *Edinburgh* was in no way a party man-ifesto, although it was privately read and approved by Lansdowne.[46] It was in effect a cry of despair from a faction that had failed to determine government response during the Famine. It is perhaps not surprising that, while many other

42 Empson vetoed any further articles by Trevelyan when the latter refused to permit any editorial control over his opinions; Empson to Trevelyan, 7 January 1848, Trevelyan to Empson, 8 January 1848, ibid., T64/368B.

43 Senior to Lansdowne, 7, 26 September 1848, Senior Papers, C215, C217. Senior expressed his belief that racial differences between those of Celtic and Saxon descent in Ulster was evident in moral attitudes, and endorsed Protestant objections to the pro-posed rate in aid for the west.

44 Ibid. Even such acts of charity as Count Strzelecki's feeding of pauper children in the schools on behalf of the British Association Senior denounced as an impediment to education.

45 [Nassau Senior], 'Relief of Irish Distress', in *Edinburgh Review*, lxxxix (January 1849), pp. 221-68.

46 Senior to Lansdowne, 2 December 1848, Senior Papers, C218.

British observers subsequently tended to gloss the Irish famine as a painful but necessary step in the road to civilization, Senior was more sceptical. Looking back from 1861 he admitted that he had been excessively fearful about the poor law and had underestimated the extent of voluntary emigration, but doubted 'whether any great alteration in the habits or feelings of the people has taken place'. Failure to adopt the measures he had consistently proposed was at the root of Ireland's continuing malaise.[47] Depopulation alone, he believed, could not solve the 'Irish problem'. With breathtaking cynicism he commented privately to Benjamin Jowett, that only a million deaths had 'scarcely been enough to do much good'.[48]

Several conclusions might be drawn. In the complex relationship between economic thinking and public policy, it is inadequate and distracting to turn primarily to the most theoretically sophisticated and articulate statements of economic theory to account for governing practice. Rather, it is vital to turn to a broader range of sources – the press and popular pamphlets, sermons and private correspondence – to build up a picture that, while lacking the intellectual coherence of orthodox thought, more accurately reflects the gamut of conflicting forces operating on political protagonists. Due consideration must be given to other ideological tendencies – all bearing the some relationship to classical economic thought, but differing from it in objectives, strategies and interpretations of both human nature and the laws of the natural world. Christian political economy, providentialism, moralism and Foxite whiggery all played important roles in the public policy debate. All must be grasped and placed in the context of the highly personalized but in the later 1840s relatively open British political world. Nassau Senior and the *Edinburgh Review* spoke not for the Whig party but for a certain faction within it, which co-existed uneasily with the remainder. In the Famine years they found their opinions swept aside by a populist middle-class tide which identified the moral failings of Irish landowners as the root of Irish evils, and which demanded policy prescriptions directed at that target. What this ideology shared with classical economics was the low priority it placed on the preservation of human life – and a wilful blindness towards the agonies of the Irish population in the midst of famine.

47 Senior, *Journals*, vol. i, pp. vii–xiii.
48 Cited in Ó Gráda, *Ireland before and after the Famine*, p. 112.

The Peculiar Opinions of an Irish Platonist:
The Life and Thought of Thomas Maguire

THOMAS DUDDY

In the opening paragraphs of *The Veil of Isis*, his undeservedly forgotten history of modern idealist philosophies, Thomas Ebenezer Webb makes the following observation about Irish philosophy:

> Ireland may claim the distinction of having produced three philosophers, each of whom formed an epoch in the history of thought. Johannes Scotus Erigena, the founder of the Scholastic System – Hutcheson, the father of the modern School of Speculative Philosophy in Scotland – and Berkeley, the first who explicitly maintained a Theory of Absolute Idealism – were all men of Irish birth, and were marked, in a greater or less degree, by the peculiar characteristics of Irish genius.[1]

Webb elaborates only a little on what he means by 'the peculiar characteristics of Irish genius', merely adding that 'the genius of the Irish People is naturally borne to dialectics'.[2] He is content to put on record the views of various commentators who have regarded the Irish 'as renowned for able logicians and metaphysicians', known in all the continental universities for their 'proficiency in the scholastic logic'.[3] He concludes that the Irish logician was as ubiquitous as the Irish soldier of fortune, and that 'like the philosophic vagabond in the Vicar of Wakefield, he disputed his way through the Universities of Europe'.[4] He goes on to note that the University of Dublin had from the beginning accommodated itself to the national bent by giving a prominent place in its curriculum to mental science. Nor, he adds, have the graduates of the Irish University been undistinguished in pursuit of the favourite study. He mentions that Dodwell, Browne, and, of course, Berkeley, were all Fellows of Trinity College, and that a number of others, including Edmund Burke, were Scholars of the House.

Webb's remarks signal a touching anxiety about the identity and status of Irish philosophy, such as it appeared in the last quarter of the nineteenth century. This anxiety is revealed in Webb's attempt to represent Berkeley as nothing

1 Thomas Ebenezer Webb, *The Veil of Isis* (Dublin, 1885), p. 1.
2 Ibid.
3 Ibid., p. 2.
4 Ibid., p. 4.

less than the founder of modern philosophy. Without Berkeley we would not have had Hume; without Hume we would not have had Kant; without Kant we would not have had Hegel. And, one supposes, without Hegel we would not have had the great divisions of thought that have marked the twentieth century. We might not have had Marxism, most notably. And so, if we ourselves are in any way inclined towards dialectics, we ought to conclude that it was Berkeley's theistic idealism which ultimately gave rise to the atheistic materialism of the Marxists and to the left-right polarities of twentieth-century political thought.

While the post-modern commentator will not wish to trace the grand dialectical trajectory that Webb did, she would be justified in arguing that the anxiety expressed by Webb concerning the identity and status of Irish philosophy ought to be making its presence felt again – and for precisely post-modernist reasons. We are living in an age of re-discovery, an age which is characterised by a determination to bring to light the work of artists, writers, and others who have been ignored for (arguably) ideological reasons. It is typical of contemporary multi-cultural thinking to encourage recuperative raids on archival materials hitherto ignored. While this has been a familiar enterprise in feminist and ethnic studies for some time, especially in areas such as literature and art, the history of philosophical studies in Ireland, especially nineteenth-century philosophical studies, remains relatively neglected. Most of the recuperative work on Irish philosophy has been done on the lesser-known eighteenth-century philosophers, particularly John Toland.[5] The only substantial contribution to nineteenth-century philosophical studies in recent years has been Dolores Dooley's book on Anna Doyle Wheeler and William Thompson.[6]

In this paper I want to look at one nineteenth-century academic philosopher whose reputation in philosophy was a modest one, but whose life and work taken together should nonetheless prompt some useful reflection on the relationship between philosophy and ideology – a relationship that may obtain even in the case of idealist or metaphysical styles of philosophising which may seem very far removed from more bloody-minded political and ideological concerns.

The apparent contrasts that often emerge in biography between the high-mindedness of the thought and the compromises of the empirical life are magnified to a salutary degree in the case of the Irish academic philosopher,

---

5 See, for example, Robert E. Sullivan, *John Toland and the Deist Controversy* (Cambridge, Mass., 1982); David Berman, 'The Irish Counter-Enlightenment,' in Richard Kearney (ed.), *The Irish Mind* (Dublin, 1985), pp. 119-40; Alan Harrison, *John Toland 1670-1722* (Dublin, 1994); Pierre Lurbe, 'John Toland, Cosmopolitanism, and the Concept of Nation,' in Michael O'Dea and Kevin Whelan (eds), *Nations and Nationalisms: France, Britain, Ireland and the Eighteenth-Century Context* (Oxford, 1995), pp. 251-9; and Desmond M. Clarke, 'Locke and Toland on Toleration,' in O'Dea and Whelan (eds), *Nations and Nationalisms*, pp. 261-71.

6 See Dolores Dooley, *Equality in Community: Sexual Equality in the Writings of William Thompson and Anna Doyle Wheeler* (Cork, 1996).

Thomas Maguire (1831-89). The compromises in question are not necessarily the result of a moral flaw in the character of an individual but the result rather of the pressure that historical developments can place on individuals who happen to occupy particularly sensitive ideological positions at a crucial moment, including even the sorts of positions that individuals may occupy within academic institutions. What is most poignantly salutary about Maguire's case is the nature of his failure to resolve what may be called 'the problem of disengagement'. This is a problem faced by the members of the intelligentsia in any society complex enough to have such a group or class in its midst. It is the problem of how to be sufficiently disengaged from the local culture to warrant being considered a member of the intelligentsia in the first place, while at the same time remaining sufficiently engaged with, or involved in, that culture to warrant being supported or at least tolerated by it. Members of the academic community, insofar as they may be regarded as intellectuals, cannot easily avoid this problem. Academics, in their capacity as paid-up, pensionable members of a professional intelligentsia, are supposed to be (at least according to the standard account) the overviewers and critiquers of the local culture, like the Socratic gadfly whose job it was to keep stinging and thereby rousing the lazy thoroughbred that was Athenian society. Or, to use a more contemporary and more business-like image, they are supposed to function like quality controllers whose job it is to identify and assess the various forces at work on and in the local culture, determining which forces are for the culture and which are against it. To perform this role effectively they have to be disengaged enough to adopt a critical, reflective stance on the culture in question; yet, they have to be close enough to the culture to understand it from within and care about the direction in which it is moving. They have to become, in Wallace Stevens's words, 'insiders and outsiders at once'.[7] The conscientious academic, in short, finds himself or herself always at the centre of a systematic dilemma about degrees of engagement and disengagement. The life and thought of Thomas Maguire presents us with a dramatic example of the tragic consequences that can ensue for the provincial academic who is duly responsive to local ideological pressures but who is less than canny about the quality of his relationship with the local culture at a critical moment in its history.

Maguire was born in Dublin in 1831 into a Catholic merchant family.[8] He attended Trinity College in 1851, graduating in 1855 as a senior moderator in Classics and Philosophy. When the Professorship of Latin became vacant in

7 Wallace Stevens, *Opus Posthumus* (New York, 1966), p. 261, quoted in Kevin Whelan, 'The Region and the Intellectuals,' in Liam O'Dowd (ed.), *On Intellectuals and Intellectual Life in Ireland* (Belfast, 1996), p. 116.

8 For biographical information on Maguire I have drawn heavily on Timothy P. Foley's 'Thomas Maguire and the Parnell Forgeries' in *Journal of the Galway Archaeological and Historical Society*, lxvi (1994), pp. 173-96.

Queen's College, Galway, in 1869 Maguire was appointed. He did not, however, remain in Queen's College, Galway, for very long. Indeed, his time at the Galway college does not appear to have been a happy or productive one. An editorial in the *Weekly Freeman* (2 March 1889) would conclude that during the

> earlier portion of his stay at the seat of learning in the Citie of the Tribes he did not distinguish himself by any assiduous attention to his duties, and rather gained a reputation as a learned man who had eschewed the midnight oil. He lived close by the town in a true bachelor's residence, and soon became remarkable for peculiar opinions.[9]

It seems that Maguire was less than regretful about leaving Queen's College, Galway, in 1880 to take up a fellowship at Trinity College, Dublin. He had the distinction of being the first Catholic to be elected to such a fellowship since 'Fawcett's Act' of 1873 had removed religious disabilities at Trinity. From 1880 to 1882 he held a lectureship in Greek and Latin at Trinity until he was appointed to the Professorship of Moral Philosophy in 1882. This would be the position that he would hold until his death, in unhappy circumstances, in 1889.

During his time as an academic philosopher, Maguire would lead a kind of double-life. As a philosopher, he was a metaphysician in the Platonic or idealist mode. All his academic publications were on idealism, transcendentalism, or Platonism. His first book, *The Platonic Idea*, was published in 1866, three years before he came to the professorship in Galway. His next substantial publication, *Essays on the Platonic Ethics*, appeared in 1870 during his stint in Galway, though it was written before he took up the professorship here. His next academic publication would not appear until 1882. This was *The Parmenides of Plato*, which is in fact an edition of the Greek text, introduced and annotated by Maguire, and intended, in Maguire's own words, 'chiefly for the Metaphysician'.[10]

Indeed, all of Maguire's academic philosophical writing is intended chiefly for the metaphysician. He is not only an expositor and interpreter of the metaphysics of Plato but also writes defensively about idealism and transcendentalism in general. He is defensive, in other words, about the idea that there exists a reality which is superior to, and somehow more real or more substantial than,

---

9 Ibid., p. 174.
10 Thomas Maguire, *The Parmenides of Plato* (Dublin, 1882), p. [v]. Maguire's other published academic or philosophical work included *Reviews: i. Mr J.S. Mill's 'Utilitarianism.' ii. Rev. Mr Barlow's 'Eternal Punishment.' iii. Mr J.S. Mill's 'Hamilton'. Reprinted from 'The Christian Examiner,' 1863-1865* (Dublin, 1867); *The External Worlds of Sir William Hamilton and Dr Thomas Brown: A Paper Read before the Dublin University Philosophical Society, 1857* (Dublin, 1868); *The Will in Reference to Dr Maudsley's 'Body and Will': An Opening Lecture, Michaelmas Term, 1883* (Dublin, 1883); *Agnosticism: Herbert Spencer & Frederick Harrison. A Lecture Delivered in Michaelmas Term, 1884* (Dublin, 1884); *Mr Balfour on Kant and Transcendentalism: A Lecture Delivered in Michaelmas Term, 1888* (Dublin, 1889).

the temporal, material world in which we conduct our practical lives. It is in fact this very idealism which makes it difficult, at first glance, to understand the other side of Maguire – the side which caused him to become 'remarkable for peculiar opinions' and to become involved in one of the most notorious conspiracies in Irish history. Maguire became remarkable for peculiar opinions in the first place because of his outspoken opposition to the Catholic hierarchy and to the Home Rule movement, and because of his explicit support for the Unionist position. He opposed Home Rule in a number of pamphlets on the grounds that it would have disastrous consequences for Irish education. In one of these pamphlets – 'The Effects of Home Rule on the Higher Education' – he argues that Home Rule would be fatal to all real education in Ireland simply because it would place education in the hands of the Bishops. Placing education in the hands of the Bishops would mean 'crushing it for at least three generations, and perhaps forever'.[11] He accuses the Roman Catholic Church of obscurantism and anti-intellectualism, and maintains that a large section of the Roman Catholic Church is conscientiously opposed to the spread of education. He refers his Protestant readers in particular to an article in the *Dublin Review* in which the dangers of higher education are spelt out. The argument of the article is that by giving Catholic youth a higher education 'you open a new and very large avenue by which the godless spirit of the times may gain admittance'.[12] The article expresses impatience with such commonplaces as 'marching with the times', 'aiming at progress', and 'growing in largeness of thought'. Here is one of most telling paragraphs from the article, quoted by Maguire:

> We are very far from meaning that ignorance is the Catholic youth's *best* preservative against intellectual danger, but it is a very powerful one, nevertheless, and those who deny this are but inventing a theory in the very teeth of manifest facts. A Catholic destitute of intellectual tastes, whether in a higher or a lower rank, may be tempted to idleness, frivolity, gambling, sensuality; but in none but the very rarest cases will he be tempted to that which … is an immeasurably greater calamity than any of these, or all put together, viz. deliberate doubt on the truth of his religion.[13]

The article identifies the absence of higher education as a powerful preservative against apostasy. Those who watch over souls are advised not to withdraw that preservative 'until they are satisfied that some other very sufficient substitute is provided'.[14]

11 Thomas Maguire, *The Effects of Home Rule on the Higher Education* (Dublin, 1886), p. 10.
12 Quoted in Maguire, *The Effects of Home Rule,*' p. 5, from 'Catholic Higher Education in England' in *Dublin Review*, xx, p. 192.
13 Ibid., pp. 5–6.
14 Ibid., p. 6.

Having quoted passages like this from the *Dublin Review* article, Maguire then moves closer to home when he reports a revealing story about the Archbishop of Tuam, a story which he claims he heard during his stint at Galway. The Archbishop is said to have closed down a particular school, and when one of the local people asked him how and where he was to educate his children, the Archbishop is said to have replied, 'What do *they* want with school? Let them learn their Catechism'. Thus, concludes Maguire, salvation and enlightenment are perceived to be incompatible, 'and the Ultramontane logic is triumphant'.[15]

It was with such material that Maguire sustained his anti-clericalism. If his anti-clericalism had gone no further than this we could interpret his attitude to the hierarchy and even to Home Rule as evidence of a principled attempt by an Irish intellectual to disengage himself from the pressures, expectations, and demands of the local culture – as an attempt, in other words, to evaluate and even transcend the presumptions of that culture. One could even begin to see Maguire as a heroic practitioner of liberalism and pluralism in a society in which it was not politically expedient to be such. After all, we still expect our intellectuals to be critical of clericalism and also of a certain kind of patriotic or protectionist nationalism. Maguire made the mistake, however, of confusing disengagement with counter-engagement. Having rejected the demands of the local culture, he went uncritically over to a neighbouring counter-culture – that of the Protestant minority. Moreover, he became a spokesman for, and put himself at the disposal of, a Unionist association. In some of his pamphlets, most notoriously in 'England's Duty to Ireland', he expresses his admiration for the Protestant and Loyalist minority. He notes, for example, that 'the vast pre-ponderance of intelligence and wealth is in the hands of the Protestants', while he describes the Parnellites as 'the most portentous gathering of knaves, dupes, swindlers, … murderers and cowards, that the world has ever seen'.[16]

Ironically, Maguire himself would turn out to be the one who was to asso-ciate himself with, and become the dupe of, knaves and swindlers. What Maguire is most famous for among historians of nineteenth-century Ireland is not his treatises on Plato or even his pamphlets against Home Rule, but his involvement in the scandal of the Parnell (or Pigott) forgeries. The story of the forgeries began in 1887 when the *Times* of London published a series of arti-cles entitled 'Parnellism and Crime', purporting to show that Parnell and members of the Irish Parliamentary Party had supported criminal conspiracy and violence during the Land War. In one article it was alleged that Parnell had

---

15 Ibid., p. 7.
16 Thomas Maguire, *England's Duty to Ireland, as Plain to a Loyal Irish Roman Catholic* (Dublin and London, 1886), p. 18. This pamphlet received a detailed response from James Pearse in his *Reply to Professor Maguire's Pamphlet 'England's Duty to Ireland' as It Appears to an Englishman* (Dublin, 1886). James Pearse was the father of Patrick Pearse.

expressed approval of the 'Phoenix Park Murders'. This article contained the text of a letter allegedly written by Parnell, in which his approval for the assassinations in Phoenix Park was indicated. A Special Commission was set up to investigate these charges, and it soon transpired that the incriminating letters were supplied by Edward Caulfield Houston, the secretary of the Irish Loyal and Patriotic Union, a unionist association which had been founded in 1885 to oppose Home Rule. It was also revealed that Houston had in turn received the letters from a journalist by the name of Richard Pigott, that Pigott had sought and been paid money for the letters – and that much of this money had been provided by Thomas Maguire.

It is not clear whether Maguire was handing over his own money, or whether he was just a bearer for the Irish Loyal and Patriotic Union. But there is no doubt as to the degree of his involvement in the affair. One newspaper at the time – the *Pall Mall Gazette* (27 February 1889) – remarked that Maguire was 'a man who more than any other respectable person seems to have been up to his eyes in the conspiracy to ruin Mr Parnell'.[17] We know now that Maguire and the other members of the ILPU were duped by Pigott. During the investigation by the Special Commission, Pigott confessed that the incriminating letters were forgeries. Shortly after making this confession he fled to Paris. He was due to appear before the Commission on 26 February 1889, but by then he had already fled to Paris and would go from there to Madrid. On 1 March, in Madrid, just as he was about to be confronted by British policemen, Pigott shot and killed himself. By this date also, as by some kind of fateful coincidence, Thomas Maguire himself was already dead. In fact, on the day that Pigott fled to Paris, Maguire was found dead in his rooms in London. The suddenness of his death just before he was to be called as a witness led to rumours that he had either been murdered or had committed suicide. These rumours were never substantiated, and all the evidence, including evidence provided by a doctor who was treating Maguire during the trial, indicate that he did in fact die of natural causes.[18]

And so ended, in ill-starred circumstances, the life of an Irish idealist, Platonist, and transcendentalist. Newspaper reports at the time of his death often made a point of signalling or hinting at the contrast between Maguire's academic profession and his involvement in the Pigott scandal. 'Tis a thousand pities', declared an editorial in the *County Gentleman*, 'that this most eminent of English Platonists should have been drawn into the toils'.[19] The *Cork Examiner* (27 February), just days before Pigott shot himself, adopted a somewhat more judgemental stance:

---

17 Quoted in Foley, 'Thomas Maguire and the Parnell Forgeries,' p. 187.

18 For detailed discussion of the rumours about Maguire's death, see Foley, 'Thomas Maguire and the Parnell Forgeries,' pp. 186-92.

19 Ibid., p. 188.

> There is not in the Ministry nor in the Times management, nor in the
> Irish Government, nor in the ranks of the Divisional Magistrates ... a
> man who will not feel in his inmost soul that yesterday a terrible and
> most memorable blow was struck at the Government of Coercion and
> Corruption. Pigott fled; Maguire, of Trinity College, mysteriously
> dead.[20]

As these comments suggest, there is perhaps something especially scan-
dalous about the involvement of a Professor of Moral Philosophy in a conspiracy such as the conspiracy against Parnell, especially when this same person is
also a metaphysician, an idealist, even a Platonist. But perhaps this should not
surprise us too much. After all, the idealist or transcendentalist could be
described as someone who is more attracted to the reality of what is otherly, to
the reality of the Other, than to the reality of the local, empirical world in
which he finds himself. This point connects suggestively with the problem of
disengagement discussed earlier. While most academics or intellectuals accept
that some measure of disengagement is necessary to earn the name of intellectual, there is often the assumption that counter-engagement, or engagement
with an alternative culture, is a brave and effective demonstration of this act of
distancing or transcendence. Going over to the other side, away from what is
local and provincial, might even be assumed to be the most significant act of
disengagement that you can manage. This is a questionable assumption, however. Academics who commit themselves to otherly traditions are not simply
reneging on the native or local culture – they are reneging on the very principle of critical disengagement itself. This is perhaps a particular danger here for
Irish intellectuals. The inadequacies of a marginalised culture still coming to
terms with the after-effects of colonisation can precipitate the local or provincial intellectual towards the Other – towards some powerfully attractive Other
who speaks an 'other' language, who speaks with an 'other' accent, who prac-
tises an 'other' religion, who has had an altogether 'other' history.

We are perhaps too accustomed these days to talking about 'the Other', as if
this Other is always marginal, always to be pitied, always worthy of our love,
always in need of special pleading. But a redeeming feature of the life of
Thomas Maguire is to suggest to us that the Other may also be powerful and
central, and all the more attractive for that. Intellectuals in historically marginal or post-colonial cultures should perhaps be prepared to perform a double
act of disengagement – relative disengagement from the local culture, the better to reflect on it, and at the same time continued disengagement from powerfully attractive neighbouring cultures, the better also to reflect on them.

20 Ibid., p. 191.

Tears and Blood: Lady Wilde and the Emergence of Irish Cultural Nationalism

MARJORIE HOWES

The mid nineteenth-century movement known as Young Ireland marked the emergence of an Irish nationalism that was more ethnic and cultural than civic and constitutional. Although the movement fizzled out in the abortive rising of 1848, its cultural and political legacies were extensive. The poetry of Young Ireland was arguably the most popular body of literature in Ireland for the rest of the century,[1] and Young Ireland's nationalism played a key role in structuring later movements. Critics such as David Lloyd and Seán Ryder have sketched out its major related features: Young Ireland was overwhelmingly bourgeois, organized around the production of identity, and heavily gendered, equating true nationalist subjectivity with masculinity.[2] These general features, far from rendering Young Ireland ideologically simple or monologic, determined the shape of its complexities and contradictions. The purpose of this essay is to examine one particular writer's engagement with them, and in so doing to illuminate some aspects of Young Ireland's cultural nationalism that have been previously neglected by critics.

Young Ireland was associated with a group of figures that included Thomas Davis, John Blake Dillon, Charles Gavan Duffy, William Smith O'Brien, James Clarence Mangan, Lady Wilde and several other women poets. It originated in and emerged out of Daniel O'Connell's Repeal Association. Deliverer of Catholic Emancipation and campaigner for repeal of the Union between Great Britain and Ireland, O'Connell dominated, and indeed could be said to have invented, popular nationalist politics during the 1820s, 1830s and early 1840s in Ireland. His primary method was a peaceful, pragmatic constitutionalism. When *The Nation* began publication in 1842, its leading minds were part of O'Connell's movement. Various disagreements developed, mainly over the question of violence and the issue of the non-

---

1 Chris Morash, Introduction, *The Hungry Voice: The Poetry of the Irish Famine* (Dublin, 1989), p. 30.
2 For extended discussions of these features, see David Lloyd, *Anomalous States: Irish Writing and the Post-Colonial Moment* (Durham, NC, 1993) and *Nationalism and Minor Literature: James Clarence Mangan and the Emergence of Irish Cultural Nationalism* (Berkeley, 1987); and Sean Ryder, 'Gender and the Discourse of "Young Ireland" Cultural Nationalism' in *Gender and Colonialism*, ed. T.P. Foley, L. Pilkington, S. Ryder and E. Tilley (Galway, 1995), pp. 210-24.

denominational colleges the British government proposed to set up in Ireland. Young Ireland was more idealistic, more influenced by German romanticism, less shaped by Irish Catholicism, and tended to conceptualize the Irish nation in cultural rather than constitutional terms. They were more willing to advocate physical force openly and more hospitable to the 'godless colleges' than O'Connell. In 1846 these tensions led to a split between Old and Young Ireland.[3]

Wilde was born Jane Elgee in 1821, to a conservative, middle-class, Protestant family in Wexford. She married William Wilde in 1851, and became Lady Wilde when he was knighted in 1864. As a young woman, she was part of the second generation of nationalist poets that rose to prominence in the late 1840s, after Thomas Davis's death in 1845. She published poetry and prose in *The Nation* under the pen name Speranza, and was noted among her contemporaries as one of Young Ireland's most violent, emotional and inflammatory writers.[4] She published *Poems by Speranza* in 1864, and wrote a number of other essays and books during her life.[5] After the failure of the 1848 revolution, both she and William became disillusioned with Irish nationalism; later she concentrated increasingly on other literary projects and on her aspirations to run a literary salon. In the late nineteenth century, she was generally acknowledged as an important, if eccentric, figure in the Dublin literary and social scene. When her son, Oscar Wilde, toured the United States in 1882, headlines in New York's *Irish Nation* lamented, 'Speranza's Son … Phrasing about Beauty while a Hideous Tyranny Overshadows His Native Land'.[6] Ten years later,

3 On Young Ireland's origins, development, and intellectual structures, see Richard Davis, *The Young Ireland Movement* (Dublin and Totowa, NJ, 1987); George Boyce, *Nationalism in Ireland* (London, 1991), pp. 154-91; David Cairns and Shaun Richards, *Writing Ireland: Colonialism, Nationalism and Culture* (Manchester, 1988), pp. 22-41; Seamus Deane, 'Poetry and Song 1800-1890' and 'The Famine and Young Ireland' in *The Field Day Anthology of Irish Writing*, ed. Seamus Deane, vol. ii (Derry, 1991).

4 The authorities considered her anonymous 1848 essay, entitled 'Jacta Alea Est' ('The Die is Cast'), seditious enough to warrant prosecution, and tried Duffy for writing it, even though he was already in prison when it appeared. When Wilde disrupted his trial by standing up in the gallery and claiming authorship, the government declined to prosecute her, and four different juries refused to convict Duffy. For an account of the incident, see Richard Ellmann, *Oscar Wilde* (New York, 1988), p. 9.

5 She translated a novel, *Sidonia the Sorceress*, in 1849, translated Lamartine's *Pictures of the First French Revolution* and *The Wanderer and His Home* in 1850, published *The Glacier Land* in 1852 and *The First Temptation* in 1853. *Poems: Second Series; Translations* appeared in 1866. In 1880 she completed and published a book her husband had begun before his death, *Memoir of Gabriel Béranger*. *Driftwood From Scandinavia* appeared in 1884, *Ancient Legends, Mystic Charms and Superstitions of Ireland* in 1887, and *Ancient Cures, Charms, and Usages of Ireland* in 1890. *Notes on Men, Women, and Books* (1891) and *Social Studies* (1893) were collections of essays, all or nearly all of which had appeared earlier in journals.

6 Ellmann, *Oscar Wilde*, p. 195.

when W.B. Yeats wanted to praise the fiery eloquence of Maud Gonne's political speeches, he dubbed her 'the new Speranza'.[7]

Like many nineteenth-century women writers of sentimental fiction or parlour poetry, Wilde was considerably more visible to her contemporaries than she was to later cultural critics. Although her contributions to *The Nation* were nearly as popular as those of Davis, its most charismatic writer,[8] she has been largely neglected by studies of Irish cultural nationalism as well. To the extent that she has entered literary history, Wilde has done so primarily as a figure defined by her gendered 'excesses' – emotional, political, and stylistic.[9] These excesses are usually characterized as a surfeit of sentimentalizing emotion and an extravagant interest in violence, bloodshed and death: a constant sense that the history of Ireland was, as she wrote in a pamphlet on 'The American Irish,' 'an endless martyrology written in tears and blood'.[10] This essay will argue that Wilde's preoccupation with the dramatic shedding of these fluids reveals her particular engagements with the major structures and contradictions that distinguished Young Ireland from Old. In a letter to his constituents, O'Connell wrote: 'My plan is peaceable, legal, constitutional; it is part of that general scheme by which I incessantly contemplate the regeneration of Ireland, and her restoration to national dignity from her present provincial degradation, without a crime, without an offense, without a tear, and, above all, without the possibility of shedding one drop of human blood'.[11] In Wilde's works, Young Ireland's tenuous relation to the Irish masses, who it both idealized and distrusted, its interest in and anxieties about subject constitution, and the masculinism of its ostensibly transcendent nationalist subject, are negotiated and structured through representations of tears and blood.

7   'The New Speranza', *Letters to the New Island*, ed. George Bornstein and Hugh Witemeyer (New York, 1989), p. 61.

8   See Davis, *Young Ireland Movement*, p. 85.

9   Thomas Flanagan's *The Irish Novelists, 1800-1850* described her as 'the silliest woman who ever lived' (quoted in Ellmann, *Oscar Wilde*, p. 18), and Terry Eagleton's play *St. Oscar* (Derry, 1989) pokes fun at her vehement and sentimentalizing nationalism. While her work is included in a number of turn of the century anthologies (for a list see Morash, *Writing the Irish Famine*, p. 112), later in the twentieth century her work was seldom anthologized. Hoagland's *1000 Years of Irish Poetry* (Old Greenwich, CT, 1981) includes only her most famous poem, 'The Famine Year,' and A.A. Kelly excludes her from *Pillars of the House: An Anthology of Verse by Irish Women from 1690 to the Present* (Dublin, 1987) on the grounds that her poetry 'appears turgid to the modern ear' (p. 19). She does not appear anywhere in the first three volumes of *The Field Day Anthology of Irish Writing* (Derry, 1991). However, she is included in A. Leighton and M. Reynolds (eds), *Victorian Women Poets: An Anthology* (Oxford, 1995).

10 Reprinted in Horace Wyndham, *Speranza: A Biography of Lady Wilde* (London and New York, 1951), pp. 205-39.

11 M.F. Cusack (ed.), *The Speeches and Public Letters of the Liberator* (Dublin, 1875), vol. ii, pp. 414-15.

Tears

Wilde's nationalist poems are awash with tears – the tears of men, women and children; the tears of poets, patriots and peasants; the tears of sufferers, spectators and gods. These tears structure an important aspect of Young Ireland's construction of its project as subject constitution. David Lloyd's *Nationalism and Minor Literature* offers the most ground-breaking and insightful examination of this project. While Lloyd's work focuses mainly on issues of identity and unity in the work of James Clarence Mangan – unity as homogeneity between the individual and the nation, identity as the consistency of the subject over time – another way to think about subject constitution is as the production and organization of affect. Of course, most nationalisms are primarily 'about' feeling; the question for the critic is how particular nationalisms conceptualize and organize 'feeling.' In most accounts of nationalism, its engagement with the question of feeling takes the form of an erotics.[12] This assumption tends to produce two related narratives of the relationship between gender and nationalism, both focusing on the nationalist practice of representing the nation as a woman. In the first, the nation-as-woman is an eroticized lover, and her patriots worship her with an ecstatic heterosexual devotion. In the second, the nation is figured as an idealized mother whose purity secures her sons' faithfulness and mediates their potentially dangerous homosocial attachments to each other.[13] The distinction between these narratives is one of degree and emphasis rather than kind; both involve suppressing homosexual desire between men and presenting heterosexual love as the appropriate model of national affect. Such narratives do form an important part of Young Ireland's cultural production, but they do not exhaust the functions of gender in nationalist writing, nor do they encompass all the ways in which cultural nationalism engaged with the question of national feeling. In addition, women writers often have an especially problem-

---

12 The Introduction to *Nationalisms and Sexualities* observes, 'Whenever the power of the nation is invoked – whether it be in the media, in scholarly texts, or in everyday conversation – we are more likely than not to find it couched as a *love of country*: an eroticized nationalism' (ed. Andrew Parker, Mary Russo, Doris Sommer, and Patricia Yaeger [New York, 1992], p. 1); and influential books like George Mosse's *Nationalism and Sexuality: Middle-Class Morality and Sexual Norms in Modern Europe* (Madison, 1985) and Klaus Theweleit's *Male Fantasies, Volume I: Women Floods Bodies History* (trans. Stephen Conway [Minneapolis, 1987]) take as their starting points the assumption that the feelings associated with nationalism are best conceptualized in erotic terms.

13 See. for example, C.L. Innes, *Woman and Nation in Irish Literature and Society, 1880-1935* (Athens, GA, 1993); Elizabeth Cullingford, '"Thinking of Her … as … Ireland": Yeats, Pearse, and Heaney' in *Textual Practice*, iv (1990), pp. 1-21; Joseph Valente, 'The Myth of Sovereignty: Gender in the Literature of Irish Nationalism' in *ELH*, lxi, no. 1 (Spring 1994), pp. 189-210; and Ryder, 'Gender and the Discourse of "Young Ireland" Cultural Nationalism'.

atic relationship to such iconography.[14] While these representational patterns are not wholly absent from Wilde's work, they do not structure it in a significant way. Young Ireland also employed a different set of tropes for conceptualizing and organizing national feeling, one that was arguably more congenial to women writers. Through representations of tears, her poetry illustrates this alternative conception of cultural nationalism as subject constitution and that project's relation to gender and class boundaries.

While O'Connell wanted to achieve his political goals without shedding blood or tears, he was no less sentimental than Young Ireland; his nationalism simply imagined a different relation between nationality and feeling. O'Connell's movement relied upon a combination of feeling and reason.[15] His nationalism was largely a modernizing, Enlightenment project; several critics have argued that disciplined, mass, constitutional politics in the British isles originated with his movement.[16] He emphasized the calm rationality of his own political arguments — 'I am cool, and quiet, and deliberate; no bursts of passion sway my soul'[17] (Cusack 2: 373) — and exhorted his followers to legal, orderly agitation. On the other hand, O'Connell also employed, and was shaped by, the nineteenth-century discourses of sentimentalism and melodrama. His speeches, especially at the 'monster meetings' of the 1840s, were often calculated to arouse the passions of his audiences, and did so quite effectively. Even his written effusions, in a letter to his followers, on the death of Thomas Davis aspired to the status of a spontaneous, unmediated outpouring of feeling: 'I can write no more — my tears blind me.'[18] The main difference between O'Connell and Young Ireland, then, was that for O'Connell, although nationalism involved feeling, feeling was not the quintessential mark of national subjectivity. This was because O'Connell had little investment in Irish culture or identity as bases for political action or arrangements; his Irish nationalism was not primarily a project of subject constitution. He viewed the decline of the Irish language with equanimity, and, as Oliver MacDonagh observes, he would have found such concepts as 'anglicization' or 'mental colonialism' incompre-

---

14 For a discussion of the Irish case, see Eavan Boland, *A Kind of Scar: The Woman Poet in a National Tradition* (Dublin, 1989).

15 As a young man, the two books he was most influenced by were Godwin's *Caleb Williams* and Mackenzie's *The Man of Feeling*, representing the cults of rational improvement and sensibility, respectively (Oliver MacDonagh, *The Hereditary Bondsman: Daniel O'Connell 1775-1829* [London, 1988], p. 39).

16 See Davis, *Young Ireland Movement*, p. 2 and Terry Eagleton, *Heathcliff and the Great Hunger: Studies in Irish Culture* (London, 1995), p. 274.

17 Cusack (ed.), *Speeches and Public Letters*, vol. ii, p. 373.

18 Quoted in Oliver MacDonagh, *The Emancipist: Daniel O'Connell 1775-1829* (New York, 1989), p. 272. MacDonagh also notes that for most of his life, O'Connell's favourite writer was Thomas Moore, famous for his tearful sentimentalities on the subject of Ireland and the Irish (*Hereditary Bondsman*, p. 194).

hensible.[19] For O'Connell, nationality was a matter of location rather than feeling. 'The Irish people' simply meant all the inhabitants of Ireland, and the power and legitimacy of his movement rested on its mass character, rather than on its 'Irish' character. He liked to intone, 'I speak the voice of seven millions'.[20]

For Young Ireland, speaking the voice of the Irish was more complicated. Many critics have remarked on the doubleness that characterizes discourses of the nation; these discourses assert that the nation already exists, and at the same time they seek to create it.[21] This doubleness assumed a particularly virulent form for Young Ireland. On one hand, an anti-colonial nationalism has to work harder to illustrate the pre-existence of the nation than a statist nationalism, and in the case of Ireland, sectarian division provided glaring evidence that a unified nation did not already exist. On the other hand, Young Ireland arose under circumstances that made the task of a didactic, transformative nationalist project particularly difficult, so the possibilities for creating the nation appeared slim as well.[22] For Young Ireland, 'the Irish people' was a problematic, paradoxical entity, made up of subjects that were already, ineradicably constituted as national, and, at the same time, stood in dire need of such constitution.

Wilde's representations of tears encapsulate this ambiguity. In some instances, tears are the mark of a suffering and passive populace who lack national consciousness or feeling (these two being virtually equivalent for romantic nationalism). Such tears indicate the masses' inadequate response to their own conditions of oppression, conditions that cry out for political action. One poem asks, 'But can we only weep, when above us lour / The death-bearing wings of the angels of power'.[23] Another criticizes the 'abject tears, and prayers submissive' (p. 34) of the people who refuse to rise. In 'Who Will Show Us Any Good?' tears literally blind the masses to their true identity and interests: 'Suffering Ireland! Martyr-Nation! / Blind with tears thick as mountain mist; / Can none amidst all the new generation / Change them to glory [?]' (p. 59). Tears as the sign of colonial abjection are often gendered feminine; the

19 MacDonagh, *The Emancipist*, p. 137.
20 Cusack (ed.), *Speeches and Public Letters*, vol. i, p. 517.
21 See Lloyd, *Anomalous States*, especially 'Adulteration and the Nation,' Eagleton, *Heathcliff*, especially 'Culture and Politics from Davis to Joyce,' and Homi Bhabha's influential formulation in 'DissemiNation: Time, Narrative, and the Margins of the Modern Nation' in *Nation and Narration*, ed. Homi Bhabha (New York and London, 1990) pp. 291-322.
22 R. Radhakrishnan succinctly sums up this dilemma in the context of Indian nationalism: 'The masses can neither be bypassed (for they are the real India) nor can they be legitimated qua people' ('Nationalism, Gender, and Narrative', in Parker et al. (eds), *Nationalisms and Sexualities*, p. 89).
23 *Poems by Speranza*, 2nd ed. (Glasgow, n.d.), p. 18. Subsequent references will be cited parenthetically.

same poem describes a passive Ireland as the 'Saddest of mothers' (p. 60). Such representations fit smoothly into the main stream of literature produced by other Young Irelanders such as Davis or Mangan. Another *Nation* poet put it this way: 'Serf! With thy fetters o'erladen, / Why crouch you in dastardly woe? / Why weep o'er thy chains like a maiden, / Nor strike for thy manhood a blow?'[24] Like Wilde, 'Mary' (Ellen Downing) and 'Eva' (Mary Eva Kelly) of *The Nation* also exhorted their men to nationalist fortitude by denigrating a weak and tearful femininity as the alternative; as Seán Ryder has observed, their poetry 'differs little from that of their male colleagues in its reproduction of bourgeois nationalist gender relations – the difference being that it often articulates such relations from a woman's point-of-view'.[25]

Not all Irish woe was dastardly; Young Ireland's writers frequently invoked the tears of the suffering to describe the brutalities of English rule and the horrors of the Great Famine of the 1840s. Mary Eva Kelly's 'A Scene for Ireland' describes a starving mother's inability to feed her baby: 'She has no food to give it now / Save those hot tears outgushing'.[26] But such a literature of Irish misery still equated weeping with helplessness, and thus lent itself to appropriation by a version of imperial sentimentality, exemplified by writers such as Ernest Renan and Matthew Arnold, that constructed the Irish as sensitive, romantic, and politically inept. Thomas Moore's *Irish Melodies* illustrates the potential ease of such appropriations. Moore's work expressed enough nationalist sentiment to get him condemned by the conservative English press and quoted religiously by O'Connell. But Moore was a liberal unionist, and his poems were immensely popular in the drawing rooms of England several decades before they became household words in Ireland. Although he sometimes took up a nationalist call to armed resistance, at other times Moore's portrait of the Irish as the nation of the smile and the tear meant that Irish cultural production expresses the suffering of the Irish with such lyrical poignancy that 'Thy masters themselves, as they rivet thy chains, / Shall pause at the song of their captive, and weep'.[27] This image perfectly captures the classic mode and dynamics of imperial sentimentality, in which the empire nostalgically cathects that which it is in the process of destroying.

Wilde's works attempt to navigate between the nationalist Scylla of tears that indicate contemptible helplessness and the imperial Carybdis of tears that indicate moving helplessness that nevertheless remains helpless by transferring the imperative to nationalist subject constitution and action to the spectator or reader. Such a transfer is implicit in Young Ireland's laments for Irish suffering and their privileging of popular forms like the ballad. It also accords with

24 *The Spirit of the Nation, Part 2* (Dublin, 1843), p. 17.
25 'Gender and the Discourse of "Young Ireland" Cultural Nationalism', p. 219.
26 Morash (ed.), *The Hungry Voice*, p. 61.
27 *The Poetical Works of Thomas Moore* (New York, 1852), p. 237.

Young Ireland's project, discernible in a number of its intellectual structures, to transform the history of Irish suffering, national and individual, into a source of and blueprint for a gloriously victorious future. But Wilde theorized, more thoroughly than many of her contemporaries, the processes and mechanisms through which tears undergo this transformation. In her works tears constitute a spectacle of suffering capable of generating national feeling and spurring nationalist action; they also signify that a viewer is reacting properly to that spectacle. As this description suggests, such representations of weeping are generically related to the late eighteenth-century discourses of sensibility and their sentimental Victorian descendants, though they do not coincide completely with either. Terms like sensibility and sentimentality are notoriously hard to define; their political implications are even more slippery. Sensibility could be organized around individualistic, democratic, and liberal principles, or it could be mobilized in the service of 'natural' social and political hierarchies.[28] The politics of sentimentality are similarly uncertain and in contention.[29] The various formulations of these discourses shared a conviction of the immediately political significance of feeling, and a concomitant conception of feeling as the basis of the social bond. Thus when Edmund Burke attacked the French Revolution, whose excesses are widely supposed to have irrevocably tainted the vocabulary of sensibility after the 1790s, he did it by claiming sensibility's terms as his own without acknowledging them, lamenting the elimination of natural sentiments and affections as the basis for a hierarchical and harmonious social order.[30]

Burke, Wilde, and various Victorian sentimentalists shared a double interest in feeling as a spectacle to be observed, and as the response that a particular kind of spectacle should produce in the ethically and politically enlightened observer. The tears of the suffering object and the tears of the observing subject go together; the former produces the latter. Wilde's often millenarian vocabulary tended to interchange an earthly observer with a heavenly one. One poem urges, 'Let us lift our streaming eyes / To God's throne above the

28 See Chris Jones, *Radical Sensibility: Literature and Ideas in the 1790s* (London and New York, 1993), Claudia Johnson, *Equivocal Beings: Politics, Gender and Sentimentality in the 1790s: Wollstonecraft, Radcliffe, Burney, Austen* (Chicago, 1995) and Anne Vincent-Buffault, *The History of Tears: Sensibility and Sentimentality in France* (New York, 1991).

29 For example, Anne Douglas argues for the reactionary nature of sentimental fiction's tendency to reinforce nineteenth-century stereotypes of women (*The Feminization of American Culture* (New York, 1988), while Jane Tompkins argues for its revolutionary potential because it re-locates the crucial scene of social and political transformation in the sphere traditionally associated with women: the heart and hearth (*Sensational Designs: The Cultural Work of American Fiction 1790-1860* (Oxford, 1985). For another discussion of Victorian sentimentality, see Fred Kaplan, *Sacred Tears: Sentimentality in Victorian Literature* (Princeton, 1987).

30 See Johnson, *Equivocal Beings*, especially the introduction.

skies, / He will hear our anguish cries' (p. 17). In 'The Voice of the Poor,' the speaker claims: 'If the angels ever hearken, downward bending, / They are weeping, we are sure, / At the litanies of human groans ascending / From the crushed hearts of the poor' (p. 14). Similarly, 'Ruins' predicts that the weeping of the poor will 'Start the angels on their thrones' (p. 40). If God and the angels could be trusted to respond with the appropriate sympathetic tears to the weeping of the oppressed, members of the Protestant Ascendancy could not. 'The Faithless Shepherds' (pp. 45-7) castigates the landed aristocracy for its cruel indifference to the plight of the poor during the famine by asserting that the Ascendancy (like many contemporary descriptions of Famine victims) are the walking dead: 'Dead! – Dead! Ye are dead while ye live / Ye've a name that ye live – but are dead.' This ethico-political (or national) death-in-life manifests itself as an absence of feeling – 'For the heart in each bosom is cold / As the ice on a frozen sea' – and a lack of sympathetic tears: 'With your cold eyes unwet by a tear, / For your Country laid low on your bier.' The absence of national feeling indicates the corruption of the current regime and presages its violent demise, just as the presence of such feeling in heaven suggests that the nationalist revolution is divinely directed or sanctioned.

'The Brothers,' subtitled 'A scene from '98' (pp. 7-9), presents a spectacle, an execution, and revolves around its potential ability to generate national feeling, measured in tears, and the nationalist action such tears should also produce. Insofar as it is cast as an exemplary or paradigmatic spectacle, the kind of scene supremely suited to produce the desired sentiments, we might also think of the poem as Wilde's equivalent to Burke's famous description of Marie Antoinette in *Reflections on the Revolution in France*. The prisoners, 'two noble youths,' are 'in pride of life and manhood's beauty' and bear their fate with exemplary heroism. Christ-like, they are 'Pale martyrs' who die for the sake of their fellow Irish. The poem emphasizes its narrative of events as a national spectacle whose significance lies primarily in its effect on its audience. The first stanza describes the 'pale and anxious crowd' who witness the execution before introducing the brothers, and positions the reader among them: 'You can see them through the gloom.' The second stanza also insists on the importance of the crowd for whom the emotional effect of the spectacle is measured in tears: 'All eyes an earnest watch on them are keeping, / Some, sobbing, turn away, / And the strongest men can hardly see for weeping, / So noble and so loved were they.' The syntax equates watching and weeping, spectatorship and sympathy: 'There is silence in the midnight – eyes are keeping / Troubled watch till forth the jury come; / There is silence in the midnight – eyes are weeping – / 'Guilty!' is the fatal uttered doom.' The crowd's lamentations are an index to their level of feeling, but tears alone are not enough; true national feeling must express itself in action. As in Wilde's other representations of weeping as the mark of colonial abjection, tears that do not generate politically conscious resistance are feminizing: 'Oh! the rudest heart might tremble at such a sorrow, / The rudest cheek might blanch at such a scene: / Twice the judge essayed to speak the word – to-morrow – / Twice faltered, as a woman he had been.' The judge is moved, but the inadequacy of his feelings, which manifests itself as feminine weakness, is structural as well as personal, springing from his position as the imperial official presiding over the brothers' conviction and execution.

Wilde's poem thus explicitly rejects, in conventionally gendered terms, the imperial sentimentality of a writer like Moore, which figures the captors weeping over the chains of their victims as a positive conception of national feeling or identity. The penultimate stanza juxtaposes the crowd's passive weeping with the active intervention imagined by the narrator, a more advanced nationalist who sounds oddly like Burke:

> Yet none spring forth their bonds to sever
> Ah! methinks, had I been there,
> I'd have dared a thousand deaths ere ever
> The sword should touch their hair.
> It falls! – there is a shriek of lamentation
> From the weeping crowd around;
> They're stilled – the noblest hearts within the nation –
> The noblest heads lie bleeding on the ground.

The crowd's tears cannot prevent the spilling of the heroes' blood. The last stanza places the spectacle in the distant past for the first time in the poem. At the same time, it figures the execution scene as a kind of perpetual present, embodied in the heads that refuse to decay and in the continued appeal of the spectacle to nationalist sensibilities:

> Years have passed since that fatal scene of dying,
> Yet, lifelike to this day,
> In their coffins still those severed heads are lying,
> Kept by angels from decay.
> Oh! they preach to us, those still and pallid features –
> Those pale lips yet implore us, from their graves,
> To strive for our birthright as God's creatures,
> Or die, if we can but live as slaves.

Having transferred the burden of reacting properly to the scene from the weeping but passive crowd to the narrator, the poem then transfers this burden to its readers. The poem itself, as well as the events it features, exists as a permanent national spectacle, waiting for the reader in whom it will inspire sentiments and actions like the narrator's. Wilde locates the power to constitute the subject of Irish nationalism simultaneously in the timeless spectacle, which should produce it automatically in anyone, and in the contingencies of the poem's particular readership.

Weeping is thus a figure for the doubleness of the nation; it can signify either the ineradicable plenitude and force of the spirit of the nation, or its devastating absence. As a way of structuring Young Ireland's anxieties about cultural nationalism as subject constitution – defined as the production and organization of feeling – this ambiguity generates a problematic that differs substantially from the problematics produced by an erotics of nationalism. The erotics of nationalism raise the threat of homosexual (as opposed to homoso-cial) bonds between men, the possibility that the patriot will choose his wife over her sexual rival, the nation, and the spectre of the woman-as-nation whose sexual betrayal or rape is equivalent to colonial conquest. The tearful strand of nationalism exemplified in Wilde work, however, grapples with the danger that the signs of national feeling are ambiguous; their meanings contin-gent on who displays them. Wilde's work manages this ambiguity by con-structing taxonomies of feeling based on gender and class distinctions. Thus Young Ireland's representations of tears also occupy the intersection between their drive towards a transcendent national unity and their need to maintain the divisions that unity supposedly transcended.

Men and Women; Leaders and Peoples

Wilde's work is structured by two hierarchies of tears – the tears of men over the tears of women, and the tears of patriot leaders over the tears of the mass-es. While O'Connell's movement was largely for and populated by men, he was well aware of the potential intersections between feminine sentimentality and political reform. He was passionately opposed to slavery, and once claimed that Thomas Moore's *Captain Rock* was to the struggle for Catholic emancipation what *Uncle Tom's Cabin* was to the abolition of slavery.[31] Maurice R. O'Connell has argued that the logic of Young Ireland's romantic cultural nationalism, which emphasized the uniqueness of peoples, militated against their sharing O'Connell's Enlightenment, universalist concern with American slavery and other instances of oppression outside Ireland.[32] I would add that this emphasis on identity, whose supposedly ungendered national subject was actually a male subject, also militated against Young Ireland embracing Stowe's 'feminine' brand of reform. Like Stowe, Wilde insists that political change begins with and depends on conversion, a change of heart. Unlike Stowe, however, Wilde does not locate this change in the feminine, domestic sphere of

31 MacDonagh, *Emancipist*, p. 17.
32 Maurice R. O'Connell, 'O'Connell, Young Ireland, and Negro Slavery: An Exercise in Romantic Nationalism', *Thought*, lxiv, no. 253 (June 1989), pp. 130-6.

the hearth, or give women any special power to effect it. In Wilde's taxonomy of tearfulness, the most ethically and politically laudable tears are mainly the privilege of middle and upper class men.[33]

Wilde's acceptance of Young Ireland's equation of true nationalist subjectivity with masculinity meant that while weeping as a sign of powerlessness or a lack of political consciousness is often feminized in her work, tears as evidence of positive national feeling are associated with masculinity: 'Meekly bear, but nobly try / Like a man with soft tears flowing' (p. 26). Similarly, while the tears of the populace often reveal their despair and pre-political stupor, the tears of patriot leaders embody the riches they can offer the nation:

> And woe to you, ye poor –
> Want and scorn ye must endure;
> Yet before ye many noble jewels shine
> In the sand.
> Ah! they are patriots' tears – even mine –
> For Fatherland! (p. 99)

This impulse towards hierarchy and differentiation within the boundaries of the nation was the inevitable companion to Young Ireland's drive towards various kinds of unity – political, aesthetic, and ethical. While the latter has received more critical attention, the former is particularly crucial to Wilde's work. Since the nation was always in the process of being forged, the nationalization of the masses was always incomplete. This was particularly true for Young Ireland, given its relative lack of organic connections to the Irish masses. O'Connell's movement, in contrast, had been more genuinely popular, with the emergent Catholic middle classes, particularly in cities and rural towns, as its backbone of support.[34] Young Ireland never achieved the popular following that O'Connell had; the enormous early success of the *Nation* depended in part upon O'Connell's Repeal Association, which distributed it. In addition, though O'Connell continued to have a popular following, the Famine destroyed his political machine.[35]

Accordingly, a number of scholars have read Young Ireland's project as an attempt to create in culture a unity that did not exist in the political sphere.[36]

---

33 Similarly, Johnson argues that, rather than feminizing culture, politics, or men, the late eighteenth-century discourses of sensibility entailed the masculinization of formerly feminine traits; those traits were legitimized only because and only insofar as they were recoded masculine (*Equivocal Beings*, p. 14).

34 Roy F. Foster observes that O'Connell's origins, which 'blended Gaelic clansmen and local Catholic gentry,' allowed him to assert his organic connection to them successfully (*Modern Ireland 1600-1972* [London, 1988], p. 300).

35 Boyce, *Nationalism in Ireland*, p. 171.

36 See, for example, Seamus Deane, 'Poetry and Song 1800-1890,' in which he argues that

Thus Young Ireland's founding premise of a unified spirit of the nation located in the Irish masses arose as the chances of them achieving such unity and politicizing the masses were actually receding. But this compensatory response created its own contradictions; it is less often observed that nationalization had to be incomplete, or it risked undoing some of cultural nationalism's other founding premises.[37] Their healthy respect for property and general economic conservatism (with a few exceptions) set limits on Young Ireland's unifying, assimilative ideals, and led them to privilege the leading role of the bourgeois intellectual. As Wilde wrote in an essay on an anthology of Irish songs, 'The utterances of a people, though always vehement, are often incoherent; and it is then that men of education and culture are needed to interpret and formulate the vague longings and ambitions of the passionate hearts around them'.[38] For Young Ireland, the relationship between leaders and peoples demanded both that the masses assimilate themselves to the model of the leaders, and that this assimilation remain perpetually deferred.

As a result, the figure of the nationalist leader carries enormous weight for Young Ireland, embodying both an ideal of unity and the continued significance and the superiority of the bourgeois intellectual. Wilde's work is obsessed with leaders – the current dearth of effective national leaders, the qualities and techniques associated with leadership, the nature of the relationship between leaders and peoples. Her poems refer to leaders with epithets such as 'poet-prophet' (p. 53), 'poet-priest' (p. 25), 'prophet-leader' (p. 39), and 'patriot leader' (p. 28); her leaders are heroic, Christ-like, or God-like. At the same time, her works constantly return to the faults of the masses who have failed to assimilate themselves to the model offered by such leaders. 'Have Ye Counted the Cost?' sneers, 'Let the masses pass on scorning, / Seek not courage in their mind; / Self-devotion, patriot fervour, / Spring not from the craven kind' (p. 34). When she became frustrated with the national movement, she blamed the populace, writing to Duffy, 'I do not blame the leaders in the least. In Sicily or Belgium they would have been successful'.[39]

Along with other Young Irelanders, Wilde subscribed to Carlyle's dictum that the history of the world is a series of biographies – the biographies of great men. She wrote biographical essays about a number of figures, including

'The political rhetoric could not be translated into action because it bespoke a unity of purpose that did not exist' (p. 1).

37 The fact that this formulation echoes the ambivalence Bhabha has identified in imperialist discourses of native assimilation reminds us once again of cultural nationalism's formal similarities to imperialism. See Homi Bhabha, *The Location of Culture* (London and New York, 1994), especially 'Of Mimicry and Man: The Ambivalence of Colonial Discourse.'

38 Quoted in Wyndham, *Speranza: A Biography*, p. 160.

39 Ibid., p. 31.

Thomas Moore and Daniel O'Connell. David Lloyd has explored Young Ireland's preoccupation with biography and autobiography, arguing that for Irish cultural nationalism the hero's biography represents a repetition of the nation's history, pre-figures its destiny, and asserts the seamless continuity of the individual with the nation.[40] Wilde's essay on O'Connell exemplifies this pattern. His life, she wrote, was 'one long gladiatorial wrestle against oppression and bigotry in which every step was a combat, but every combat a victory. ... The life of O'Connell is, indeed, the history of Ireland for nearly a century. ... He lived through all, incarnated all, and was the avenger, the apostle, and the prophet of her people'.[41] This view of Irish history as a series of gladiatorial triumphs was, to say the least, counter-intuitive, and may seem particularly perverse in the wake of the Famine. In contrast, for O'Connell, the history of Ireland was a history of Irish patience and reason in the face of British cruelty and provocation. For Wilde, O'Connell's life was part of the incomplete process of resistance as well as an image of its successful completion; it embodied a history of suffering and defeat and provided a diagram of victorious revolution. The contradictions that inhabit such a formulation are compounded by the leader's relationship to the people, whom the leader must both represent and exceed.

Wilde's works foreground the question of the leader's success or failure in transforming the masses, invariably imagining this transformation occurring when the leader breathes the spirit of the nation into the populace through his passionate oratory. Thomas Davis's essays emphasized the skill of past Irish orators and encouraged present would-be leaders to study the character of their audiences and the techniques of oratory. Wilde described O'Connell's powers as an orator using a language of the mythical and the magical: 'Never, perhaps, since sirens gave up sitting and singing upon rocks, did such witch-music fall on the ear of listener. The effect was magical – it acted like some potent spell; ... Men were charmed, subdued, enchanted – forgot everything but him, and could not choose but listen, love him, and swear to do or die for him'.[42] Although O'Connell was famous, in Parliament and in Ireland, for his oratorical skills, he was not inclined to think of himself as a siren. He theorized his effect on his audiences and his role as a leader in very different terms. O'Connell was well aware of something Benedict Anderson would theorize later: that print capitalism and increased literacy made the rise of his modern popular nationalism possible.[43] In 1839 he threatened his colleagues in Parliament by asking whether they realized 'that the Irish people almost uni-

40 Lloyd, *Nationalism and Minor Literature*, pp. 59–60.
41 Lady Wilde, 'Daniel O'Connell' in *Notes on Men, Women and Books* (London, 1891), pp. 180–97.
42 Ibid., pp. 188–9.
43 Boyce, *Nationalism in Ireland*, p. 160.

versally were now readers? – that where newspapers formerly hardly went out of the great towns, they were now to be found in every village, and almost in every cabin?'[44] O'Connell described the mass political power of the Irish as a nation using Anderson's figure for 'the secular, historically-clocked imagined community'[45] of the nation: the daily plebiscite of the newspaper. For O'Connell, the Irish people were no less a people, and no less a political force, for being apparently isolated, each in his or her own cabin. Luke Gibbons has pointed out that Anderson's argument requires some modification in relation to Ireland and other colonized nations which had important traditions of resistance in oral culture.[46] In addition, newspapers like *The Nation* were often passed around and read aloud to groups. So, while Irish newspapers were central to O'Connell's movement, and their effective circulation and cultural authority was far greater than sales figures suggest,[47] they were closely connected to oral culture. But O'Connell did not privilege speech over writing, and he explicitly theorized the importance of print culture, rather than his own siren-like powers, to his nationalist project.

Although Young Ireland consciously promoted and exploited print media, set up Repeal reading rooms, and lauded their literary projects as part of the national struggle, their rhetoric, in contrast to O'Connell's, went to some lengths to conceal their dependence on print. Cultural nationalism's representations of the nation erased the mediated national community created by print and visualized by O'Connell as each Irish citizen reading a newspaper at home, and replaced it with the physical immediacy of an orator addressing a crowd. Young Ireland's definition of the leader as orator cast him less as the people's representative than as their hypnotist, or, as Wilde put it, their siren. Although the people formed a natural and inevitable national community, they needed the leader's magical eloquence to make them aware of their nationhood and give it political force. To imagine the orator relying on logic, persuasion or choice in mobilizing the people was tantamount to recognizing the nation as constructed and contingent, so Young Ireland described its orators using a language of mystical transformation, in which the masses simply 'woke up' from the nightmare of their own ignorance and passivity. Wilde asks in one poem, 'Then trumpet-tongued, to a people sleeping / Who will speak with magic command[?]' (p. 61). Another poem calls for a leader to 'Pass the word that bands together – / Word of mystic conjuration' and predicts the result: 'And, as fire consumes the heather, / So the young hearts of the nation /

44 Cusack (ed.), *Speeches and Public Letters*, vol. i, p. 536.
45 Benedict Anderson, *Imagined Communities: Reflections on the Origin and Spread of Nationalism* (London, 1983), p. 39.
46 Luke Gibbons, 'Identity Without a Centre: Allegory, History and Irish Nationalism' in *Transformations in Irish Culture* (Cork, 1996).
47 MacDonagh, *Hereditary Bondsman*, p. 208.

Fierce will blaze up, quick and scathing, / 'gainst the stranger and the foe' (p. 31). The hearts of the masses respond automatically, irrationally and uncontrollably, like a field set ablaze, their reaction unmediated by distance, time, or thought.

As the repositories of the spirit of the nation and the instruments of that spirit's emergence in the people, poets and leaders were interchangeable in Wilde's work. 'The Young Patriot Leader' describes the hero's eloquence as an overpowering natural (and ultimately supernatural) force, capable of achieving the transformation of the heart that sentimentalists like Stowe imagined in less violently martial terms: 'As a tempest in its force, as a torrent in its course, / So his words fiercely sweep all before them, / And they smite like two-edged swords, those undaunted thunder-words, / On all hearts, as tho' angels did implore them' (p. 29). Similarly, 'A Remonstrance' asserts: 'Flashes from Poet's words / Electric light, strong, swift, and sudden, like / The clash of thunder-clouds, by which men read / God's writing legibly on human hearts' (p. 52). In Wilde's works, the words of patriot leaders and poets burn, smite, act as 'thunder crashes' (p. 24) or 'God's thunder' (p. 30); they are both physical objects with concrete effects and fetishes, magical objects with absolute power to transform listeners. The greater and more God-like the orator's transformative powers, however, the greater his distance from the masses with whom he was eventually supposed to be merged. Young Ireland's emphasis on the unmediated character of the orator's effect on the people formed the very vehicle through which they inscribed his absolute separation from them. Conversely, it was O'Connell's faith in the mediation of print that made it possible for him to imagine himself a member of the Irish nation, similar to other members.

Most of Wilde's works emphasize that the masses have yet to be transformed by the spirit of the nation. The exhortatory language of her work casts it as an attempt to generate that spirit among her readers. The didactic impulses of Young Ireland's project are well known. But in Wilde's case, representations of gender play a particularly important role in organizing those impulses. The recalcitrance of the masses, and the necessary, continued separation of the leader from them, is expressed in the discrepancy between the women poet and the male patriot leader. 'Who Will Show Us Any Good?' laments: 'Alas! can I help? but a nameless singer – / Weak the words of a woman to save; / We wait the advent of some light-bringer' (p. 61). The female poet is the pale, inadequate shadow of the true inspirer of the nation, the patriot leader. The doubleness of the nation, which exists eternally yet remains to be created, is mapped onto a gender gap between them.

The first poem in *Poems by Speranza*, 'Dedication. To Ireland' (pp. iii–iv), introduces the volume by emphasizing this discrepancy. The opening stanza, written entirely in the conditional tense, details how the speaker would like to inspire the nation, but also implies that she cannot:

My Country, wounded to the heart,
Could I but flash along thy soul
Electric power to rive apart
The thunder-clouds that round thee roll,
And, by my burning words uplift
Thy life from out Death's icy drift,
Till the full splendours of our age
Shone round thee for thy heritage –
As Miriam's, by the Red Sea strand
Clashing proud cymbals, so my hand
Would strike thy harp,
Loved Ireland!

The second stanza confesses: 'I can but look in God's great face, / And pray Him for our fated race, / To come in Sinai thunders down, / And, with His mystic radiance, crown / Some Prophet-Leader, …' The poem turns on the speaker's gender, which renders her an inferior substitute for a true poet-leader: 'The woman's voice dies in the strife / Of Liberty's awakening life; / We wait the hero heart to lead, / The hero, who can guide at need.' The poem's last stanza affirms the efforts made by the 'woman's hand' of the speaker, while insisting on their limited efficacy. Even the reference to Miriam indicates that she will never achieve the status of a true poet-prophet. Miriam was Moses' sister, and her only prophecy was a song of praise for Moses after he parted the Red Sea. Later, she was punished by God for complaining that Moses had too much power; Wilde's speaker is unlikely to incur punishment for a similar offense.

Like the other women writers of *The Nation*, in general Wilde did not explicitly critique or resist the major structures of Young Ireland's cultural nationalism. Instead, I have been arguing that she inhabited their contradictions in a particular way. Wilde emphasized a sentimental rather than an erotic model of national feeling, but did not make the claims to specifically feminine power that other sentimental literatures did. She used Young Ireland's gender conventions to mediate a bourgeois nationalism's necessary but problematic separation from the people, embodied in the weak feminine tears of the masses and the worthy, masculine tears of the true patriot. Similarly, rather than explicitly assert the worth of the woman writer, Wilde employed the figures of the woman poet and the male patriot to inscribe the doubleness of the nation and the ambiguous status and potential the masses had for Young Ireland. But if Wilde found a despairing, pre-national people problematic, she hardly found a mobilized, nationalist people less so, as is illustrated in her representations of blood.

Blood

O'Connell struck (or, perhaps more accurately, failed to strike) an uneasy balance between threatening revolutionary violence and condemning it.
Although the British political classes viewed him as a figure who deliberately
aroused the passions of the mob, O'Connell feared and distrusted the masses
who supported him, hated social unrest, and condemned revolutions and
agrarian secret societies.[48] His speeches and essays counselled legal agitation,
orderly mass demonstrations, and non-violence: 'Let there be no riot, no outrage, no violation of the law, and above all, no despair. We are eight millions'.[49]
He repeatedly insisted that 'the best possible political revolution is not worth
one single drop of human blood'.[50] Much of O'Connell's pacifist politics was
based, however, on the implicit threat of a mass uprising. His speeches sometimes employed martial language, especially when he wanted to whip up popular feeling at the monster meetings of the early 1840s. The meetings themselves, which scholars have compared to people's festivals, religious revivals, and
theatrical spectacles, bristled with potential mass violence, and encapsulated
the tensions between violence and non-violence in the movement. They were
elaborately staged, with much pomp and pageantry, and audiences responded
passionately to O'Connell's famed oratorical skills. Crowds were often organized into ranks and marched in step, in a display of quasi-military discipline
that suggested their potential to become a real army.[51] It was this combination
of O'Connell's ability to mobilize the passions of the masses and his skill in
controlling them, in the manner of an inspired military leader, that many contemporary observers found particularly threatening.

In some respects, Young Ireland's warlike rhetoric simply meant that they
stated plainly what O'Connell had been careful to suggest obliquely. However,
the devastation of the Famine, England's largely uncaring and inept handing of
the crisis, and the French Revolution of 1848 radicalized some of the remaining
nationalists by the late 1840s. Wilde began contributing to *The Nation* just after
the Famine began, and as the crisis worsened nationalist writers confronted the
issue of how to represent death and suffering on an unprecedented, and nearly
unrepresentable, scale. Blood, like tears, can illustrate the violent abjection of a
colonized people, and the 'excessive' carnage in Wilde's work is, in part, a
response to the ethical imperative to render the excessive carnage of the Famine
adequately.[52] Like tears, blood has other functions in Wilde's work as well.

48 MacDonagh, *Emancipist*, pp. 229–31, and *Hereditary Bondsman*, passim.
49 Cusack, *Speeches and Letters*, vol. ii, p. 394.
50 Ibid., p. 441.
51 See MacDonagh, *Emancipist*, pp. 229–31, and Davis, *Young Ireland Movement*, p. 41. Some
    peasants in the south of Ireland actually interpreted an 1828 meeting and the agitation
    surrounding it as preparation for a rising (Boyce, *Nationalism in Ireland*, p. 141).
52 For an insightful discussion of these issues, see Chris Morash's *Writing the Irish Famine*

While Wilde's representations of tears were inflected by the dominant dis-courses of feeling, her representations of blood were informed by the major impulses of contemporary religious discourses, the importance of which, as Maria Luddy has shown, can hardly be overestimated as a shaping force in the lives of publicly active nineteenth-century Irish women.[53] Her preoccupation with blood, violence and death was structured by a Protestant millenarianism in which the apocalypse signals the end of this world, judgment, and the beginning of the new millennium. Chris Morash has pointed out that Irish Protestantism was heavily indebted to millenarian thought in the nineteenth century, and that interest in millennial prophecy was especially high in the late 1840s. Morash argues that although millenarian thought among most Protestants was reactionary and anti-Irish, it also offered Young Ireland a way of narrating the Famine that exposed the massive suffering it caused while also casting it as an apocalyptic harbinger of a utopian world.[54] In addition, Young Ireland's conception of the nationalization of the masses as a magical transfor-mation, their fetishistic emphasis on the power of words, and their vagueness about how revolutionary change was actually to come about are all character-istics Eric Hobsbawm associates with millenarian movements.[55]

Like her interest in biography, Wilde's millenarianism was a way of writing the history of the nation and the individual as both a record of oppression and a blueprint for victory. The cataclysmic nature of the suffering involved becomes an index to the radical nature of the transformation it heralds. Poems such as 'Foreshadowings' (pp. 17-19) graft the vocabularies and structures of millenarian thinking onto a discourse of nationalist resistance. The poem begins, 'Oremus! Oremus! [Let us pray!] Look down on us, Father!' and con-flates the horsemen of the apocalypse with imperial coercion and famine: 'On rushes the war-steed, his lurid eyes flashing / There is blood on the track where his long mane is streaming, . . . There's a tramp like a knell – a cold shad-ow gloometh – / Woe! 'tis the black steed of Famine that cometh.' 'Signs of the Times' (pp. 21-23) claims, 'By our prophets God is speaking, in Sinai's awful thunders, / By pestilence and famine, in fearful signs and wonders,' and describes the rough beast that slouches towards Ireland as a successor to the French revolution: 'On its brow a name is written – France read it once before, / And like a demon's compact, it was written in her gore – / A fearful name – thrones tremble as the murmur passed along – / RETRIBUTION, proud oppressors, for your centuries of wrong.' The signs of a better world are literal-ly 'written' – both determined and predicted – in violence, blood and gore.

(Oxford, 1995) and his Introduction to *The Hungry Voice*.

53　Maria Luddy, *Women and Philanthropy in Nineteenth-Century Ireland* (Cambridge, 1995).

54　Morash, *Writing the Irish Famine*, chaps 4 and 5.

55　Eric Hobsbawm, *Primitive Rebels: Studies in Archaic Forms of Social Movement in the 19th and 20th Centuries* (New York, 1965), chaps 4-6.

The Irish might be suffering horribly, but God – and the nationalists whose divine sanction was indicated by the interchangeability of the earthly and heavenly avengers that her poems constantly invoke – would judge the oppressors and avenge their crimes.

Analyses of cultural nationalism often associate its more violent-minded formulations with its nostalgic, mythologizing, backward-looking impulses.[56] But Young Ireland's nostalgia for lost origins and pristine pre-colonial culture did not prevent them needing, and embracing, however ambivalently, a modernizing, nineteenth-century narrative of progress. Hobsbawm points out that millenarianism is the most 'modern' of 'primitive' social movements, and can be fairly easily harnessed in the service of modern political revolutions. Wilde's bloody millenarianism coexists with her commitment to progress, most often imagined as the 'onward march of nations' (p. 69) through history. 'Who Will Show Us Any Good?' asserts, 'Ireland rests mid the rush of progression, / As a frozen ship in a frozen sea,' and laments, ' we alone of the Christian nations / Fall to the rear in the march of Man' (p. 61). In fact, her bloody rhetoric offers an alternative, apocalyptic narrative of progress rather than a backward-looking resistance to it. 'The Year of Revolutions' asks, 'Shall we, oh! my Brothers, but weep, pray, and groan, / When France reads her rights by the flames of a Throne? / Shall we fear and falter to join the grand chorus, / When Europe has trod the dark pathway before us?' (p. 35). The apocalypse of the Famine and the nationalist apocalypse it prefigures propel Ireland forward along the path of civilization.

Wilde imagined violence and bloodshed as both the mark of oppression and a sign that the nationalist cause was advancing. But while the tears that indicate the weakness of the masses become the enlightened tears of the patriot or reader/spectator, her representations of blood usually revolved entirely around the masses, organizing her conception of the masses' role, once mobilized, in nationalist politics. This conception was the logical complement to Young Ireland's impulses to limit (as well as to achieve) the merging of leaders and peoples. Her version of O'Connell's disciplined army, that is, of the Irish people mobilized as an effective political force, was a raging mob. She assumed that mass politics was by nature violent and irrational, so when she imagined the successful transformation of the masses, she emphasized the unthinking and bloodthirsty propensities of the masses so transformed. Often, the mobilized populace becomes part of the landscape itself, taking the form of some blindly powerful and destructive force. 'Signs of the Times' lists the 'signs apocalyptic' (p. 21) of a coming upheaval, comparing disturbances among the people to surging oceans and tempest-tossed forests: 'When mighty passions, surg-

56 See, for example, Richard Kearney, 'Myth and Motherland' in *Ireland's Field Day* (Notre Dame, IN, 1986), pp. 61–80.

ing, heave the depth of life's great ocean – / When the people, sway, like forest trees, to and fro in wild commotion' (p. 21). 'Forward' threatens, 'And the heaving myriad surges, / To and fro in tumult swaying, / Threaten death to all who vainly would oppose them in their might' (p. 31), while 'The Year of Revolutions' exhorts, 'On, on in your masses dense, resolute, strong' (p. 36). Wilde's descriptions of violent nationalist mobs as blazing fields, human oceans, wind-swept forest, thunder clouds and other powerful natural phenomena fit them into millenarian narratives of upheaval. They also embody Young Ireland's anxious conceptualization of mass politics as irrational and bloody.

Wilde's conception of mass politics as crowd violence made a transition from tears to blood an inviting figure for the nationalization of the masses. 'France in '93' (pp. 53–55) compares the French bread riots of the 1790s to the cry of the starving Irish during the Famine, and describes the transformation of the abject people into a savage agent of crowd violence. The first stanza presents the lower classes as crude and lacking national consciousness: 'Hark! the onward heavy tread – / Hark! the voices rude – / Tis the famished cry for Bread / From a wildered multitude.' The 'wildered multitude' signifies its helplessness and despair by weeping: 'Thousands wail and weep with hunger.' The second stanza traces their transformation into 'an armed multitude.' The armed multitude has exactly the same 'heavy tread' and 'voices rude' as the despairing crowd in the first stanza. The only visible mark of their transformation is that they have stopped shedding tears and begun shedding blood: 'Bloody trophy they have won, / Ghastly glares it in the sun – / Gory head on lifted pike. / Ha! they weep not now, but strike.' Young Ireland's didactic impulses notwithstanding, they have not been enlightened; they have simply become enraged.

The poem gleefully addresses the guilty, aristocratic victims of the crowd's revenge, threatening and taunting them, as in 'Calculating statesmen, quail; / Proud aristocrat, grow pale; / Savage sounds that deathly song' or 'What! coronnetted Prince of Peer, / Will not the base-born slavelings fear?' Throughout, the poem emphasizes the violent savagery of the revolution it depicts. In contrast to O'Connell's conception of violence in politics, the crowd's power lies not in threat or disciplined action but in their blind, uncontrollable hunger for violence: 'Blindly now they wreak revenge – / How rudely do a mob avenge!' The poem emphasizes hunger as the source of the riot, repeating words like 'famished' and 'bread.' In Wilde's apocalyptic reading of the Famine, the masses' hunger for food – which represents their colonial subjugation – and their hunger for violence – which represents their mobilization as an effective political force – become indistinguishable. The dismembered bodies of aristocrats become strange fruit, to borrow a phrase from a later description of mob violence: 'Ghastly fruit their lances bear – / Noble heads with streaming hair.' The speaker imagines the carnage of the riot in terms of a

savage 'harvest' of aristocratic blood: 'Royal blood of King and Queen /
Streameth from the guillotine; / Wildly on the people goeth, / Reaping what
the noble soweth.' Thus the lines 'Hunger now, at last, is sated / In halls where
once it wailed and waited' have multiple referents: food, blood, blood as food.
While national feeling among the male patriot leaders manifests itself as tears,
national feeling among the masses manifests itself as a blind bloodlust as deep
and instinctive as the hunger for which it is a metonym.

Current criticism often theorizes cultural nationalism's project of subject
constitution as the formation of a centered subject whose autonomy prefigures
national autonomy, and whose national feelings are embodied in unmistakable
signs, such as love of country. Wilde's work illustrates that, at the same time,
Young Ireland's bourgeois nationalism also produced different, more unsettling
versions of national subject constitution, particularly in relation to the Irish
masses. In this version, the signs of national feeling are ambiguous, their meanings contingent and shifting. This subject's bodily integrity is tenuous – defined
through shedding tears, spilling blood, even ingesting blood – and its autonomy dissolves into the unreasoning mind of the crowd. These divergent conceptions of subject constitution marked Young Ireland's ambivalence about the
Irish masses; subject constitution as the achievement of individual integrity,
autonomy and stable signification was the province of the elite. The necessary
complement to Young Ireland's drive towards unity, their dreams of assimilation, and their faith in the people as the embodiments of the spirit of the
nation was their reliance on class and gender hierarchies, their will to separate
bourgeois leaders and intellectuals from the populace, and their fear that the
masses could not be constituted as national subjects, or that they could only be
constituted as threatening, ambiguous kinds of national subjects. As a woman
writer engaging with a deeply masculinist tradition, Wilde had cause to be particularly sensitive to the latter set of impulses – those that emphasized disjunction, distrust and hierarchy. The major tropes and patterns of Wilde's work
embody, rather than resist, many of Young Ireland's gender conventions.
Through those conventions, however, Wilde illustrated with particular clarity
the disintegrative and divisive aspects of the contradictory formulations that
distinguished Young Ireland from Old.

'Grimmige Zeiten': The Influence of Lessing, Herder and the Grimm Brothers on the Nationalism of the Young Irelanders

EVA STÖTER

'I speak French to my generals, Italian to my sweetheart, Hungarian to my groom and German to my horse' said Frederick the Great – according to John Mitchel, who quotes him in *The Nation* of 9 August 1845, adding:

> He, the most potent soul of Germany, in his time thought his fatherland could not too soon forget its own speech, and learn that of the Gaul; and, now, that man is hardly to be found on the Right of the Rhine, who does not boast the supremacy of his German literature over every other, and there are few elsewhere who will not concede its equality.[1]

The purpose of this essay is to explore how the changes in German cultural thought, brought about by Herder, Lessing and the Grimm brothers, influenced the nationalism of the Young Irelanders, in particular Thomas Davis.

Johann Gottfried von Herder (1744-1803) was born in Prussia and studied theology in Königsberg where he attended Immanuel Kant's lectures on geography. The way in which Kant connected climatic and physiological factors with human society considerably influenced Herder's thinking and found its expression in works such as his essay 'Auch eine Philosophie der Geschichte zur Bildung der Menschheit' ('Philosophy of the History of Mankind') in which he explores humankind's attachment to the soil, and the impact climatic factors might have on a community and its way of living. During his extensive travels around Europe Herder met some of the most eminent figures of his time. In 1770, for example, he met Lessing in Hamburg, an encounter which led to the termination of Herder's engagement as a private tutor. Herder stayed in Strasbourg where he met Goethe, with whom he began a friendship that lasted almost a lifetime. Patrick O'Neill was later to call Herder the 'high priest' of the German Ossianic cult, as Herder enthusiastically tried to prove the authenticity of Macpherson's poems, motivating him to read old Scottish and Irish texts, and to study Gaelic in order to translate the Ossianic 'original'.[2]

---

1 *The Nation*, iii, no. 148, 9 August 1845, p. 715.
2 P. O'Neill, 'Ossian's Return: The German Factor in the Irish Literary Revival' in W.

According to Herder there exists an inherent essence which is the drive behind human development and which controls birth, creation and death. He claims that 'genetic power is the mother of all the forms upon earth',[3] and politicises this idea by claiming that 'man has never existed without political organisation. It is as natural to him as his origin'.[4] In other words, the pure state of nature is already a political one even without human activity. 'The most natural state is a community with its own national character'[5], proclaims Herder, a state is something organic and natural as long as no 'patched up fragile conceptions known as state-machines'[6] are imposed upon it. Two doctrines naturally evolve from this philosophy – doctrines that also had a crucial impact on nineteenth-century nationalism. Firstly is the conviction that self-determination and independence are indispensable for the development of a country, and secondly is the conviction that there exists such a thing as a spirit (*Volksgeist*) and character of a nation. This character is common, according to Herder, to all people who share the same cultural heritage, and it can be developed with the help of the proper education. The individual is to be addressed as a single human being, as a part of one national unity and as a representative of humankind. However, the thought of independence and self-determination was less than pleasing to German aristocratic society. Herder had to establish a solid foundation for his theories, which he claimed to find in the works of one of his most eminent predecessors, Gotthold Ephraim Lessing, and in the most unshakeable touchstone of Western culture – the Bible.

Lessing (1729-81) was a central figure in the German Enlightenment and is probably best known for his very impressive play *Nathan der Weise* ('Nathan the Sage') – a piece advocating religious tolerance and generosity in times of savage prejudices against the Jewish community in Germany. Lessing asserts in his work *Die Erziehung des Menschengeschlechts* ('The Education of Mankind') that humanity can reach its fulfilment through the education of both the head and the heart. He sets education and revelation as co-termini, and argues that God set up one *Volk* (that of Israel) as a role model for man. For this reason the 'barbaric' folk of Israel were given Moses as a teacher, who had the task of educating them and leading them from childhood to adulthood – a process which ideally should have culminated in a condition where people perform good deeds for goodness' sake and not for fear of punishment. In this Herder found a useful reference to a community which – through freedom and proper

Zach and H. Kosok (eds), *Literary Interrelations 2: Comparison and the World* (Tubingen, 1987), pp. 207-20; Goethe also translated passages of Macpherson's opus.

3 J.G. von Herder, *Reflections on the Philosophy of the History of Mankind* (Chicago, n.d.), p. 22.

4 Herder in F.M. Barnard, *Herder's Social and Political Thought: From Enlightenment to Nationalism* (Oxford, 1965), p. 55.

5 Barnard, *Herder's Social and Political Thought*, p. 59.

6 Ibid., p. 59.

teaching – finally arrived at its goal of becoming a self-determined nation, respected by all other members of the human family. 'Law should rule and not the Legislator,' proclaims Herder, 'a free nation should freely accept and honour it; the invisible, reasonable and benevolent forces should guide us, and chains should not enslave us: this was the idea of Moses'.[7]

In an 1845 edition of Thomas Davis's *National and Historical Ballads*, similar imagery to Herder's and Lessing's is used in order to describe Davis's role in Irish politics and literature. 'Novalis used to lament bitterly the severance of poetry from philosophy, and surely not without abundant cause' asserts the editor in the preface, and continues by saying that the divorce of poetry from life and action was even more deplorable. A man of action such as Solon was, in the author's words, 'a poet, as well as a statesman and sage', just as Moses and David were poets, 'as well as prophets and kings.'[8] Thomas Davis was one of these men who combined the poet and the prophet with the statesman and the teacher. The religious leader Moses was thus transformed into a national spokesperson.

Davis himself used this literary 'secularization' of religious motives quite frequently in his speeches. In his famous address before the College Historical Society of Trinity College in 1840, Davis very skilfully combines Biblical images with political issues. He repeatedly employs the image of a chosen people and – ultimately – regards political independence as a kind of spiritual resurrection. He says about the Irish nation:

> I have thought I saw her spirit dwelling … rising … and thought that God had made her purpose firm and her heart just; and I know that if He had, small though she were, His angels would have charge over her 'lest at any time she dash her foot against a stone'.[9]

Obviously, nothing can happen to a 'spirited' *Volk* with a purpose, and once a nation finds its destiny, celestial help is going to follow. It is indirectly suggested here that the nation's leaders are capable of guiding their people on the way to independence, like Moses who brought his chosen folk to the fulfilment of their destiny. 'Christianity' is replaced by 'Nation', and the Bible replaced by a national literature. The term 'spirit' gradually loses its religious meaning and is instead defined in terms of cultural heritage and social bonds.

The combined forces of a secular nationalistic 'religion', and the idea of nations as naturally-grown units, enabled the Young Irelanders to create a new definition of progress which was geared especially towards the political and

7 Ibid., p. 65.
8 Thomas Davis, *National and Historical Ballads, Songs and Poems by Thomas Davis*, ed. T.W. Rolleston (Dublin, 1846), p. 17.
9 Thomas Davis, *Prose Writings*, ed. T.W. Rolleston (London, 1889), p. 41.

religious situation in Ireland. Progress was no longer something that was defined in relation to English industrialism and the modernization of society, but took on the form of a spiritual process. A nation could progress spiritually without the latest technology, without the influence of a foreign government, and without losing its traditions. This spiritual growth, however, would have to be catalysed through education. Not surprisingly, Davis calls education 'the apostle of progress',[10] and declares that the right type of knowledge functions as an almost divine tool for the betterment of humanity. Exactly what kind of education Davis had in mind becomes apparent right from the start of his speech when he asserts to his audience: 'The power of self-education, self-conduct, is yours: "Think wrongly if you will but think for yourselves"'.[11] What is demanded here is an independence from structures and a maturity of thought. The second part of this sentence – 'think wrongly if you will but think for yourselves' – is taken directly from Lessing, as acknowledged by the editor of the 1889 edition of Davis's work, T.W. Rolleston, who was an expert on Lessing. Patrick O'Neill points to another literary borrowing made by Davis, this time from Herder: 'Calling for the revival of the Irish language,' O'Neill writes, 'he [Davis] pointed to Germany's success in stopping "the incipient creeping progress of French" for "no sooner had she succeeded than her genius, which had tossed in a hot trance, sprang up fresh and triumphant"'.[12] Davis's use of this particular quotation has a very political resonance, considering the fact that in 1840, France – and in particular Adolphe Thiers – had demanded vast regions on the Rhine, demands which led to widespread demonstrations in Germany, including the singing and writing of anti-French national songs and ballads. Transferred into an Irish context, this allusion suggests that the Irish should resist the encroachment of English culture.

Davis pushes things even further when he assures the students of Trinity College that continental philosophy, which, in his words, 'proclaims the unlimited right and innocence of free inquiry and self-government of mind',[13] was moving among them. Later Davis would ask whether the men he addresses are 'like the young men of Germany; as students, laborious; as thinkers, profound and acute'.[14] If Davis subsequently claims that universities are unfit to develop the real powers of the 'head or heart',[15] he echoes Herder's reflection that it is not an intellectual training that is most needed in order to secure proper progress of mankind but, as Herder phrases it, an 'education of the heart'[16]

10 Ibid., p. 42.
11 Ibid., p. 2.
12 O'Neill, 'Ossian's Return', p. 219.
13 Davis, *Prose Writings*, p. 41.
14 Ibid., p. 2.
15 Ibid., p. 21.
16 R.T. Clark, *Herder: His Life and Thought* (Berkeley, 1969), p. 287.

which would improve the understanding of human nature itself. This clash between the sensitive heart and the state-imposed mechanical structuring of data leads to the ultimate battle between, what he calls, the Irish 'mind-chieftains' and Trinity College. When Davis exclaims 'Look back on those who have been the mind-chieftains in the civil strife of Ireland – Swift, Lucas, Grattan'[17] the term 'mind' seems to function as a vehicle for cultural transmission, while 'chieftain' represents the notion of tribal community, which was also one of Herder's main points. For Herder and Davis respectively, it was language and education that qualified social heritage to be 'transmittable' from one generation to the next. On the other side of Davis's education scale lies Trinity College; that seems – thanks to his new ideas on pedagogy – 'to have lost the office for which it was so long and so well paid – of preventing the education of the Irish', as Davis so poignantly remarks in his 'historical' speech.[18] This idea about a more practical education, the demand for deeds instead of words, reflects Lessing's belief that Christ was one of the first practical teachers. 'Christianity ... is justified not by arguments about its letter but by the living demonstration of its spirit', asserts Lessing,[19] and traces of this philosophy can be found in both Herder's and Davis's theories.

However, in his later and even more politically radical essays, Davis explicitly mentions Prussia as a 'model' after which Irish education could be shaped. Herder's conviction that a nation could survive the collapse of its governmental organisations as long as it maintained its distinctive linguistic and cultural knowledge is echoed in various passages of Davis's work. As Davis says,

> if Ireland had all the elements of a nation, she might, and surely would, at once assume the forms of one, and proclaim her independence. Wherein does she now differ from Prussia? ... Why can Prussia wave her flag among the proudest in Europe, while Ireland is a farm? ... The difference is in knowledge.[20]

A nation, in other words, starts to be perceived as something that exists more in peoples' heads than in state structures; an inherent part of humanity, not a cultural construct. As Elie Kedourie puts it in his book, *Nationalism*,' it is very often truer to say that national identiy is the creation of a nationalistic doctrine than that nationalistic doctrine is the emotion or expression of national identity'.[21]

17 Davis, *Prose Writings* , p. 6.
18 Ibid.
19 Clark, *Herder*, p. 276.
20 Thomas Davis, *Essays Literary and Historical*, ed. D.J. O'Donoghue (Dundalk, 1914), p. 225.
21 E. Kedourie, *Nationalism*, (Oxford, 1993 [1960]), p. 141.

Before long nationalistic discourse was absorbed into mainstream European politics, and Herder's most valuable idea – that of tolerance between 'naturally' developed nations – evaporated into meaningless slogans. Even the realm of the fairies was used as an instrument for political propaganda. Herder's collection of folk tales, for example, was taken as an insult by the authorities as, for the first time, the knowledge of the 'primitive' people was to constitute a crucial part of the essence of a whole nation. Once more, Herder strove to justify his ideas and daringly proclaimed that Solomon's 'Song of Songs' was, in fact, nothing other than a collection of folk songs (justifying his belief that such lore contains wisdom). In 1773, Herder had collected numerous English and German folk-ballads whose publication was delayed. When the final collection appeared in 1778 with ballads from English and German it also contained material from Estonian, Lithuanian, Greenlandic, Inuit and Greek poetry, as well as original poems by Goethe and Herder. Gavan Duffy later used this literary model of combining the old with the new in his collection of national ballads; including old Irish tales as well as some of Davis's works so as to assure the reader that the 'spirit of the folk' remained among them and could still be passed on by men of exceptional talent and dedication. Ballads and folk tales were soon to be considered as vehicles for the transmission of the cultural essence of a people. The entire field of comparative studies, including the area of comparative linguistics, became increasingly important during the nineteenth century as a means to study parallels and differences between various nations. A complete system was set up which could allegedly prove whether or not two nations were related. This new-found interest in comparative studies manifests itself in another significant nineteenth-century Irish-German connection, that between the brothers Grimm and the Irish 'man of the fairies', the Cork born antiquarian and folktale collector Thomas Crofton Croker.

Both Jacob (1785-1863) and Wilhelm (1786-1859) Grimm were influential philologists and folklorists. Both had studied law in Marburg and were dismissed from their respective lecturing jobs at the University of Göttingen due to their participation in the demonstrations of *die Göttinger Sieben* (The Göttinger Seven), a group of intellectuals who protested against various aspects of Metternich's politics, in particular his censorship laws. The brothers wrote several distinguished works. For example, in his *Deutsche Grammatik* (German Grammar) Jacob Grimm described the fundamental laws of the German language, and developed the theory that the thorough exploration of language gives an insight into the relationship between different peoples. The Grimm Brothers' collection of German fairy tales (*Kinder und Hausmärchen*) contributed further to the notion that comparative studies deepen the understanding of what is characteristic for one people and their relationship to others. The work of most importance in the context of this paper is their German dictionary (*Deutsches Wörterbuch*), which was published in 1854, and skilfully combined the central issues of religion, nation and literature. Jacob Grimm declares in the preface that thanks to the great poets of Germany, who displayed the *Sprachgewalt* (power of the language) to the people, German cultural heritage survived all 'fiendish subjugation' – a remark which is strikingly similar to Herder's 'stopping of the incipient creeping process of French', which Davis had used in his address. Obviously, the Grimms saw the dictionary not only as a reference work which would contribute to the manifestation of a new nation, but also as a bulwark against foreign influences who were 'infiltrating' the fatherland, invited into the country by francophile aristocrats and German bureaucracy rather than the 'ordinary' people.[22] In a remark about the 1848 revolution in Germany and its failure, Grimm claims that it was this uprising that evoked in the people the desire for ideas which, as he phrases it, 'unite and not divide Germany',[23] and that German language, history and literature is now, even a short time later, all the more highly valued. As with Mitchel in the quotation at the beginning of this paper, the Grimm brothers declared the need for a national literature which would include folk tales and ballads. Jacob Grimm believed that the establishment of linguistic science was a lucky coincidence which added to the overall aim of creating a national consciousness, although the publication of this book of words would have, according to him, never been possible without the help of the common people – the *Volk*.

In an article published in 1946, John Hennig describes Jacob Grimm as 'one of the first on the continent to demand the linking of the book study of Celtic languages with the study of the living tradition of Gaelic'[24] – a combination of linguistic science and literature which encouraged fairytale collections to be regarded as character studies of a folk. The Irish folklorist, T. Crofton Croker, adapted this system of comparing the national characters of people through studying their respective folklores, as is revealed by his correspondence of 1826–28 with Wilhelm Grimm. In one letter Croker addresses Grimm as follows:

> The collection of Welsh legends which appears in this volume will, I doubt not, prove acceptable to you, as from their similarity with those current in other countries, they afford an additional proof that the Fairy creed must have been a completed and connected system. I have taken some pains to seek after stories of the elves in England; but I find that the belief has nearly disappeared, and in another century no traces of English fairies will remain, except those which exist in the works of Shakespeare, Herrick, Drayton and Bishop Corbet.[25]

22 J. and W. Grimm, *Deutsches Wörterbuch* (Munich, 1984 [1854]), Band 1, p. xxviii.
23 Ibid., p. vii.
24 J. Hennig, 'The Brothers Grimm and T.C. Croker' in *Modern Language Review*, xli (1946), p. 50.
25 T.C. Croker, *Fairy Legends and Traditions of the South of Ireland* (New York, 1971 [1825-8]), Part 2, p. v.

With this comparative-system, Wilhelm Grimm was able to establish that the Irish, in his experience (which was purely derived from books) drank too much, were slightly dull, but also cunning; whereas Croker was able to suggest that the English were an inferior race due to their lack of leprechauns.[26] Fortunately, the Germans had their *Kobolde* (goblins), which were regarded as equally respectable as their Irish counterparts.

Nevertheless, Croker, as a progressive person, deeply lamented that superstitions should exist in his country and remarked that his aim had been 'to bring the twilight tales of the peasantry before the view of the philosopher' which may be a noble but rather vague undertaking. One of the Corkman's greatest fears was that superstitions should 'retard the progress of civilisation',[27] which caused him to copy a newspaper article of July 1826 reporting that an Irish mother had killed her infant as she had thought it to be a fairy child.[28] Thus it is suggested that the transmission of cultural heritage is only a good thing if it does not block the coming of a new age. On the other hand, the traumatic experience of a society undergoing change can be softened by tradition – a device which Thomas Davis himself used for his type of nationalism.

I shall end by quoting Walter Rix, who identifies the more emotional links between Germany and Ireland. He claims, for example, that Jacobsen developed his idea of a German national anthem against the background of Thomas Moore's songs, 'feeling that Germany and Ireland were in the same position'. He recites Paul Heyse's poem 'Die Pfälzer in Irland', and finally quotes a poem by Friedrich Engels' friend Georg Weerth which might be taken as an indication of the emotional closeness between the two countries (but which is hopefully not representative of the quality of Irish-German cultural relations). It goes:

> One did not understand the other –
> But they shook hands like a brother
> And became comrades in joy and woe –
> For poor devils were the two.[29]

---

26 Hennig, 'Brothers Grimm', p. 45.
27 Croker, *Fairy Legends*, p.vii.
28 Ibid.
29 W.T. Rix, 'Ireland as a Source', in W. Zach and H. Kosok (eds), *Literary Interrelations: Ireland, England and the World, vol. 1: Reception & Translation* (Tübingen, 1987), p. 31.

The Iron Cage of Femininity:
Visual Representation of Women
in the 1880s Land Agitation

NIAMH O'SULLIVAN

In describing the domestication of women in *A Vindication of the Rights of Woman* (1792), Mary Wollstonecraft presciently consigns a certain category of women – what she called 'ephemeron trifflers' – to the cage.[1] She compared such married, bourgeois women to members of 'the feathered race': snared birds who 'have nothing to do but to plume themselves and stalk with mock majesty from perch to perch'.[2] This analogy was translated into a political reality in the form of an actual enclosure, a separate, contained space devised for women in the House of Commons. The Ladies' Cage, as it was known, was a method of isolating women, not only from the inconceivable – participation in public life – but even from their passive presence in the Visitors' Gallery. Women, as if they constituted a dangerous species, were quarantined, according to the *Illustrated London News*,

> on the utmost sufferance extended even to the point of suffering on their part. ... High up above the Speaker's Chair and over the Reporters' Gallery there has been scooped a small suite of apartments, which have been fitted up on the architectural principle which applies to ... the cages in which oriental women are, or used to be generally confined.[3]

The heavily decorated, latticed metal screen protected those in the chamber from any awareness of those in the cage, and for those in the cage it filtered their viewing and hearing of public proceedings, effectively reinforcing their unenfranchised state in emphatic physical terms. This concept of isolating women extended beyond the literalness of the Ladies' Cage to a form of perceptual deprivation which severely incapacitated them in their social behaviour.

Yet, as a barrier, it may well be that the cage, marking a boundary between inside and outside, possessed the same ambiguity which Lady Mary Wortley Montagu discerned in the wearing of the veil by oriental women. While the veil did indeed deny visibility to women, it also 'allowed the "masquerader" to claim the power of sight while remaining unremarked, the paradigmatic voyeuristic scenario'.[4] Anna Parnell used the same argument in 'How They Do

---

1 Mary Wollstonecraft, *A Vindication of the Rights of Woman* (London, 1992), p. 21.
2 Ibid., p. 60.
3 *Illustrated London News*, 12 February 1870, p. 174.
4 Wendy Frith, 'Small-pox and Seraglios: A Monument to Lady Mary Wortley Montagu'

Plate 1 'The Ladies'Gallery, House of Commons', *Illustrated London News*,
12 February 1870.

it in the House of Commons,' a series of articles written in 1880 for the journal, *Celtic Monthly*.[5] Her first attempt at political reporting stylistically prefig-
ured her remarkable book, *The Tale of a Great Sham*, oscillating between
humour and observation, with only hints of the scathing contempt to come.[6]
From the high vantage point of the Ladies' Cage, she gives a bird's eye view of
the proceedings, noting wryly that

> the ladies are certainly much better off than male visitors, who are sub-
> jected to very severe discipline by the attendants, not being allowed to
> speak ... and above all, not allowed to go to sleep.

in Gill Perry and Michael Rossington, *Femininity and Masculinity in Eighteenth-Century
Art and Culture* (Manchester and New York, 1994), p. 109.
5 Anna Parnell, 'How They Do It in the House of Commons: Notes from the Ladies'
Cage' in *Celtic Monthly*, iii, no. 5 (May 1880), pp. 469-72; iii, no. 6 (June 1880), pp. 537-
41; iv, no. 1 (July 1880), pp. 17-21.
6 Anna Parnell, *The Tale of a Great Sham* (Dublin, 1986). The manuscript for this publication is now in the National Library of Ireland, NLI, MS 12144.

Anna Parnell goes on to argue that, contrary to what one might expect, there was resistance to reforming suggestions concerning the removal of the grating which screened the women from view, not because of any modesty on behalf of the women, but because they would prefer to endure the auditory and visual deprivation of the cage as 'they value the freedom ensured to them by what at first sight would appear to be intended as a restraint'.[7] In fact, Parnell gleefully acknowledges that the women are so 'invisible' that they are not asked to leave when there is a call for strangers to withdraw from the chamber; 'not being visible', she maintains, 'they can very easily be supposed not to exist'.[8] When Mr Biggar, for example,

> ejected the Prince of Wales and so made a thrill of horror run through the backbone of the Empire ... the ladies were present all through, and thus enjoyed ample compensation for any disadvantages imposed on them by their position in ordinary times, so that it is not after all hard to understand why they so contentedly submit to imprisonment and seclusion.[9]

Anna Parnell uses these articles to expound on the phenomenon known as Irish Obstruction, in which the smallest parliamentary party in history held the House of Commons in frustrated thrall, a brilliant strategy of circumvention, the intricacies of which are keenly appreciated by Parnell herself. Indeed, Anna Parnell's own contribution to Irish politics could also be described as one of attempted circumvention. Ironically, not only did she need to circumvent the House of Commons but also the original obstructionists themselves.

At a time when the separation of the spheres was being consolidated in advanced metropolitan countries, women in Ireland were still not fully domesticated within the home, as is clear from the numerous images of women outworkers found in popular illustrations of the period. As the site of production shifted dramatically in the industrialising world, the sexual division of labour became entrenched; as the social and economic value of men's work increased, that of women correspondingly decreased, constituting what Engels called 'the world-historic defeat of the female sex'.[10] Wielding his relative wealth, man now controlled the household, reducing women to virtual slave status – object of his desire, mother of his children. Engels used the metaphor of capitalist relations to describe the contract between husband and wife, and it is not surprising, therefore, that the economic modernization programme of the Land

---

7 Parnell, 'How They Do It,' p. 469.

8 Ibid.

9 Ibid.

10 Friedrich Engels, *The Origin of the Family, Private Property, and the State* (New York, 1972), p. 120.

League should display a profound instability and ambivalence when it came to considering the position of women within its campaign.

Anticipating that the imprisonment of the men under the extensive powers of Coercion was now only a matter of time, Michael Davitt persuaded a reluctant leadership to adopt the idea of a Ladies' Land League as suggested by Fanny Parnell. Davitt admits that his proposal was

> laughed at by all except Mr Egan and myself, and vehemently opposed by Messrs Parnell, Dillon and Brennan who feared we would invite public ridicule in appearing to put women forward in places of danger.[11]

He regained the upper hand with his colleagues by reminding them that 'We were engaged in virtual revolution. Our purpose should be to make confusion worse',[12] and so he justified the formation of the Ladies' Land League with the dubious compliment that 'No better allies than women could be found for such a task'. He briefly redeemed himself, in relation to the women, by proclaiming that 'They are in certain emergencies, more dangerous to despotism than men,' only to equivocate with limited confidence:

> They have more courage, through having less scruples, when and where their better instincts are appealed to by a militant and just cause in a fight against a mean foe. The fight was to save the homes of Ireland – the sacred, domestic domain of a woman's moral supremacy in civilised society.[13]

This allusion to the domestic is significant. It allowed the men to temporarily embrace women in the struggle. Women saving homes was, apparently, acceptable, women saving Ireland was not. This contestation of women's position in late nineteenth-century society is evoked powerfully in the pictorial press of the day in a range of conflicting images which locate the debates concerning gender and citizenship on either side of the domestic door-step. 'The Daily Farewell' (*Graphic*, 20 November 1880) poignantly illustrates the separation of the spheres, as we observe a resident landlord leaving his family in the safety of the home, to be escorted to work by armed guards; It is clear, however, that the family awaiting the return of another landlord, will not be so fortunate:

> Hark! did I hear a distant gun?
> A cry a groan, an angry word ...

11 Michael Davitt, *The Fall of Feudalism in Ireland* (London and New York, 1904), p. 299.
12 Ibid.
13 Ibid.

Plate 2 'The Land Agitation in Ireland – A Resident Landlord: The Daily Farewell',
The Graphic, 20 November 1880.

Like 'The Daily Farewell', 'Awaiting His Return' (*Graphic*, 1 January 1881)
also shows three generation of women, rooted helplessly to the threshold;
while a visit from 'Rory of the Hills' (*Illustrated London News*, 22 January
1881) reveals, in no uncertain terms, the fate of this man who has resisted,
what the accompanying report called, the 'illegal mandate of the Land
League'.[14] The French journal, *L'Univers Illustré*, which carried the same illustrations, recognized, significantly, that what these images are really concerned
with is 'the inviolability of the home'.[15] It is not difficult to imagine from
these illustrations the lengths to which women might in time be prepared to
go to protect the home. It is, thus, on the spatial boundary between inside
and outside, symbolising the personal and the political, the public and the
private, that the tensions of gender and domesticity are tantalisingly teased
out.

For Davitt the land question was but a stepping stone towards the resolution of the national question; it is doubtful if he, or his already reluctant colleagues, who considered women's involvement in the Land League a dangerous experiment, would have admitted women into the more revolutionary
political struggle of national import.

Historically, the New Departure was always described in binary terms,

14 *Illustrated London News*, 22 January 1881.
15 *L'Univers Illustré*, 2 April 1881.

Plate 3 'The New Year in Ireland: Awaiting His Return', *The Graphic*, 1 January 1881.

comprising moral and physical force factors. In fact it possessed a problematic third dimension turning on gender which is rarely fully acknowledged. Two years into the Land League, the already unique combination of revolutionary, agrarian and constitutional factions was dramatically transformed by the admission, not only of individual women, but of women as a category. Indeed, weeks into the Ladies' Land League Anna Parnell sardonically observed at a public meeting 'that we have succeeded today in getting rid of the men nearly

Plate 4 'Disturbed Ireland; A Visit from Rory of the Hills', *Illustrated London News*, 22 January 1881.

entirely – and I am sure that we all feel much more comfortable in consequence'.[16]

It is strikingly obvious from Anna Parnell's speeches and writings that her style of leadership would be emphatically different from that of her brother and his colleagues. Despite disparaging and misleading descriptions of 'fanatics' haranguing the masses, Anna Parnell particularly disliked the emotionalism of mass meetings which she regarded 'as a peculiarly male form of political demagoguery which incited crowds to frenzied cheers regardless of the content of the speech'.[17] The tactics of the women were more educative than rhetorical, but no less effective for that. Preferring to assemble at evictions where practical solidarity could be displayed and useful discussion encouraged the women avoided the cult of personality in favour of collective action.

Inspirationally, the women took a long-term view of the situation. Their role in nurturing good foundations in their children's education is pointedly exercised by the establishment of the Children's Land League in 1881, thereby demonstrating the inclusive tactics of the women in politicising those for whom they had responsibility. The main function of the Children's Land League was to teach Irish history, using the M.F. Cusack (the Nun of

16 Reported in *The Nation* newspaper, 19 February 1881 and quoted in Margaret Ward, *Unmanageable Revolutionaries: Women in Irish Nationalism* (Dingle, 1983), p. 16.

17 Ward, *Unmanageable Revolutionaries*, p. 23.

Kenmare's) *Irish History for Students*, supplemented with some useful nationalist mnemonics:

> A is the army that covers the ground
> B is the buckshot we're getting all round
> C is the crowbar of cruellest fame
> D is our Davitt, a right glorious name
> E is the English who've robbed us of bread
> F is the famine they've left us instead ...

This was not quite what was intended in bestowing upon women the responsibility for the moral education of children. Predictably, Bishop Gilooly of Elphin remonstrated, declaring that such a development would 'train up the youth as rebels and communists'.[18]

The politicisation of the women inevitably caused consternation in the church, as if only a miracle could reverse the seemingly inexorable breach of women of the public domain. As if made to order, such a miracle took place within a few days of the founding of the Land League in the form of the famous apparition of the Virgin Mary at Knock. Whatever about its scientific status, the moral or political message of the apparition was clear. On the one hand the cluster of individuals who concerned themselves with the apparition at Knock clearly put God on the nationalist side, and on the other hand, the role of the church in enshrining the apparition clearly contributed, Marina Warner argues, to the subjugation of women:

> The Virgin of Knock is silent, so the message is interpreted that a good woman is a woman of few words, submissive, obedient and resigned; the Mother set forth as the ideal woman works in the kitchen and is idolised as saintly by her children. But the credit for 'planning' and 'striving' goes to 'Father'. 'Mother' is granted her pedestal worship to make up for the contempt in which her essential and unceasing labour is held.[19]

In effect, Knock introduced new parameters to the concept and practice of motherhood. Indeed, given church teaching on the innate inferiority of women, whose 'place was the seclusion of home', the existence of the Ladies' Land League not surprisingly troubled Archbishop McCabe's social, if not pastoral conscience. His infamous pastoral of 1881 denounced the Ladies' Land

---

18 Quoted in Jane Cote, *Fanny and Anna Parnell: Ireland's Patriot Sisters* (London, 1991), p. 192.
19 Marina Warner, 'What the Virgin of Knock Means to Women', *Magill* (September 1979), p. 39.

League, ordering women to desist from political involvement and demanding to know if a whole nation was sheltering under women's petticoats. He was greatly alarmed about the woman who 'so far disavows her birthright of modesty as to parade herself before the public gaze in a character so unworthy as a Child of Mary'.[20] This allowed Michael Davitt to make a perceptive connection between the Land League and what we might call the 'erotic economy' of women:

> the tens of thousands of Irish girls who had been driven to shame and ruin in foreign cities in being evicted from Irish homes ... never once appealed to the moral indignation or political thoughts of this Castle bishop. He was only aroused from his peaceful pastoral slumbers on the question of modesty, when ladies, belonging to the families at least as respectable as his own, felt called upon to face an infamous law and system in defence of the homes of Ireland and to run the risk of imprisonment in a struggle for righteousness. [21]

Acutely conscious of gender as an inhibiting factor in her contribution to public life Anna Parnell maintained that 'if the Irish landlords had not deserved extermination for anything else, they would have deserved it for the treatment of their own women,' arguing that the landlords of Ireland dishonoured their pathetic obligations to female relatives who had annuities secured on landed estates, in effect treating their ladies as they would their tenants, by insisting on the primacy of their own profits.[22] Not only did she have an unusual understanding of the connection between the sexual oppression of women and the exploitation of workers but, a contemporary, Andrew Kettle, a prominent League secretary, described her as having

> a better knowledge of the lights and shades of Irish peasant life, of the real economic conditions of the country, and of the social and political forces which had to be acted upon to work out the freedom of Ireland than any person, man or woman[23]

– a remarkable tribute given the prejudicial circumstances of the time.

The credibility and fearlessness of the women of the Land League lay in the fact that they were, as women, untainted by historical power and excluded from future power, rendering them potentially very radical indeed. Interestingly, they are criticised for what they are supposed to be inherently

20 Maria Luddy, *Women in Ireland 1800-1918: A Documentary History* (Cork, 1995), p. 263.
21 Davitt, *The Fall of Feudalism*, p. 314.
22 Parnell, *Tale*, p. 86.
23 Quoted in Ward, *Unmanageable Revolutionaries*, p. 14.

incapable of doing, that is, following the logic of the principles established by the men. The long-missing manuscript, *The Tale of a Great Sham*, was a serious gap in the historiography of the movement allowing suggestions of, predictably, incompetence or extravagance to mar the record of the women's stewardship. When it finally appeared, Anna Parnell's account of the period was, ironically, a searing attack on the male leadership, especially its inconsistency and timidity.

In carrying on what the men had started, but had either not the courage or intention of following through, the Ladies' Land League went into directive leadership. Instead of maintaining a semblance of continuity, they actually set out to achieve the original objectives of the League only to be accused by Charles Stewart Parnell of 'extremism and extravagance'. In time-honoured fashion what the men seem to have wanted was to disempower the women but, as Foster says, have them 'continue as workhorses'.[24] The commitment of the women to the original revolutionary principles was seen, both then and subsequently, as such an embarrassment that it was necessary to discredit the contribution of what St John Ervine disparagingly called 'Miss Parnell's band of harridans'.[25]

Within a year of its formation, the Ladies' Land League constituted over 500 branches. Like the men before them, the women toured the country, travelling under very poor conditions, attending evictions; resisting land-grabbing; organising boycotts; forming new branches; building houses for the evicted; dealing with legal and agricultural matters; negotiating with the clergy and the armed forces; addressing public meetings; and raising and dispensing large amounts of money. On the arrest of William O'Brien they even assumed the publishing of the *United Ireland*, drawing on Miss Lynch's governess' French to negotiate with French printers. Unlike the men, however, they set up exemplary systems for recording data on every estate, landlord and tenant as well as documenting developments and morale around the country.

The tenacity of the Ladies' Land League, and its assertion of a female presence in a revolutionary public space, gave the lie to the separation of spheres, and the attempts of both the 'Victorian' nationalism of the catholic church, and the official Victorianism of the state, to quarantine women within the home. As the land war progressed it became apparent that home was not a haven in a heartless world but was actually infiltrated by violence. In 'The Reign of Terror in Ireland', Norah's attempt to block the penetration of the shadowy form, personifying, disintegration, is, we can see, doomed to fail. Nor was it simply a case, moreover, of woman as perpetual victim; the incongruity of domestic space became gradually apparent as successive images showed women on their

24 R.F. Foster, *Charles Stewart Parnell: The Man and his Family* (Sussex, 1979), p. 277.
25 Quoted in C.L. Innes, *Woman and Nation in Irish Literature and Society 1880-1935* (Athens, GA, 1993), p. 113.

Plate 5 'The Reign of Terror in Ireland', *The Graphic*, 18 December 1880.

socialite rounds or even in the privacy of the boudoir resorting to the gun to protect themselves against the intrusions of the outside world.

The Ladies' Land League thus fundamentally challenged the prejudiced oxymoron of rational woman. Its suppression, therefore, by the government in December 1881, with the ensuing arrests and harassment, was nothing compared to the savagery of the men's resumption of power following their release from prison. Shaken by the confidence of the women, and the extremes of loyalty and distrust which they had inspired – and in an attempt to wipe their own revolutionary record clean – the men besmirched the women with exaggerated criticisms, in an effort to re-erect the gender shibboleth to women's political position. Fraisse and Perrot maintain that in the dialectic which

Plate 6 'Irish Society in 1882: Going to a Ball', *The Graphic*, 8 July 1882.

opposed family and civic values, the very foundation of the civic community depended on the active repression of femininity.[26] Ultimately, on the issue of women in public life Gladstone and Parnell were as one.

Less restrained in her views on physical force than her sister, it has been argued, Fanny Parnell, author of the 'Marseillaise of the Irish Peasant,' here photographed – alias Annie Oakley – in American western costume, uses what Lyn Innes calls 'the rhetoric of martyrdom, of bloodshed as fertilising the land for future revolution'.[27]

26 Genevieve Fraisse and Michelle Perrot, *A History of Women in the West: Emerging Feminism from Revolution to World War*, vol. iv (Cambridge, MA and London, 1993), pp. 18-19.
27 Innes, *Woman and Nation*, p. 111.

Plate 7 'The Reign of Terror in Ireland; A Lesson in the Art of Self-Defence',
The Graphic, 5 February 1881.

In 'Hold the Harvest' she too declares that God is on the peasant's side as
she incites the peasantry to

> Rise up! the answer to your prayers shall come, tornado-borne,
> And ye shall hold your homesteads dear, and ye shall reap the corn.

This invocation of prayer – the call to heaven – acquires more significance
in view of M.F. Cusack's linking of unmanageable women with the lethal
threat of collective violence; 'Women and the mob,' she quotes, 'must have
some kind of religion; it is necessary for them, because we wish to keep
them in some subjection, and we know of no other means to effect this
end.'[28] This necessity to control women and the mob becomes an explosive
issue when women actually become the mob. And so, the constructed docil-
ity of women is challenged by a long tradition of women as firebrands.
Fraisse and Perrot have observed that women often played a 'galvanising' role

28 M.F. Cusack, *Woman's Work in Modern Society* (Kenmare, 1875), p. 132.

Plate 8 Fanny Parnell as Annie Oakley

in uprisings, but were relegated to the sidelines as soon as associations took control of events – they were emphatically excluded from the institutions of revolution – initially there was

> room for both sexes, neither being organised, but once it was succeeded in establishing an effective political structure, a structure that excluded women even though it was supposed to represent the sovereign people from whom it drew its legitimacy, the new insurrectional economy could afford to dispense with the earlier balance of gender relations.[29]

So, while the executive of the Ladies' Land League sought to maintain their position *in* control there were groups of women, especially in the West of Ireland, who, it could be argued, were emphatically *out* of control. One of the first physical skirmishes of the Land War was the Battle of Carraroe in which the local process server was prevented from serving notices to quit, and was set

29 Fraisse and Perrot, *A History of Women*, pp. 18-19.

upon by a group of highly indignant women and boys who incurred a number of bayonet wounds while the body of men who marched with them stood back from the onset; we hear of Mrs Mackle who succeeded in throwing a shovelful of burning turf upon Sub-inspector Gibbons – the resulting attack by the constabulary finally roused the men to action, and they retaliated with stout blackthorns and stones forcing the police to retire from the fray. This, we are informed by Fraisse and Perrot, is the stock pattern. They cite the role of peasant women in the French Revolution – taking the initiative, the women led the first onslaught, but once the rebellion was underway, the men took over, and the women resumed their conventional roles. Maternity and paternity are key determinants in militant engagement – the fact that the typical male militant was a family man in his forties, and the typical female militant was under thirty or over fifty, would suggest that the former is actively engaged while she is left holding the proverbial baby; unencumbered by children, however, in her youth or later middle age, she is, at least, as militantly active as he.

Having assuaged their position through the land courts, the larger farmers distanced themselves from the League, leaving a mutual sense of identification between the women and the poorer sections of the peasantry who had yet to gain from the Land War. In a sense, neither the women nor the peasantry had anything to lose and so, inevitably, there were escalating incidences of the latter taking matters into their own hands. The result was a dramatic increase in agrarian 'outrages', for which women, regardless of whether they were victims, onlookers or perpetrators, were largely blamed. Using abusive language, rocks, scalding water and sticks the women, often in large groups, 'mostly barefooted' and 'all poorly clad with blue lips and hungry looks',[30] prided themselves on intercepting the hated process-server, disrupting evictions and defending the moral economy; indeed, it was the women of Lough Mask who prevented the process server from carrying out his work in the Boycott affair.

According to James Daly of the *Connaught Telegraph*:

> God or nature never intended ... that the manhood of any nation could be so cowardly and demoralized as to intrench themselves behind the fair sex. ... We do not see how any man or body of men having Celtic blood coursing in their veins can be found to descend to or condescend to female leadership. ... We ... enter our solemn protest against having the responsibility of Irish affairs vested in women.[31]

Anne Digby's study of Victorian values deals with the concept of moral insanity, devised by Victorian psychiatry to police unusual female behav-

---

30 *Connaught Telegraph*, 15 May 1880, quoted in Donald E. Jordan, *Land and Popular Politics in Ireland* (Cambridge, 1994), p. 296.

31 *Connaught Telegraph*, 12 February 1881.

iour.[32] It is highly significant that instead of using the existing law,[33] under which the male Leaguers were imprisoned, male disapproval of the Ladies' Land League was signalled by the invocation of an ancient statute dating to the fourteenth century and subsequently used to curb prostitution. Once imprisoned the women were denied political status and treated with unparalleled harshness; while the *Illustrated London News* (unfairly) accused the male Parnell of getting fat on the food from the Governor's table, the women were being humiliated by the application of a misogynistic law which allowed the men to avail of their accomplishments and then apostatise them in solitary confinement. The imprisonment of Irish women in this way suggests intense male discomfort with their crossing of the threshold – the social borderland – into confrontational behaviour.

32 See Clarissa Campbell Orr (ed.), *Women in the Victorian Art World* (Manchester, 1995), p. 5.
33 The Protection of Person and Property Act, 1881, which gave the authorities power to arrest on suspicion, was known as the Coercion Act.

The Aryan Myth: A Nineteenth-Century Anglo-Irish Will to Power

EDWARD A. HAGAN

Standish James O'Grady has frequently received an obligatory nod or footnote in histories of the Irish revival. Not noted, however, is the pattern of insistence throughout his work that the Irish are Aryans. This constant reference seems to have been a way in which O'Grady legitimated revival of the ancient bardic literature of Ireland.[1] Study of the ancient Irish required a larger context, a more respectable (and oddly mystical though thought to be scientific) justification than any inherent, strictly Irish value it might have.

O'Grady's consistent passing reference to the Aryan Myth actually reveals how central that myth was to Irish nineteenth-century discourse. Indeed the pages of both the *Dublin Review* and *Dublin University Magazine* give ample evidence that the whole subject of primitive Aryan origins was a central concern of Irish intellectual activity. The Aryan Myth is actually much more: it is a touchstone for seeing the nature of the Protestant-Catholic divide – political, social, and religious – as it played itself out in the nineteenth century as well as a way of seeing a difference between the work of Joyce and Yeats in the twentieth century. Yes, it is really important to recognize Yeats's Protestant roots and Joyce's Catholicism.

---

1 The point here is that O'Grady was working within a nineteenth-century intellectual context that venerated Aryan origins. O'Grady's Aryan references reflect the 'invention' of Celtic Ireland – a Romantic concept that grew out of philological studies. Robin Flower, lecturing in 1927, has to clear away this 'new literature, largely poetical and not unjustly described as Neo-Celtic, which has imported a latter-day mysticism into the handling of the old matter. Flower thus shows that the intellectual context of O'Grady's endeavours to resuscitate early Irish literature made it difficult to recover a genuine picture of the early Irish: '… it is another matter when criticism begins to interpret the past in the light of these modern imaginations, and it is plain that much of the critical writing on Irish and Welsh subjects since the rise of the Romantic school has been dominated by this "Celtic" prepossession. The picture of Celtic literature drawn by Ernest Renan and Matthew Arnold – neither of whom, I believe, knew any Celtic language – does not carry any conviction to those who read the original texts in their own setting, for it rests upon an artificial selection of subjects and episodes and, of necessity, can tell us nothing of those subtle and characteristic effects which the peculiar turn and idiom of a language lend to the handling of a subject' (Robin Flower, 'Ireland and Medieval Europe', the Sir John Rhys Memorial Lecture, British Academy 1927 in *Proceedings of the British Academy*, vol xiii (1927), pp. 5-6).

O'Grady is particularly valuable because he sums up the Protestant Ascendancy so well. He saw himself as part of it and was involved in its politics. (He served as secretary of a Landlords' meeting during the Land War.) He was a leading article writer for the conservative Dublin *Daily Express* for approximately 25 years – from 1873 to 1898. He was educated at Trinity College, and his work shows the influence of its chief intellectual organ, the *Dublin University Magazine*, to which he contributed several articles in the 1870s. The range of subjects covered in the review from its inception in 1833 fits well with O'Grady's interests.

O'Grady is known mostly for his 1878 and 1880 two-volume 'bardic history'. In 1881 in his *History of Ireland: Critical and Philosophical* he traced a clear line between bardic literature and nineteenth-century enthusiasm for Aryan researches. O'Grady thought he could make a contribution to Aryan research by arguing that Irish bardic literature 'still lingers in the mountains which gave it birth. It is near the well-head'.[2] Thus early Irish literature offered Aryan researchers the opportunity of studying a stage in the development of Aryan culture that has become submerged in other countries. It is worth noting that O'Grady, at least in this instance (he was not always consistent or logical), believes in a common Aryan, blood-linked development of race. It is possible therefore to argue from one group of Aryans to the other.

It is also important to note that the 'well-head' is in the mountains and thus follows the commonly-accepted Aryan doctrine that the original Aryan race had its 'original seat among the highest elevations of Central Asia …'[3] Such thinking also included the notion, discussed often in the *Dublin University Magazine*, that the Vedas in the original Sanskrit are seminal Aryan documents.

O'Grady even saw that the Irish could bolster the argument for a more westerly origin for the Aryans – a sort of sub-plot of the search for the Aryans. R.G. Latham, an English philologist, had argued in his 1851 study, *Man and His Migrations*, that the original Aryans had a more westerly home. Leon Poliakov, the author of *The Aryan Myth* – which was published in 1971 and is subtitled *A History of Racist and Nationalist Ideas in Europe*, notes that the British could not brook the notion of Indian origins; perhaps their colonial interest made it difficult for them to accept an Indian origin for their ancestors, the Aryans. (O'Grady was naïve in thinking the British would be more comfortable with an Irish origin for the British Aryan ancestors.)

O'Grady maintained his belief in the Aryan nature of the Irish throughout his life, and his last work, *Arcadia*,[4] a utopian vision of Ireland, propounds a

---

2 Standish James O'Grady, *History of Ireland: Critical and Philosophical*, vol. i (London and Dublin, 1881), p. 53.
3 T.C. Irwin, 'The Origin and Source of Language' in *Dublin University Magazine*, lix (1862), pp. 749-55.
4 I have most of the unpublished manuscript of *Arcadia*.

dim view of Christianity that follows the pattern of nineteenth-century ethnology:

> That universal and absolutely right and natural feeling of our Aryan
> ancestors has been obscured in more modern Europe by the prevalence
> of Semitic fanaticisms, the devotion to divers gods and demons made in
> the likeness of corrupt mankind; but it has been here always neverthe-
> less; and always will be. The love of Nature, the all-Mother, has ever lain
> deep in the European heart.[5]

It is important to note that O'Grady's words are anti-Catholic – the obvious
reference to worship of images as well as the fact that the term 'Semitic fanati-
cisms' is consistent with the view of St Peter as a kind of religious reactionary
presented in the *Dublin University Magazine*.[6] At the same time O'Grady
alludes to nature as the 'all-Mother'. In Aryan tracts India is often called
'Mother' of the Aryans, and there is a whole gender issue here that requires
further study. Suffice it to say that O'Grady is a sufficient indicator of the
prevalence of the Aryan myth in Anglo-Irish thinking and that such thinking
was popular, at least in part, because of its anti-Catholic undertones. John
Rhys, writing in 1888, is quite pointed in connecting Aryans and Protestantism:

> How, then, is it that the Aryan-speaking nations of Europe are so differ-
> ent, and how is it that they do not hopelessly stagnate, as the nations of
> the East? The answer is doubtless to be sought, to some extent at least,
> in the ever-acting stimulus supplied by the antithesis between the Aryan
> and the Anaryan elements in the composition of all the great nations of
> Europe ... after he [the pure Aryan] had slowly and reluctantly adopted
> Christianity, he eventually broke loose from the older forms of it, and
> developed a very different one in Protestantism which, making less of
> the priestly element, now prevails in all the countries where the Aryan
> blood is most copious.[7]

In Ireland, of course, there were doubts about the copiousness of Aryan
blood among the 'native Irish,' a taint that Ernest Renan's *Poetry of the Celtic
Races* had partially alleviated and had even 'helped' the Anglo-Irish to see the

---

5 Standish James O'Grady, 'Chap. 6: "Children and Animals"', typescript, pp. 5-6 (Standish
   DeCourcey O'Grady Collection).
6 See F.R. Conder, 'The Founder of Aryan Christianity' in *University Magazine*, xciii
   (1879), pp. 59-77.
7 John Rhys, 'Race Theories and European Politics' in *New Princeton Review*, v (1888), pp.
   1-17.

native Irish as their fellow Aryans. (This fact helps to explain how O'Grady and other Anglo-Irish writers became 'Irish' for the first time.) The Aryan myth made possible a reconstruction of Anglo-Irish consciousness. The Ascendancy was under attack in the nineteenth century, and Protestantism had lost its informing power. O'Grady, following Carlyle, knew that his class had to find 'new clothes,' if it was going to maintain itself as an aristocracy. The Aryan Myth in the guise of Irish bardic literature was a suit that he tailored for Anglo-Irish resuscitation.

It is important to understand what the myth involved, and Poliakov offers a useful summary: the 'basic elements of the myth [were]: the emphasis on biology, the deserved triumph of the strongest, the pre-eminence of youth, the superiority of the Whites'.[8] Thus throughout Europe there grew up a kind of belief in an Aryan Manifest Destiny – *essentially a competitive ideal* – although there were those, O'Grady among them, who sometimes visualized a peaceful, rural, agricultural Aryan ideal. Dominance and religious progress were key ideas in the Aryan ideal as it developed in the nineteenth century despite the efforts of Max Muller, a German who was Professor of Philology at Oxford, and Ernest Renan to disavow the militarism that necessarily resulted from such an emphasis and that they themselves had engendered.[9]

In Ireland the Aryan myth offered O'Grady and other Anglo-Irish thinkers the opportunity of re-establishing the feudal relationship of the Ascendancy with the native Irish population – a way out of the Protestant-Catholic opposition. The Aryan Myth could be a new, Anglo-Irish 'will to power'.

However, not everyone was seeing the virtues of Schopenhauer for Irish thinking. Catholic writers in the *Dublin Review*, founded in 1836 soon after the *Dublin University Magazine*, could not buy the anti-Catholic bias of the Aryan myth and saw immediately that it required a progressive view of history in which the coming of Christ, while certainly an important event, was not a culmination of all human history. For Catholics, the only new event could be the Final Judgment – a world view that did not allow for the great, civilizing historical mission of the Aryans, the leading edge of progressive evolution. In criticizing two books by Edward Clodd (a protégé of Max Muller's) significantly entitled *The Childhood of Religions*, the reviewer in the *Dublin Review* delineates the difference in the Catholic position from the author's:

> [Clodd's] theory on this point is very nearly the same as that of Auguste Comte, the chief difference being that, unlike Comte, he wishes to stop at the monotheistic stage, instead of going on to the Comtist ideal of perfection in which pure philosophy is to rule the world. Like Comte, he sees in fetish worship the beginning of religion on earth, instead of

8 Leon Poliakov, *The Aryan Myth*, trans. Edmund Howard (New York, 1974), p. 197.
9 Ibid., p. 206.

regarding it as we do, as the lowest point of degradation of religion, not the starting point in its upward progress.[10]

That upward progress did not continue beyond the coming of Christ in the Catholic view. W.E. Addis, a Catholic writing in the October 1880 issue of the *Dublin Review*, in criticising Ernest Renan's *Lectures on the Influence of the Institutions, Thought, and Culture of Rome, on Christianity and the Development of the Catholic Church*, points directly at his fellow Christians, 'the Protestant orthodoxy,' and says that it 'is losing its hold on society, and giving way beneath the powerful solvents of foreign infidelity'.[11] Addis was specifically pointing to the threat posed by Renan – whom Poliakov calls the 'chief sponsor of the Aryan myth in France' – but he was also alluding to Max Muller and other German critics who espoused a dim view of a so-called 'Semitic Christianity'. (F.R. Conder's 1879 article in the *[Dublin] University Magazine*, is entitled 'The Founder of Aryan Christianity' and lionizes St Paul – the Protestant Aryan hero – as opposed to St Peter – the Catholic Semitic hero.) The views of the German critics were rooted in the Aryan doctrine that saw Christianity as but an epoch in the larger and more important history of the Aryans. The Semites had contributed monotheism, but (Renan argues) they 'have nothing further to do that is essential'.[12]

It was for this reason that in 1863 Renan published a new Bible, his *Life of Jesus*, that placed Christianity in the proper Aryan context. A series of Aryan Bibles followed by Jules Michelet, Louis Jacolliot and others. All denied divinity to Christ and placed him in the role of martyr by Semites or Jews, not in the role of deity. All agreed in seeing a glorious Aryan past. Poliakov describes this:

> Jacolliot was able 'to ascribe the origins of the Bible to the highlands of Asia and to prove that, the influence and memories of the birthplace having been prolonged throughout the ages, Jesus Christ had come to regenerate the new world as Iezeus Christna had regenerated the old'. The Old Testament was regarded by Jacolliot as no more than a collection of superstitions, the Jews as a degraded and stupid people, and Moses as a 'fanatical slave charitably educated at the court of Pharaohs'.[13]

Addis's article is a fascinating Catholic polemic: he argues that Rome's domination of the Western World was divinely approved because it made pos-

---

10 'The Childhood of Religions' in *Dublin Review* o.s., xci (1882), pp. 331-54.

11 W.E. Addis, 'The Truth and the Falsehood of M. Renan's Lectures' in *Dublin Review*, lxxxvii (1880), pp. 333-59.

12 Ernest Renan in Poliakov, *Aryan Myth*, p. 207.

13 Poliakov, *Aryan Myth*, p. 209.

sible the destruction of the Temple of Jerusalem and, with it, the demise of the conservative Judaizers led by Peter, who in Addis's estimation would have kept the Church within narrow Jewish bounds. Thus the Church was forced to become 'catholic' – a Church for everybody – and the Roman empire was the structure divinely prepared for spreading the Church to all peoples.[14]

Addis thus attacks the nationalism that was ironically being fuelled by the transnational Aryan doctrine. (We do know how it finally worked itself out in Nazi Germany.) His argument is that:

> Rome did Christianity another service, and that one more important still. Her universal empire had destroyed the spirit of patriotism; Syria, Cyprus, Asia Minor, had lost even the memory of freedom, the republics of Greece which would have crushed Christianity had vanished, even at Rome patriotism survived only in a few of the ancient families. Hence room was made for a religion 'which was from the first the denial of any earthly country'. More than this, the absence of political struggle, the fact that politics had ceased to create enthusiasm or even interest, threw men back on themselves, and made them willing ears to moral and religious teaching.[15]

Addis thus has propounded one of the Catholic ideas that has always mitigated Irish nationalism although the British and the Protestants have been incapable of recognizing that the Roman Church wanted Irish Catholics to be Roman Catholics first. (George Bernard Shaw pointed out this blindness in his preface to *John Bull's Other Island*.) In short, the Roman Church was the cure for Irish nationalism if only the power structure would see it.

More importantly, Addis was laying the groundwork for a way out of the Protestant-Catholic opposition. He saw that Renan's Aryan doctrines and Protestantism promoted nationalism whereas the Roman Catholic Church staunchly opposed it. Addis says, 'Protestantism has always exhibited itself as a national religion; or to put it more accurately, the different religions which have been known under the common name of Protestant, have always been national'.[16] Furthermore, among Irish Catholics there was a long memory of acts that did not suggest that Protestantism made Christians more civilized. While barbarism was not limited to the acts of some Irish Protestants, George

---

14 K.L. Urlichs made the same point in *Dublin Review* in 1839 – some 41 years before Addis. 'The Romans', he argues served 'as an instrument of Providence to render the human race, (saving the inhabitants of Palestine,) by the universality of Grecian and Roman elements, ripe and ready for the Christian religion'; K.L. Urlichs, 'Roman History' in *Dublin Review*, vii (1839), p. 69.

15 Addis, 'M. Renan's Lectures,' p. 337.

16 Ibid., p. 345.

Crolly, writing in the *Dublin Review* in 1847, compares them unfavorably with the 'conventional savages' of the nineteenth century, who demonstrated greater 'civility': 'The remains of the dead were in general treated with respect by pagan nations, as well as by the patriarchs and the Jews'.[17] Irish Catholics thus were open to more positive views of foreign 'others' while the Aryan Myth was confirming the inherent superiority of the Ascendancy over those 'others'.

Addis's article is typical of many that appeared in the *Dublin Review* for many years. Staunchly polemical, the journal usually opposed the prevailing rage for Aryan researches on the grounds that they denied the supernatural nature of the Christian religion.[18] Catholics emphasized divine revelation, and, in taking credit for 'religious evolution,' the Aryan enthusiasts were making religion a human invention that the Aryans were perfecting. Thus, the *Dublin University Magazine*, the journal associated with Trinity College, enthusiastically catalogued the human progress of the Aryans with frequent discussions of India, Sanskrit, and progress in the study of philology, and with numerous articles on Germany, which are suggestive of real adulation for all things German.

A curious adjunct to the journal's interest in all Aryan subjects is the frequency with which it published articles on theosophy and mysticism throughout the nineteenth century. Ernest Boyd has told us that in the 1890s the Irish Theosophical Society was important because it was a place for Irish intellectuals to meet.[19] The interest in the occult by the Ascendancy class is consistent with an interest in Aryan doctrine since it is precisely Aryan doctrine that many occult systems parallel. For example the Theosophical Society of India to this day preserves as its central dogma the reconciliation of all religious dogma in an evolution back to an original unity that bears a great deal of resemblance to the notion of Aryan origins in the mountains of India.

---

17 George Crolly, 'The History and Antiquities of Ireland' in *Dublin Review*, xxiii (1847), p. 483.

18 W.S. Lily, in reviewing in the *Dublin Review* a number of books on the East including collections of translations of sacred Eastern texts edited by Max Muller, argues for divine inspiration of Eastern sacred books and therefore denies that they are solely of human invention. Unlike the derogatory remarks typical of the Aryan progressive advocates, Lily quotes Cardinal Newman to argue the merit of the Eastern sacred books: 'surely the spirit in which we should approach these "Sacred Books" is clear enough. Hidden in every one of them we should delight to trace "something [Newman says] that could lift up the human heart from the earth to a higher world, something that could make men feel the omnipresence of a higher power ..."The most degraded fetish worshipper seems to me wise and venerable beside the Atheist, equipped with all the culture of this enlightened age. The votary of Mumbo Jumbo, at least, has retained that power of looking up to something higher than faith and reason supply, which is lacking to the Materialist of nineteenth-century Europe, into whose soul, as he gropes amid the beggarly elements of corruption, death has entered' (W.S. Lilly, 'The Sacred Books of the East' in *Dublin Review*, xci [1882], p. 31).

19 Ernest Boyd, *Ireland's Literary Renaissance* (New York, 1918), pp. 212-213.

That the Anglo-Irish Ascendancy was interested in both the occult and the Aryan myth is a conjunction of interests that may reveal the insecurities of a ruling class that was losing its grip. It is not hard to see how these fascinations indicate that the Ascendancy was compensating for its loss of power, purpose, and ideology. O'Grady accused the aristocracy of losing its way, and indeed its shocked inaction during the famine and subsequent vacillation during the land wars qualified the class as defunct and in need of an injection of new life.

Study of the occult held out the illusory promise of secret knowledge. Hope of secret and powerful knowledge drove many Anglo-Irish intellectuals (most notably AE) to espouse theosophical studies in the hope of connecting with the well-head of original knowledge.

The Catholic view of the Church as being for everyone fits quite well with James Joyce's pluralism. Given the prevalence of the Aryan myth, it is not surprising that a Catholic Joyce would create a polygenetic hero of *Ulysses* with a bit of everyone in him – Irish, Semite, Hungarian, Catholic, Jew, Protestant. One meaning of HCE is 'Here Comes Everybody'. Vincent Cheng's recent book, *Joyce, Race and Empire*, has clearly presented Joyce's internationalism. It is worth noting that Joyce's Catholic heritage qualified him to see the world more as Addis did than as O'Grady would have had him do. As a recent reviewer, Daniel Schenker, of a book on Joyce noted, 'Joyce's dissent from the Church was not rooted in an essential hostility or indifference toward religion. Joyce's complaint against the Church was more that it was not *religious enough*'.[20]

Yeats's 1894 play, *The Land of Heart's Desire*, on the other hand, may be read as a compendium of much nineteenth-century Anglo-Irish, Protestant/Aryan thinking, but Yeats's irony undoes its will to power. The play's conflict is between the ambiguously attractive, youth-endowing, faery religion of 'old' Ireland and a stultifying Catholicism. Mary Bruin, the play's central character, is described as being 'too much in the old book'[21] – a reference to the ancient Irish religion but, not inconceivably, by extension to the Aryan Bibles as well. Mary chooses life with the faeries over the continued entrapment of life with her mother and father and Shawneen of a husband. Yeats shows the flaws of Irish domestic life, complete with the negative figure of a priest who has no real spiritual understanding and who cooperates in giving power to the faery child who succeeds in taking away Mary Bruin. The priest removes a crucifix from sight, and Yeats is specific: it is a crucifix, not simply a cross, and thus the priest is removing the image of Christ crucified – a Catholic object of veneration.

The play embodies a Rosicrucian view of the cosmos (and therefore is quite consistent with Aryan thinking). The faery child refuses wine and asks for

20 Daniel Schenker, review of *Ulysses and the Irish God*, by Frederick K. Lang in *Studies in the Novel*, xxvii (1995), p. 226.

21 W.B. Yeats, 'The Land of Heart's Desire' in *The Collected Plays of W.B. Yeats* (New York, 1952) p. 35.

milk, which is given to her once she is carried across the threshold and thus into power over the Bruin household. For Rosicrucians (and we know that Yeats was steeped in Rosicrucianism in the 1890s) a key act in the life of Christ is the wedding feast of Cana where Jesus changed water into wine. Rosicrucians believe that Christ came to dull the senses of some humans (not the apostles, to whom he imparted esoteric knowledge that Rosicrucians claim to possess), and thus the act of changing water into wine suggests his stultifying power.[22] Since the fifth epoch of humanity is the Aryan Epoch, Rosicrucians view Christ enigmatically.[23] While he dulled human consciousness with wine (in the play Shawn Bruin fetches wine saved from a Spanish, and therefore Catholic, wreck for his mother), Christ also took his apostles up on the mountain and gave them secret knowledge. (Mountains are the original home of the Aryans.) It is this secret knowledge that the Rosicrucians claim possession of: it is remarkably similar to the Aryan progressive view of religion. Moreover this version of Christ's work helps to explain how Catholicism is a Semitic fanaticism while at the same time Christianity was progress for the select Aryans who heeded St Paul and moved away from the Semitic St Peter.

Rosicrucians see the Christian epoch much as the espousers of the Aryan Bibles did: it was a Semitic stage in the evolution of the Aryan story. Rosicrucians believe that humans live several lives and seek to return to an original unity. The third epoch of Rosicrucian history is the epoch of milk drinking. In asking for milk, the child in *The Land of Heart's Desire* is seeking return to that earlier stage in the evolution back to original oneness.

Yeats thus has worked out in *The Land of Heart's Desire* a dramatic return of a passionate woman to a more attractive, but not particularly attractive, previous dispensation or epoch. Further devolution or retrogression is required. Notably her salvation involves rejection of marriage governed by the church to her husband, rejection of the greasy till, rejection of an unimaginative, restricted, prudish life, and a return to the ancient religious traditions of Ireland. Yeats's dramatic resolution thus recapitulates the pattern of nineteenth-century glorification of an Aryan past – in his Ireland this vision secures a reborn, newly unified Irish triumph over the death of the Ascendancy class. Of course, Yeats's vision of triumph is ironic – Aryan 'improvement' results not in dominance, but in the restoration of ambiguity.

22 Max Heindel, *The Rosicrucian Cosmo-Conception or Mystic Christianity* (Oceanside, CA, and London, 1937), pp. 165-72.
23 Max Heindel's description of the Rosicrucian 'Cosmo-conception' bears extraordinary resemblances to the Aryan Myth. He specifically labels Christianity as Aryan and progressive: '… as Christianity is the religion of the most advanced Race, it must be the most advanced Religion, and because of the elimination of this doctrine [the laws of Consequence and Rebirth] from its *public* teachings, the conquest of the world of matter is being made by the Anglo-Saxon and Teutonic races, in which this phase has been carried the furthest' (ibid., p. 168).

Celticism: Between Race and Nation

CHRIS MORASH

'What', asked Douglas Hyde in 'The Necessity for De-Anglicising Ireland' (1892), 'lies at the back of the sentiments of nationality with which the Irish millions seem so strongly leavened?' The answer, he declares, is racial memory:

> I believe that what is largely behind it is the half unconscious feeling that the race which at one time held possession of more than half Europe ... is now – almost extirpated and absorbed elsewhere – making its last stand for independence in this island of Ireland; and do what they may the race of today cannot wholly divest itself from the mantle of its own past.[1]

A passage like this forces us to interrogate the relationship between nationalism and racialism on this island. This is, after all, the man who became the first President of Ireland, a moderate when compared, for instance, with Arthur Griffith, Vice-President of Sinn Féin in the first Dáil, who wrote in 1913 that no Irishman needed an excuse for 'declining to hold the negro his peer in right'.[2]

To raise the issue of race in such a context is to ask awkward questions, liable to expose the person who asks them to charges of being a revisionist heretic of the worst kind. When they have been raised (and it has not been often), it has usually been with the proviso that, as Luke Gibbons puts it in his essay 'Race against Time: Racial Discourse and Irish History', 'not all the concepts of Irishness which emerged under the aegis of cultural nationalism were dependent on racial modes of identity',[3] although he admits that those which

---

1 Douglas Hyde, 'The Necessity for De-Anglicising Ireland', in *The Field Day Anthology of Irish Writing*, vol. ii, ed. Seamus Deane (Derry, 1991), pp. 528-29.
2 Arthur Griffith, 'Preface to the 1913 Edition' in *Jail Journal* by John Mitchel, ed. Thomas Flanagan (Dublin, 1982), p. 370.
3 Luke Gibbons, 'Race Against Time: Racial Discourse and Irish History' in *Transformations in Irish Culture* (Cork, 1996), p. 156. Gibbons points particularly to George Sigerson as a proponent of a non-racial version of Irish identity. I would maintain that Sigerson is in fact working very firmly within a racialist tradition, but is also registering its 'excess', as when he writes: 'It has been too much the custom to speak of the Irish as altogether Celts, and then to construct the usual theory. Even in the days of the native chiefs there were Norse and Anglo-Saxon settlers amicably established in various parts of Ireland. Then, again, the Danes forced themselves upon its ports, and surely

did found in it a powerful corrective to the discontinuous narrative of Irish history. While it is certainly the case that any sort of axiomatic linking of nationalism and racialism is too crude, it is equally misleading to suggest that race is somehow a disposable accessory in nationalist discourse. To do so is to establish a model in which, as Etienne Balibar puts its, 'the core of meaning contrasts a "normal" ideology and politics (nationalism) with an "excessive" ideology and behaviour (racism), either to oppose the two or to offer the one as the truth of the other.'[4]

In order to avoid either a simplistic linking or an equally simplistic dissociation of racism and nationalism, we need to turn to the concept of 'excess', which Balibar argues needs to be developed further if we are to do other than provide the relationship between nationalism and racism with alibis. 'Racism', Balibar argues is not an 'expression of nationalism'. Nor is it a 'perversion' of nationalism, 'for there is no pure essence of nationalism'. Instead, he maintains, it is:

> ... a *supplement of nationalism* or more precisely *a supplement internal to nationalism*, always in excess of it, but always indispensable to its constitution and yet always still insufficient to achieve its project.[5]

Since this idea is the key to my argument here, it is worth saying a few words about the 'supplement' and 'supplementarity'. The terms direct us, of course, toward Jacques Derrida, particularly those passages in *Of Grammatology* which deal with language and Nature in Rousseau. For Derrida, writing in Rousseau's texts appears as a 'supplement' to Nature, which is to say, it supplants or replaces Nature, thereby indicating that Nature is not present; at the same time, it is in excess of nature, 'adding itself, it is a surplus, a plenitude enriching another plentitude'.[6] In short, if we can paraphrase Derrida, (never an easy or a wise thing to do), the supplement is never enough, for it can never fully supplant the imagined plentitude of full presence; and yet it is always too much, in excess of its object. The supplement is both impoverished and exorbitant.

Keeping in mind Balibar's insistence that the racial supplement is 'internal to nationalism' (whereas Derrida insists upon its exteriority), we might begin

bequeathed some portion of their characteristics to the inhabitants, after they had lost sovereign rule' (George Sigerson, *Modern Ireland* [Dublin, 1868], vol. ii, p. 240). Indeed, the praise here for a hearty racial mix is very similar to the argument put forward by Comte Arthur de Gobineau in his *Essay on the Inequality of the Races*.

4 Etienne Balibar, 'Racism and Nationalism' in Etienne Balibar and Immanuel Wallerstein, *Race, Nation, Class: Ambiguous Identities* (London, 1991), p. 46.

5 Ibid., p. 54.

6 Jacques Derrida, *Of Grammatology*, trans. Gayatri Spivak (Baltimore, 1976), pp. 144–5.

to understand race as that which reminds us of the absence on which an aspiration to nationhood is founded in a colonial situation. 'The bulk of the Irish race really lived in closest contact with the traditions of the past and national life of nearly eighteen hundred years', writes Hyde, 'until the beginning of this [the nineteenth] century'.[7] The 'national life', which for Hyde is the true life of 'the bulk of the Irish race', has existed for almost two millennia (thus, not insignificantly, making the origin of the 'Irish race' coincide exactly with the birth of Christ). Its continued existence is the justification for the founding of the nation state. At the same time, however, the absence of the 'national life' provides the occasion for Hyde's lecture. To put it more simply, the logic of such an argument is that the nation is and always has been, and the nationalist will do everything possible to bring it into existence.

The absence on which his project is founded resurfaces when Hyde claims that in the nineteenth century, the 'Irish race' 'lost all that they had – language, traditions, music, genius, and ideas. Just when we should be starting to build up anew the Irish race and the Gaelic nation ... we find ourselves despoiled of the bricks of nationality'.[8] Who is speaking here? The 'Irish race' and 'the Gaelic nation' (again, they are synonymous terms here) are both absent, in so far as they need to be 'built up anew'. Like Didi and Gogo in *Waiting for Godot*, each gives the other the impression that they exist; which is to say, race and nation are written in Hyde's text in a relation of supplementarity, neither providing a firm basis for the other's existence, but each necessary to the other. Hence, Hyde is forced to formulate a metonymic figure for this unstable relation – 'language, music, genius, ideas' – of which the most privileged term is 'language'.

By inserting 'language' between 'race' and 'nation', Hyde is working within one of the most important, and one of the most contested, aspects of nineteenth-century race theory. For instance, James Cowles Prichard, an influential early ethnologist, wrote in 1831:

> ... among the investigations which belong exclusively to our own species [is] an analysis of languages. ... This resource, if properly applied, will furnish great and indispensable assistance in many particular inquiries relating to the history and affinity of nations.[9]

Prichard wrote those words in a book entitled *The Eastern Origins of the Celtic Nations Proved by Comparison of Their Dialects with Sanskrit, Greek, Latin and Teutonic Languages: Forming a Supplement to Researches into the Physical History of*

---

7 Hyde, 'The Necessity for De-Anglicising Ireland', p. 530.
8 Ibid.
9 James Cowles Prichard, *The Eastern Origins of the Celtic Nations, [etc.]* (London, 1831), p. 3.

Mankind. Prichard's study of the 'Celtic nations' was, as the subtitle suggests, a part of a larger project, *Researches into the Physical History of Mankind*. The 'Celtic nations' find themselves treated as a 'supplement' to the rest of mankind because, unlike the rest of humanity, which could be adequately differentiated along physiological lines, Pritchard found that when he encountered the 'Celtic race' the criteria of difference he had been able to use elsewhere did not quite work, and he needed to turn towards language. In Prichard's *Eastern Origins of the Celtic Nations*, as in Hyde's speech sixty years later, the terms 'nation', 'race' and 'language' have a habit of sliding into one another as if they were synonymous. At the most basic level, this is because nationalism, comparative ethnology, and comparative philology are all developing along roughly similar trajectories at the same time, emerging from their roots in the Enlightenment to proliferate in all of their nineteenth-century effusiveness. Moreover, Prichard's *Eastern Origin of the Celtic Nations* appears just at the moment when comparative philology is beginning to establish itself as a master discourse. While the technique of, as he puts it, comparing 'respective vocabularies or stocks of primitive words or roots, and secondly, the peculiarities and coincidences in their grammatical structure',[10] in order to establish the relation between two languages may sound arcane enough to be innocent, with the work in the 1830s and 1840s of the first generation of modern comparative philologists – such as Franz Bopp, J. Kaspar Zeuss and Hermann Ebel – philology was beginning to offer race theory what looked like a stable and coherent system of classification.

'We must therefore infer', writes Prichard of the consequences of comparing linguistic roots, 'that the nations to whom these languages belonged emigrated from the same quarter',[11] and thus shared the same gene pool – thereby making for Pritchard the link between language and bodies. In so doing, he brings together two discursive fields in what was to be become one of the century's most powerful and unstable constellations. While only a handful of comparative philologists could claim to understand the details of the monumental works of figures such as Bopp and Zeuss, the basic structures of difference and relation linking the languages of the world were quickly assimilated by the more accessible writings of ethnographers, so that by the time Josiah C. Nott and G.R. Glidden produced *Types of Mankind* in 1854, the volume contained parallel charts showing the various linguistic groups of humanity, collated with charts showing physical types, making clear for the general reader the identity of the two means of classification. 'Philology', as Matthew Arnold puts it in his *Study of Celtic Literature* in 1867, 'carries us towards ideas of affinity of race which are new to us'.[12]

10 Ibid., p. 27.
11 Ibid., p. 22.
12 Matthew Arnold, *The Study of Celtic Literature* (London, 1910 [1867]), p. 72.

As these two competing notions of race – race as physical difference and race as linguistic difference – came together, there was a proliferation of race theory. 'Discussions upon race are interminable', writes Ernest Renan in the early 1860s, 'because the word "race" is taken by philological historians and by physiological historians in two totally different senses'.[13] Renan's use of the word 'interminable' here should be taken literally; it can not be terminated. It is in a constant state of play, because it is the function of a gap between two different discursive fields. And yet, at the same time, physiological racialism and linguistic racialism required each other. If this was true as a general principle, it was particularly true when race theory turned its gaze from the more general fourfold division of the world into black, yellow, white and red races, to internal differences within the 'white race'. Hence, Hyde and other Irish nationalists who sought in race theory some form of stability were in fact locating their project at one of the most unstable fissures in an unstable structure.

We see this fissure opening up, for instance, in the work of one of the most widely read English theorists of race in the latter part of the nineteenth century, John Beddoe. In a paper read before the Anthropological Society of London on 14 June 1870, entitled *The Kelts of Ireland*, Beddoe presented the results of his attempts to apply his 'Index of Nigrescence' to Ireland. The 'Index' was a method for charting racial difference based on hair type. Beddoe's research methodology involved walking purposefully around a particular region looking at the inhabitants' hair colour, and then, once he had a big enough sample, 'subtracting the red hair from the dark brown *plus* twice the black hair'[14] to produce a percentile figure for the area.

Where Beddoe's method had produced fairly regular results in Egypt, for instance, his 'Nigrescence' map of Ireland showed no perceptible pattern whatsoever. His conclusions are thus less than resounding:

> My ideas respecting the physical history of the Keltic race, are, as follows: Whether the original clan or sept which broke away from the Aryan race in Central Asia, carrying with it the parent language of the Keltic tongues, was dark or fair, I do not pretend to know; but ... its descendants [were] variously crossed with those of the people they had conquered or intermixed with on the way. ... Ireland, having been peopled mainly by successive strata of grey-eyed, brown or darkish haired Gaelic Kelts, more or less mixed probably with Kumric Kelts, Iberians, Ligurians and Finns or other aborigines, was invaded by the fair Northmen.[15]

13 Ernest Renan, 'What is a Nation?' in *The Poetry of the Celtic Races and Other Studies*, trans. W.G. Hutchison (London, n.d.), p. 73.
14 John Beddoe, *The Kelts of Ireland* (London, 1870), p. 4.
15 Ibid., p. 11.

There is not much in the way of racial purity here, with everyone from Iberians to Finns adding their drop of blood to the Celtic cocktail. What is worth noting, however, is that while Beddoe is attempting to work with race as a purely physiological phenomenon, he can only identify what he calls 'the original clan or sept which broke away from the Aryan race' in terms of its language, 'the parent language of the Keltic tongues'. What that original 'Celtic' race looked like ('fair or dark'), it is impossible to say; their language, however, is a different matter. In short, instead of physiology providing the material basis for discerning racial difference, with language as its cultural overlay (or, we might say, physiology providing the signified to the signifier of language), the situation here is reversed. From the point of view of a physiological ethnologist, it is language which is the stable term, and physiology which is arbitrary and shifting.

However, from the philological point of view, the opposite was the case. In spite of the work of Bopp and Zeuss, the philologist and geologist (and later President of Queen's College Cork), William K. Sullivan would write in 1859 of the absence of an agreed methodology in ethnology of language, turning for his point of reference to zoology. 'If a naturalist included the ox and the goat in the same genus', he writes despairingly, 'because they had eyes, were covered with hair, had four legs, a tail, and generally two horns, he would not depart more from the principles of a true natural classification than do many ethnologists in their classification of languages'.[16] In an effort to introduce a 'true natural' basis for the classification of linguistic races into the Irish debate, Sullivan promoted the work of Zeuss in a series of articles written in the late 1850s, and translated one of the leading German comparative philologists whose work seemed to fix the place of the Celtic once and for all, Hermann Ebel.

Ebel concludes, in accordance with what was a growing consensus, that the Celtic languages belong precisely in the centre of an Indo-European line, 'with the Italic on one side and the German on the other, and through both with other already established twigs of the European bough'.[17] Philological work like Ebel's which placed the Celtic races in the centre of the Indo-European line looked like it was going to provide some kind of stability for race theory as it had a bearing on Ireland. This was certainly the case with John Beddoe, who found that after several weeks spent counting heads in Ireland, the only thing he could say for sure about the 'Kelts of Ireland' was that they were Indo-European, or Aryan. However, as Beddoe's comments suggest, placing the

16 William K. Sullivan, 'On the Influence which the Physical Geography, the Animal and Vegetable Productions, etc. of Different Regions, Exert upon the Languages, Mythology, and Early Literature of Mankind, with Reference to Its Employment as a Test of Ethnological Hypothesis', *Atlantis*, ii (January 1859), p. 147.

17 Hermann Ebel, 'The Position of the Celtic', trans. William K. Sullivan, *Atlantis*, iv (January, 1864), p. 339.

Celts so firmly in the middle of the Aryan family tree also meant that a Celtic heritage ceased to be a purely Irish possession. For instance, the Swiss ethnologist and race theorist, Adolphe Pictet, author of the two-volume *Indo-European Origins, or the Primitive Aryas. An Essay in Linguistic Palaeontology* of 1859, was a vociferous proponent of the idea that the Celts were Aryans, part of the 'race destined by Providence some day to dominate the entire globe'.[18] Pictet's Celtophilia was not, however, the product of any great love of Ireland; instead, in the Celts of the 'La Tène' civilization based at Lake Neuchâtel during the late Iron Age, Pictet found an Aryan genealogy and lineage for his own culture. A similar impulse can be detected both in the work of the German Celticists, such as Bopp, Zeuss and Ebel, with relation to the Celtic Iron Age 'Hallstatt' culture, and in the later generation of French comparative philologists, including Henri Martin, d'Arbois Jubainville and Camille Jullian, who in turn influenced more mainstream French historians, most notably Michelet. Indeed, when Matthew Arnold claimed that English poetry owes its 'style', 'melancholy' and 'natural magic' to 'the Celtic part in us',[19] he was simply adopting a strategy which had already been deployed throughout Continental Europe.

In other words, while establishing the Celtic race as one of the key members of the Aryan family made it possible for Hyde, for instance, to speak of the Celts as 'the race which at one time held possession of more than half Europe',[20] it also means that George Sigerson, in his influential introductory essay to *Bards of the Gael and Gall*, will write that early Irish literature 'enables us to gain some glimpse into the homes of other nations – Teutons as well as Celts – whose lamps were extinguished'.[21] On a similar note, Hyde concludes 'The Necessity for De-Anglicising Ireland', with a list of what he calls 'dispassionate foreigners' – Zeuss, de Jubainville, Heinrich Zimmer, Kuno Meyer, Ernest Windsich, and Graziado Ascoli – whose view of the 'Gaelic nation', he claims, encompasses issues of 'greater importance than whether Mr Redmond or Mr MacCarthy lead the largest wing of the Irish party for the moment, or Mr So-and-So succeed with his election petition.'[22] Placed in its Indo-European context, Hyde's Gaelic nation spills over and exceeds the geographical unit of Ireland. The spatial and temporal sweep of the Celtic race, properly understood, makes the business of real politics in Ireland mundane, parochial, diminished. 'In vain', writes Joseph Dunne of Ireland in 1916, 'do we look elsewhere for similar literary records to take us back to one of the earliest stages of

---

18 Adolphe Pictet, *Indo-European Origins, or The Primitive Aryas. An Essay in Linguistic Palaeontology*, 2nd ed., (London, 1877), p. 8. Cited in Jacques Barzun, *Race: A Study in Modern Superstition* (London, 1938), p. 38.
19 Arnold, *The Study of Celtic Literature*, p. 113.
20 Hyde, 'The Necessity for De-Anglicising Ireland', p. 528.
21 George Sigerson, *Bards of the Gael and Gall* (Dublin, [1897]), p. 22.
22 Hyde, 'The Necessity for De-Anglicising Ireland', pp. 532-3.

Aryan culture, coeval in some respects with that of the Heroic age, and in some details even with the civilization of the original inhabitants of western Europe'.[23] A Celtic racial heritage, rather than being a unique feature of Irish difference, turns out to be something that Ireland shares with most of western Europe – including, of course, the coloniser, England.

Let me conclude, then, by reiterating that racialism as an ideology functions as a 'supplement' to nationalism. It is not simply the case that race provides the missing stability that a colonial nationalism lacks in terms of a continuous history. Race may appear to offer continuity; however, as Derrida writes of the supplement, 'it produces no relief, its place is assigned in the structure by the mark of an emptiness'.[24] 'The excess it [racialism] represents in relation to nationalism', writes Etienne Balibar, 'and therefore the supplement it brings to it, tends both to universalize it, to correct its lack of universality, and to particularize it, to correct its lack of specificity':

> In other words, racism actually adds to the ambiguous nature of nationalism, which means that, through racism, nationalism engages in a 'headlong flight forward', a metamorphosis of its material contradictions into ideal contradictions.[25]

Theories of race – and in particular theories of a Celtic race – were being developed simultaneously in a parallel series of discourses (comparative philology, ethnology, anthropology, biology) which were in themselves in the process of drawing up their own narratives throughout the nineteenth century. Philological race theory depended upon physiological race theory, while at the same time physiology relied upon philology; each part used the other as an alibi. The net result was a system without a centre, in which the boundaries would stretch if pushed at any point – and pushed they were, thereby producing a monstrous proliferation of texts. By the end of the nineteenth century, the field of race theory as a whole was vast, and Celticism one of its most extensive parts. Indeed, racialism was capable of subsuming theories of the nation-state which were being formulated in this island, and thus constituted a threat to the stability of the national unit, while at the same time helping to make possible the state's existence. Running the trace of this racial supplement in the genealogy of Irish nationalism thus emerges as an urgent project in any attempt to salvage nationalism's emancipatory potential for the future.

23 Joseph Dunne, *The Study of Celtic* (Dublin, 1916), pp. 5, 7.
24 Derrida, *Of Grammatology*, p. 145.
25 Balibar, 'Racism and Nationalism', p. 54.

Notes on Contributors

ANGELA BOURKE is a Lecturer in the Department of Irish at the National University of Ireland (NUI), Dublin. She is the author of *Caoineadh na dTrí Muire: Téama na Páise i bhFilíocht Bhéil na Gaeilge* (1983), a book of short stories, *By Salt Water* (1996), and many essays on the Irish oral tradition.

THOMAS A. BOYLAN teaches in the Department of Economics at NUI, Galway. He is a graduate of NUI, Dublin, and of Trinity College, Dublin. He is the author (with Tadhg Foley) of *Political Economy and Colonial Ireland: The Propagation and Ideological Function of Economic Discourse in the Nineteenth Century* (1992) and (with F. P. O'Gorman) of *Beyond Rhetoric and Realism in Economics* (1995).

THOMAS DUDDY teaches in the Department of Philosophy at NUI, Galway. He is the author of *Mind, Self, and Interiority* (1995) and numerous papers on the philosophy of mind, ethics and aesthetics. He is currently working on a history of Irish philosophy.

TERRY EAGLETON is the Warton Professor of English Literature at the University of Oxford and is the author of many books, including *Heathcliff and the Great Hunger: Studies in Irish Culture* (1995). He has written plays on Oscar Wilde and James Connolly, and an Irish novel, *Saints and Scholars* (1987). In 1997 he was awarded an honorary DLitt by the National University of Ireland.

TADHG FOLEY teaches in the Department of English at NUI, Galway. He is a graduate of NUI, Galway and of the University of Oxford. He is the author (with Thomas A. Boylan) of *Political Economy and Colonial Ireland: The Propagation and Ideological Function of Economic Discourse in the Nineteenth Century* (1992). He is the co-editor of *Gender and Colonialism* (1995).

LUKE GIBBONS is a graduate of NUI, Galway, and he teaches in the School of Communications at Dublin City University. He is the co-author (with Kevin Rockett and John Hill) of *Cinema and Ireland* (1988), the author of *Transformations in Irish Culture* (1996) and of the forthcoming *The Colonial Sublime: Edmund Burke and Irish Romanticism*.

PETER GRAY is a Lecturer in Modern History at Southampton University. He is the author of *The Irish Famine* (1995). His second book, *Famine, Land and Politics: British Government and Irish Society 1843-1850*, will be published in 1998.

EDWARD A. HAGAN is a Professor of English at Western Connecticut State University. He received his MA and PhD from SUNY at Stony Brook and his BA from Fordham University. He is the author of *High Nonsensical Words: A Study of the Works of Standish James O'Grady* (1986).

JUDITH HILL is an architect and architectural historian. She is the author of *The Building of Limerick* (1991) and *Irish Public Sculpture: A History*, published by Four Courts Press, Dublin, 1998.

MARJORIE HOWES, who received her PhD from Princeton, teaches at Rutgers University, New Brunswick, and is the author of *Yeats's Nations: Gender, Class, and Irishness* (1996), which won the ACIS (American Conference for Irish Studies) Michael J. Durkan prize for the year's best book in literary and cultural criticism. She has published essays on nineteenth-century Irish literature, on postcolonial theory, and has edited a section of volume 4 of the *Field Day Anthology*.

TERRENCE McDONOUGH teaches in the Department of Economics at the National University of Ireland, Galway. He is a graduate of the University of Massachusetts at Amherst. He is the co-editor of *Social Structures of Accumulation: The Political Economy of Growth and Crisis* (1994). He is also the author of articles in the areas of political economy, economic history, the history of economic thought and economic policy.

CHRIS MORASH is the author of *Writing the Irish Famine* (1995) and has edited a collection of Famine poetry, *The Hungry Voice* (1989). He has published essays on nineteenth-century Irish writing, and has contributed to reference works including the *Oxford Companion to Irish Literature*, *Blackwell's Companion to Irish Culture* and the *World Encyclopedia of Contemporary Theatre*. He is currently writing a history of Irish theatre. He is a Lecturer in the Department of English, NUI, Maynooth.

WILLA MURPHY is a Lecturer in English and Religious Studies at St Patrick's College, Dublin City University. She is the editor of *The Endless Knot: Literature and Religion in Ireland* (1997), a special issue of the journal *Religion and Literature*.

NIALL Ó CIOSÁIN lectures in the Department of History, NUI, Galway. He is the author of *Print and Popular Culture in Ireland 1750-1850* (1997), and has published articles on printing, popular culture and the Great Famine.

MARGARET PRESTON is currently completing her PhD in History at Boston College, on Irish women and philanthropy. In 1991 she received her MA in history from NUI, Dublin. Her most recent publication, in *New Hibernia Review*, is entitled 'The Good Nurse: Women Philanthropists and the Evolution of Nursing in Nineteenth-Century Dublin'.

NIAMH O'SULLIVAN is a Lecturer at the National College of Art and Design, Dublin. She is working on the biography of the Irish-American painter and illustrator Aloysius O'Kelly and is curating an exhibition of his work for the Hugh Lane Gallery of Modern Art in 1999.

SEÁN RYDER lectures in the Department of English at NUI, Galway. He is the co-editor of *Gender and Colonialism* (1995). He has published articles on aspects of early nineteenth-century Irish cultural nationalism and is editing the poems of James Clarence Mangan for Oxford University Press.

SANDRA F. SIEGEL writes on British literary culture and Anglo-Irish relations and teaches at Cornell University. She is the author of *William Butler Yeats: Purgatory* (1986). The essay included here belongs to her forthcoming book on Oscar Wilde.

EVA STÖTER, who holds an MA in Anglo-Irish Literature from NUI, Maynooth and an MA in Drama Studies from NUI, Dublin, is a PhD student in the Department of English, NUI, Maynooth.

Index